JOKES

LEMON FRESH TOILET HUMOUR

Published in 2012 by Prion
an imprint of the Carlton Publishing Group
20 Mortimer Street
London W1T 3JW

ISBN 978-1-85375-875-1

10 9 8 7 6 5 4 3 2 1

Printed and bound in Great Britain by CPI Group (UK) Ltd, Croydon CR0 4YY

JOKES

LEMON FRESH TOILET HUMOUR

**HUNDREDS OF JOKES GUARANTEED TO
CHEER UP ANY BATHROOM EXCURSION**

PRION

Are you sitting comfortably?

A bathroom break is the perfect opportunity to clear your head of the day's woes, so why not savour the peace and enjoy a good chuckle at the same time?

This book contains a huge collection of funnies specially compiled for those precious solitary moments in your bathroom. There's no particular order, so you can just flick through and find a random gag or hilarious story to turn your trip to the bathroom into a real 'sitcom'.

Auntie Lou

Graffiti on the wall of a ladies' loo:

My husband follows me everywhere!

Written just below it: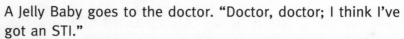

I do not!

A Jelly Baby goes to the doctor. "Doctor, doctor; I think I've got an STI."

The doctor is surprised, "You can't have an STI, you're a Jelly Baby!"

"But, doctor, I've been sleeping with Allsorts."

Two women were standing at a funeral.

"I blame myself for his death," said the wife.

"Why?" asked her friend.

"I shot him," said the wife.

A policeman pulls over a car for swerving and asks the driver to take a breathalyzer test.

"I can't do that," says the man. "I'm an asthmatic. The breathalyzer could bring on an attack."

So the policeman suggests a urine sample.

"Can't do it," says the man. "I'm a diabetic, so my urine always has strange stuff in it."

"Well," says the angry policeman, "why don't you just get out of the car and walk along this white line?"

"Sorry," says the man, "but I can't do that either."

"Why not?" asks the officer.

"Because I'm drunk."

A defence lawyer says to his client: "I've got good news and bad news. The bad news is your blood test came back and the DNA is an exact match with the sample found on the victim's shirt."

"Damn," says the client. "What's the good news?"

"Your cholesterol is down to 140."

Two chimps in a bath. One says, "Oh, oh, ah, ah, ee, ee!"

The other one says, "Put some cold water in then."

Three cowboys are sitting in the bunkhouse. "That smart-arse Tex," says the first. "He's going to start bragging about that new foreign car he bought as soon as he comes in."

"Not Tex," says the second. "He's just a good ol' boy. When he walks in, I'm sure all he'll say is, 'Hello.'"

"I know Tex better than any of you," says the third. "He's so smart, he'll figure out a way to do both. Here he comes now."

Tex then swings open the bunkhouse door and shouts, "Audi, partners!"

A man walks into a doctor's office. "What seems to be the problem?" asks the doc.

"It's... umm... well, I have five penises," the embarrassed man finally admits.

"Blimey!" says the doctor. "How do your underpants fit?"

"Like a glove."

Three Irishmen, Paddy, Sean and Shamus, were stumbling home from the pub late one night and found themselves on the road which led past the old graveyard.

"Come have a look over here," says Paddy, "It's Michael O'Grady's grave, God bless his soul. He lived to the ripe old age of 87."

"That's nothing", says Sean, "here's one named Patrick O' Tool, it says here that he was 95 when he died."

Just then, Shamus yells out, "Good God, here's a fella that got to be 145!"

"What was his name?" asks Paddy?

Shamus stumbles around a bit, awkwardly lights a match to see what else is written on the stone marker and exclaims, "Miles, from Dublin."

An Englishman, a Frenchman and a German survive a plane crash. They are stranded on a desert island and, knowing that nothing but certain death is to be their fate, God grants them one last wish. The Frenchman asks for a huge, sumptuous dinner washed down with an excellent Burgundy; the German asks if he can make the after-dinner speech; and the Englishman clasps his hands together and says: "Please, God, let me die before the German starts."

The ambitious coach of a girls' athletics team starts giving his squad steroids. Their performance soars, and they go on to win the county and national championships. The day after the nationals, Penelope, a 16-year-old hurdler, comes into his office.

"I have a problem," she says, "Hair's starting to grow on my chest."

"Oh my God!" yells the coach. "How far down does it go?"

"Down to my balls," she replies.

Two peanuts walk into a bar.
One was a salted.

The other night I ate at a real family restaurant.
  Every table had an argument going.

What's black and white and eats like a horse?
  A zebra.

Have you noticed since everyone has a camcorder these days,
no one talks about seeing UFOs like they used to.

Two drums and a symbol fall off a cliff.
  Ba-boom, tsshhh.

Maurice Gibb dies. Doctors say it was a TRAGEDY. He only had
a NIGHT FEVER and they had every faith in him STAYING ALIVE.

What's the difference between a mechanic and a herd of
elephants?
  The mechanic charges more.

What do you call a supermodel with a swollen toe?
  A golf club.

An Aussie walks into his bedroom with a sheep under his arm
and says: "Darling, this is the pig I have sex with when you
have a headache."
  His girlfriend, lying in bed, says: "I think you'll find that's a
sheep."
  The man replies: "I think you'll find I wasn't talking to you."

How many men do you need for a Mafia funeral?
  Just one. To slam the car boot shut.

Scientists have discovered a food that diminishes a woman's sex drive by 90 per cent: it's called a wedding cake.

How do you get a twinkle in a blonde's eye?
  Shine a flashlight in her ear.

A set of jump leads walks into a bar. The barman says, "I'll serve you, just don't start anything."

How is sex like air?
  It's not a big deal unless you're not getting any.

What do you get when you mix a laxative with holy water?
  A religious movement.

A man applies for a job in a Florida lemon grove but seems to have no experience whatsoever.

  The foreman is puzzled and asks the man, "I'm not sure that I can employ you because you just don't have the experience. Have you ever picked lots of lemons before?"

  At this the man gets up and shouts, "What are you talking about? Don't you recognize me? I'm Harry Redknapp!"

The Prime Minister was out walking on a beautiful snowy day, when he saw that somebody had urinated on the Downing Street lawn to spell out "The PM is a d*ckhead". Infuriated, he called on the secret service to figure out who had done it. In a few hours, they came to him and told him that there was some bad news and some worse news.

"The bad news is that the urine is from the Chancellor."

"Al? How could he do this to me? What could be worse than this?"

"The handwriting is your wife's."

An efficiency expert concludes his lecture with a note of caution.

"You need to be careful about trying these techniques at home," he says.

"Why?" asks a man in the audience.

"I watched my wife's routine at breakfast for years," the expert explains. "She made lots of trips between the fridge, cooker, table and cabinets, often carrying a single item at a time. One day I told her, 'Honey, why don't you try carrying several things at once?'"

"Did it save time?" the guy in the audience asked.

"Actually, yes," replies the expert. "It used to take her 30 minutes to make breakfast. Now I do it in ten."

A pompous priest is seated next to a redneck on a flight across the US. After the plane is airborne, drink orders are taken.

"I'll have a Jack Daniels and Coke," says the redneck.

When it's the priest's turn to place his order he looks at the redneck in disgust and says, "I'd rather be savagely ravaged by brazen whores than let alcohol touch these lips."

The redneck hands his drink back to the flight attendant and says, "Me, too. I didn't realize we had a choice!"

A funeral service is being held for a woman who has recently died. Right at the end of the service the bearers pick up the coffin and begin to carry it to where it will enter the cremation chamber and get burned. As they turn a corner in the chapel the coffin hits the wall and there is a loud, audible "OUCH!" from inside it. They drop the casket to the floor and it turns out that, wonder of all wonders, the woman is actually alive. The woman lives for two more years and then dies – for real this time. Everyone goes through the same ceremony but this time, as the bearers round the corner, the woman's husband shouts out, "Careful, you lot: watch out for the wall!"

A man goes to a barbershop for a shave. While the barber is lathering him up, he mentions the problems he has getting a close shave around the cheeks.

"I have just the thing," says the barber, taking a small wooden ball from a nearby drawer. "Just place this between your cheek and gum."

The man places the ball in his mouth and the barber proceeds with the closest shave the man has ever experienced.

After a few strokes, the client asks in garbled speech, "But what if I swallow it?"

"No problem," says the barber. "Just bring it back tomorrow like everyone else does."

A man goes to his doctor with a banana stuck in each ear and grapes stuck up his nose. He tells the doctor, "I feel terrible."

The doctor replies, "Of course you do; you're not eating properly."

Two guys are trying to get in a quick eighteen holes, but there are two terrible lady golfers in front of them hitting the ball everywhere but where it's supposed to go.

The first guy says, "Why don't you go over and ask if we can play through?" The second guy gets about halfway there and comes back, not really running but walking quite fast. The first guy says, "What's wrong?"

His friend catches his breath then says: "One of these two women is my wife and the other one is my mistress. There is no way I could be seen with both of them! You'll have to go."

The first guy laughs: "Yes, I can see that could be a problem! You're right, I'll go over." He gets about halfway there and comes back. The second guy says, "What's wrong?"

"Small world," the first guy says with an apologetic grin.

A man goes to the doctor with a piece of lettuce up his nose.

"That looks nasty," says the doctor.

"Nasty?" replies the man. "That's just the tip of the iceberg..."

Why did King Kong join the army?

He wanted to know about gorilla warfare.

A farmer is in court fighting for a large insurance claim following a serious road accident he didn't cause. He is being questioned by the insurance company's lawyer and is being given a hard time because of his conflicting statements.

The lawyer asks, "So, Farmer Brown; you are trying to claim substantial damages from the person you claim caused the accident, yet I have a sworn statement from the police officer who was present at the scene claiming that when asked how you were feeling immediately following the accident you said, and I quote, 'I'm fine, officer; in fact I've never felt better in my life!'"

There is a gasp around the courtroom. "Now, is this or is this not true, Farmer Brown?" continues the brief.

"Well, yes, but...' the farmer starts, but he is interrupted by the barrister: "Just a simple yes or no answer will suffice, Farmer Brown."

"Yes," says Farmer Brown.

After a while, it was the turn of the lawyer for the farmer's insurance to question him. "So, Farmer Brown, tell us the exact circumstances surrounding your statement of good health that my learned friend just made you discuss," the barrister says to the farmer.

"Well, sir, as I was trying to say," Farmer Brown explains, "I had just had this horrific accident and I was lying in the middle of the road injured. My horse had been injured too, and so had my dog. So, after a little while a policeman comes up to the horse, sees it struggling for life and shoots it. Then he walks over to my dog, hears it howling and shoots it. Then he walks over to me, bleeding on the floor, and says, 'How are you, sir?' Now what the hell would you have said in those circumstances?"

A farmer decides it's time to get a new cock to look after his hens. The old one is a bit of a ragbag and, despite doing a reasonable job, the farmer figures he hasn't got all that long to go, so he may as well replace him sooner rather than later. He buys a new cock and lets him out in the barnyard to mix it up with the hens and sort it out with the old rooster. Now, the old rooster is pretty wise, and not the sort to take anything lying down, so he thinks to himself, "I'll have the last laugh here: I'm not ready to become Chicken McNuggets quite yet." So he walks up to the new cock and says, "So you think you're good enough to take over, then, do you? Well, I'll tell you what: instead of fighting and all that stuff, if you can beat me in a simple running race – just ten times around that old hen-house – I'll just leave quietly and not cause any fuss at all. I'll leave all the hens to you." "Old man, you've got yourself a deal", says the young rooster, puffing himself up and checking himself out in a mirror. "I'll even tell you what", continues the youngster with growing confidence, "you can have a half-lap head start – I know I'm going to win, after all!"

So the race starts with the old rooster a good half-lap in front of the younger one. The old one has still got some strength left so he keeps good pace for the first lap – he's not lost any distance. By the end of the second lap he is flagging just a little and by the end of the third the young rooster is noticeably gaining on him. By the time the fourth lap is over the old cock's lead has slipped seriously and at the end of the fifth the younger rooster can reach out and touch the older one. Still they run. At this point the farmer hears some noise from the chicken run. He walks out of the house, does a double-take, runs back in again and comes out with his shotgun. He stands and looks at the two roosters running for all they are worth around the hen-house, takes aim and BANG! blows the young rooster away. As he turns and walks away he mutters to himself, "Unbelievable: that's the third gay rooster I've bought in as many weeks!"

A 75-year-old golfer comes back home after a game. "How was your golf game, dear?" asked his wife. "Well, I was hitting pretty well, but my eyesight's gotten so bad I couldn't see where the ball went," the man said, sounding dejected.

"You are seventy-five years old, Jack," said his wife gently. "I'll tell you what: why don't you take my brother Scott along?"

"But he's 85 and doesn't even play golf anymore," protested Jack.

"Yes, but he's got perfect eyesight. He could watch your ball for you,' Tracy pointed out. The next day Jack teed off with Scott looking on. Jack swung, and the ball disappeared down the middle of the fairway.

"Do you see it?" asked Jack.

"Yup," Scott answered.

"Well, where is it?" yelled Jack, peering off into the distance.

"I forgot."

A tourist in Egypt gets chatting to a man in a bar.

"What do you do for a living," asks the traveller.

"I'm a camel castrator," replies the Egyptian.

"Really? How do you go about castrating a camel?" asks the bewildered tourist.

"Well," says the man, "you go behind him and spread his legs. Then you take a big rock in each hand and smack his testicles between the rocks."

"Bugger me! That must hurt," asks the tourist.

"Not if you keep your thumbs out of the way."

At the start of World War One, a father tells his son he has to go and fight for his country. Nodding, his son asks his father to bring him back a German helmet from the battlefields. "You know," says the boy, "one with a spike on top."

And so weeks later the man is out on the mud-soaked fields of Flanders when he spies a German helmet lying in the mud. Bending down to pick it up, he finds it stuck fast; as he grasps the spike for a better grip, he realizes there is a German soldier still attached to it.

"If you pull me out of ze dirt, you can take me prisoner," says the soldier, through the mud.

"If I pull you out," says the Brit, "can I have your helmet for my son?"

"Ja – be my guest!" the German replies.

But, after half an hour, he's still only managed to get the Kraut out up to the waist. "I'm bloody knackered," he says, catching his breath.

"Vud it help," replies the German soldier, "if I took my feet out of ze stirrups?"

A man walks into a bar with a roll of tarmac under his arm and says, "Pint please, and one for the road."

A man approaches a beautiful woman in a supermarket and asks, "You know, I've lost my wife here in the supermarket. Can you talk to me for a couple of minutes?"

"Why?" she asks.

"Because every time I talk to a beautiful woman, my wife appears out of nowhere."

What's another name for push-up bras?
False advertising.

Four blokes are making the most of a fine Sunday with a round of golf. During the fourth hole they discuss how they actually got away from their wives for the day.

First bloke: "You have no idea what I had to do to be able to come out golfing this weekend. I had to promise my wife that I'll paint every room in the house next weekend."

Second bloke: "That's nothing, I had to promise my wife that I'd build her a new deck for the pool."

Third bloke: "Man, you both have it easy! I had to promise my wife that I'd remodel the kitchen for her."

They continue to play the hole when they realized that the fourth bloke hasn't said a word. So they ask him. "You haven't said anything about what you had to do to be able to come golfing this weekend. What's the deal?"

The fourth bloke replies: "I just set my alarm for 5:30 am. When it goes off I give the wife a nudge and say, 'Golf course or intercourse?' So she says: 'Remember to wear your sweater, dear.'"

A tour bus driver is driving with a coach load of OAPs when he is tapped on his shoulder by a little old lady. She offers him a handful of peanuts, which he gratefully munches up. After about 15 minutes, she taps him on his shoulder again and she hands him another handful of peanuts.

When she is about to hand him another batch again he asks her: "Why don't you eat the peanuts yourself?"

"We can't chew them because we've no teeth", she replied. "We just love the chocolate around them."

A tiny zoo in Suffolk is given a very rare species of gorilla by an eccentric explorer. After a couple of weeks, the gorilla starts to go wild: it won't eat, can't sleep, becomes violent and causes all sorts of problems. The zoo owner calls the vet in who determines that the gorilla is a female and, what's more, she's on heat. The only way to calm her down is to have someone mate with her. Sadly, there are no other gorillas of her species in captivity, so another solution will have to be found. It is then that the owner remembers Jimmy, the cage cleaner. Jimmy is a bit dumb but he has a reputation for having sex with anything, so the owner decides to offer him a proposition: would he like to have sex with the gorilla for £500? Jimmy says he's interested, but that he'll need the night to think it over. The next day he says he'd be willing and that he'd accept the offer, but only if the owner meets three conditions. "First" he says, "I don't want to kiss her on the lips." The owner says that's fine. "Second" Jimmy says, "You must never, ever tell anyone about this." That's fine, the owner says again. "And third," says Jimmy, "I'm going to need another week to come up with the money.

Standing at a urinal, a man notices a midget is watching him. The man doesn't feel uncomfortable until the midget drags a small stepladder over to him, climbs it, and proceeds to admire his privates close up. "Wow!" says the little fella. "I bet you don't have any problem with the ladies."

Surprised and flattered, the man thanks the midget and starts to move away. But the little man stops him. "I know this is a strange request, but can I take a closer look?"

Before the man can stop him, the wee man reaches out and tightly grabs the man's testicles. "OK," he shouts. "Hand over your wallet or I'll jump."

A priest was driving along and saw a nun on the side of the road. He stopped and offered her a lift which she accepted.

She got in and crossed her legs, forcing her gown to open and reveal a lovely leg.

The priest had a look and nearly had an accident. After controlling the car, he stealthfully slid his hand up her leg. The nun looked at him and immediately said, "Father, remember psalm 129?"

The priest was flustered and apologized profusely. He forced himself to remove his hand. However, he was unable to remove his eyes from her leg. Further on while changing gear, he let his hand slide up her leg again. The nun once again said, "Father, remember psalm 129?"

Once again the priest apologized. "Sorry Sister, but the flesh is weak." Arriving at the convent, the nun got out, gave him a meaningful glance and went on her way. On his arrival at the church, the priest rushed to retrieve a bible and looked up psalm 129. It said, "Go forth and seek, further up you will find glory."

Moral: Always be well informed in your job, or you might miss a great opportunity.

An Olympic relay champion is given a box of brand new Olympic condoms upon leaving the Games. Once he's home, he tells his girlfriend about his haul of rubbers.

"Olympic condoms? What makes them so special?"

"There are three colours," he replies. "Gold, silver and bronze."

"What colour are you going to try tonight?" she asks.

"Gold, of course," he replies.

"Why don't you wear silver?" says his girlfriend. "It would be nice if you came second for a change."

Two best friends crash their plane in a desert. Ten days later, hunger finally gets them. John pulls down his pants and says, "I am cutting my dick off so that I will have something to eat." "Think about your sexy wife," says Mike. "Why the hell should I think about my wife?" blasts John. "Well, I thought we might have enough meat for two if you thought about your wife," replies Mike.

A woman meets a gorgeous man in a bar. They talk, they connect, they end up leaving together. They get back to his place and as he shows her around his apartment, she notices that his bedroom is completely packed with sweet cuddly teddy bears. Hundreds of cute little bears on a shelf all the way along the floor. Cuddly medium sized ones on a shelf a little higher and huge enormous bears on the top shelf along the wall.

The woman is a bit surprised that a man would have such a collection of teddy bears, especially one so extensive, but she decides not to mention this to him and is actually quite impressed that he can so freely express his sensitive side.

She turns to him, they kiss and then they rip each other's clothes off and make hot steamy love. After an intense night of passion with this sensitive man they are lying together in the afterglow, the woman leans in to him and whispers, "Well, how was it?"

The man says: "Not bad, help yourself to any prize from the bottom shelf."

Three blokes, an Englishman, a Frenchman and a Welshman, are out walking along the beach. They come across a lantern and a genie pops out of it. "I will give you each one wish!" cries the genie.

The Welshman says, "I'm a farmer, my dad was a farmer, and my son will also farm. I want the land to be forever fertile in Wales."

With a blink of the genie's eye, 'FOOM' – the land in Wales is for ever made fertile for farming.

The Frenchman is amazed, "I want a wall around France, so that no one can invade our precious country," he says.

Again, with a blink of the genie's eye, 'FOOM' – there is a huge wall around France.

The Englishman asks, "I'm very curious. Please tell me more about this wall."

The genie explains, "Well, it's about 150 feet high, 50 feet thick and nothing can get in or out."

The Englishman says, "Fill it up with water."

A man goes to the doctor with a strange problem. "Doctor, whenever I break wind there is no smell at all. It's really strange and no matter what I eat, I get the same result – no smell whatsoever!" The doctor has a cursory investigation and then asks the man if he can possibly break wind there and then. The man drops his trousers and pants and farts extremely loudly. The doctor sniffs at the air a couple of times and immediately says, "Oh yes, this is a common one. I know exactly what the problem is," and he walks out of the room. He comes straight back with a six-foot pole with a large brass hook on the end. "Jesus Christ, doctor; what the hell are you going to do with that pole?" asks the man.

"I'm going to open the bloody window," says the doctor, "You've got a blocked nose!"

Nikos, a Greek man, was sitting in a bar talking to a young tourist. "So," he says, "you see that wall out there in that field?" He points to a huge stone wall separating two fields. "Can you see how well it's built? I spent a year of my life moving stones from down in the valley up to those pastures and carving them so they fitted. That's the strongest fence between here and Athens! And do they call me Nikos the wall-builder? No; they do not!"

Then he continues, "So, you see the bar here? The one you are leaning on right now?" and he raps it with his knuckles. "Can you see how well it's built? I spent a year of my life cutting and sanding and waxing this bar. This is the finest bar between here and Athens! And do they call me Nikos the bar-builder? No, they do not!"

Then he continues, "So, you see the pier out there in the water?" He points to a long, solid pier that stretches out into the deep, deep water. "I spent a year of my life putting that pier together. I cut down the trees, I nailed the boards and I dug the holes for the poles. It almost killed me, and it is the finest pier between here and Athens! And do they call me Nikos the pier-builder? No, they do not!" Then he looks around and checks the bar before he continues, "So I fuck ONE lousy sheep...!"

A cowboy rides into town. He has a big black stallion, a large stetson hat and two shining silver pistols. He ties his stallion to the hitching post and enters the saloon.

He walks straight up to the bar and orders two shots of whiskey, which he quickly necks. Then he looks around and sees that his horse has been stolen.

He says, "If my horse isn't returned within ten seconds, the same thing will happen here that happened in Dodge City."

Everyone in the saloon gasps, and ten seconds later the horse trots back up outside the saloon. Another cowboy steps up to the bar and asks: "Just what did happen in Dodge City, mister?"

The cowboy replies, "I had to walk home."

A man decided he wanted to become a hunter, so he set about getting himself all the equipment. Last on his list was a dog, so he went off to see the local dog breeder. The dog breeder took him out to the woods with the dog so the man could see what a top hunting dog it was. The dog breeder snapped his fingers at the dog and shouted, "GO!" The dog ran off at top speed and they could hear much crashing in the undergrowth. The dog came running back, out of breath, and barked once. "What does that mean?" said the man. "One bark means that the dog saw one rabbit in the woods," said the dog breeder. The man thought this was cool, but that he'd better see it again in case it was a scam. Again, the dog merchant snapped his fingers and shouted, "GO!" The dog ran off at top speed and they could hear more crashing of undergrowth. The dog came running back, out of breath, and barked twice. "What does that mean?" said the man. "Two barks mean that the dog saw two rabbits in the woods," said the dog breeder. The man asked to see it one more time, and the dog breeder snapped his fingers at the dog and shouted, "GO!"

The dog disappeared again, but this time he came back carrying a stick and began to hump the dog breeder's leg. "What the hell does that mean?" asked the man, astonished. "Well, that means he just saw more fucking rabbits than you can shake a stick at!"

A man and a woman meet at a bar. They get along so well that they decide to go to the woman's house. A few drinks later, the man takes off his shirt and then washes his hands. He then takes off his trousers and washes his hands again. The woman has been watching him and says, "You must be a dentist." The man, surprised, says, "Yes! How did you work that out?" "Easy," she replied, "you keep washing your hands." One thing led to another and they make love. After, the woman says, "You must be a good dentist." The man, now with boosted ego, asks, "Sure, but how did you work it out?" The woman replies, "I didn't feel a thing."

If computer manufacturers made toasters:

Every time you bought a fresh loaf of bread, you would have to buy a toaster, or at least renew your licence for it.

Toaster 98 would weigh 15,000 pounds (hence requiring a steel-reinforced worktop), draw enough electricity to power Birmingham, take up 95 per cent of the space in your kitchen and would claim to be the first toaster which lets you control how light or dark you want your toast to be.

This toaster would secretly interrogate your other appliances to find out who made them and send the details back to Microsoft.

It would have a protection device that will not let you toast bread.

It will give you advice you don't need, such as "Don't put your hand in the boiling water, only pasta," and would monitor your behaviour in the kitchen to record your bread-related habits to serve you better.

It would have a reset button, the only place worn out in an otherwise shiny toaster.

Everyone would hate toasters, but nonetheless would buy them since most of the good bread only works with their toasters.

While attending a convention, three psychiatrists take a walk. "People are always coming to us with their guilt and fears," one says, "but we have no one to go to with our problems. Since we're all professionals, why don't we listen to each other?"

The first psychiatrist confesses, "I'm a compulsive gambler and deeply in debt, so I overcharge patients as often as I can."

The second admits, "I have a drug problem that's out of control, and I frequently pressure my patients into buying illegal drugs for me."

The third psychiatrist says, "I just can't keep a secret."

A coachload of OAPs is out on a day trip travelling around the country. Suddenly, without warning, one of the old ladies leaps into the air. "I've just been molested!" she screams.

The coach driver stops the coach, "But we're down a country lane in the middle of nowhere!" he says. "Did any one else see anything?"

All the other old folk on the coach shake their heads, and as things settle down the driver heads off again.

A couple of miles along the road, the same old lady leaps into the air, "I've been molested again! Stop the coach!"

This time, the driver, wondering if she might be a little bit senile, walks back to her seat and has a look underneath.

To his amazement, there's an old, bald chap curled up in the footwell, squinting up at him.

"What the hell are you doing?" asks the driver.

"I haven't got my glasses and I'm looking for my toupée," the old geezer replies, "I almost had it twice, but it got away both times!"

On the farm lived a chicken and a horse who loved playing together. One day, the horse fell into a bog and began to sink. So off the chicken ran to get help. Running around, he spied the farmer's new Harley motorbike. Finding the keys in the ignition, the chicken sped off with some rope hoping he had time to save his friend's life. After tying one end to the horse and the other to the rear of the bike, the chicken drove forward and, with the aid of the powerful bike, rescued the horse.

A few weeks later, the chicken fell into a mud pit and soon he too began to sink. The chicken cried out to the horse to save his life. The horse thought a moment, walked over and straddled the large puddle. He told the chicken to grab his "thing" and he would lift him out. The chicken got a good grip with its beak and the horse pulled him up and out, saving his life.

Moral? When you're hung like a horse, you don't need a Harley to pick up chicks.

A brunette, redhead and blonde went to a fitness spa for some fun and relaxation. After a stimulating healthy lunch, all three decided to visit the ladies' room and found a strange-looking woman sitting at the entrance who said: "Welcome to the ladies' room. Be sure to check out our newest feature: a mirror which, if you look into it and say something truthful, will reward you with a wish. But be warned, if you say something false, you will be sucked into the mirror and live in an black, empty void for all eternity!"

The three women quickly entered and upon finding the mirror, the brunette said, "I think I'm the most beautiful of us three," and in an instant she was surrounded by a pile of money.

The redhead stepped up and said, "'I think I'm the most talented of us three," and she suddenly found the keys to a brand new Jaguar in her hands.

Excited over the possibility of having a wish come true, the blonde looked into the mirror and said, "I think..." and was promptly sucked into the mirror.

A man walks into a pub with a neck brace, orders a pint and asks the landlord, "Who's in the lounge?"

The landlord replies, "There's 15 people playing darts."

The man says, "Get them a pint, too." Then he asks, "Who's upstairs?"

The landlord replies, "150 people at the disco."

The man says, "Get them pints too."

"That'll be £328, please," says the landlord.

The man replies, "Sorry, I haven't got that much money on me."

The landlord remarks, "If you were at the pub down the road, they'd have broken your neck."

"Just been there," says the man.

A soldier arrives in a small town late one night and cannot find a free hotel room, until a manager takes pity on his tired state and tells him: "Well, I may have something. There is this guy who comes here on business and he always sleeps in the same room. He's snoring so much we have to put him apart from the other guests, but there's a spare bed in his room."

"That's fine: I'll take it," says the soldier, relieved.

"But what about the snoring? Let me tell you, this man snores very loudly!"

"I'll deal with the snoring: trust me."

The manager leads the soldier to the room. Indeed, the guy's snores can be heard two corridors away. The soldier thanks the manager and enters the room.

The following morning, he goes to pay the bill.

"So, did you have a good night's sleep after all?" the manager sneers.

"Never better: you run a very good hotel," the soldier replies.

"How did you manage to sleep through the snoring?" the manager asks, baffled.

"The guy didn't snore!"

"How come?"

"It's quite simple," the soldier explained. "'Just before going to bed I woke him up, kissed him on the cheek and said, 'Goodnight, beautiful'. He spent the whole night awake watching me."

Why do the French never play hide-and-seek?
   Nobody wants to look for them.

A priest thinks his sermons need modernizing a bit, so he decides to preach on waterskiing instead of the usual fire and brimstone or condemnation of sex. He tells his wife, who thinks it's a great idea despite the priest's inexperience with the subject matter, but is sorry she won't be able to hear his new-style sermon because she has a sick friend to see. On his way to church the priest has second thoughts. "I don't know a thing about waterskiing and I can't relate it to anything," he said to himself. "I'll just stick to what I know," and proceeded to preach his usual sermon on the sinfulness of sex. After the service, and before the priest gets home, one of the lay readers walks past the priest's house. The priest's wife is back and out doing some gardening. "Great sermon today," says the lay reader. "That's a surprise," said the wife, "because he only tried it twice, and he fell off both times!"

The General arrived at his office on a Sunday morning and discovered that none of his private aides was there. Grimly, he remembered it had been one aide's birthday party the previous evening and he had no doubt as to what condition they were in.

At around ten o'clock, five aides arrived, unshaved and in rather piteous attire. They salute as smartly as they can and brace themselves for the General's grilling.

"I presume you were at Smith's birthday party last night, weren't you?"

"Sir, yes, Sir," one aide answers.

"And you couldn't get up early enough this morning to get to the office because you were too drunk!' thundered the General.

"Er, no, sir," the aide said timidly, looking at his friends.

"So what is your excuse, young man?" the General wondered, sitting down, a dangerous, vicious smile on his lips.

"I can explain. You see, we did run a little late, I admit.

We ran to the bus but we missed it; we hailed a cab but it broke down; we found a farm and bought eight horses but they dropped dead; we ran ten miles, and now we're here. It's just a logistical problem, really, General, Sir!"

The General eyed him suspiciously, but as he hadn't heard such a good one for a long time, he let the men go. An hour later, the last aide showed up, in the same dishevelled state.

"Sorry, Sir,' he said. "I ran late; tried to catch a bus but missed it; I hailed a cab but..."

"Let me guess,' the General interrupted. 'The cab broke down, so you bought a horse in a farm but it died on you, so you ran for ten miles. Do you really think I'm going to swallow this?"

"Er, no, Sir; you see, there were so many dead horses on the way that it took for ever to go around them."

One of Bill Gates' marketing assistants approached an applicant in a market research panel and said, "Excuse me. If Microsoft made a version of Windows which only crashed once a year, would you buy it?"

The customer's eyes glistened and he seemed to be making the sign of the cross: "Oh, yes!"

The marketing assistant carried on: "... and if Microsoft made a version of Windows which crashed every five minutes?"

The customer glared at him and said, "And what kind of customer do you think I am?"

"We've already established that," the guy said. "We're just haggling over the frequency."

One day, a mechanic was working under a car when some brake fluid accidentally dripped into his mouth. "Wow," said the mechanic to himself. "That stuff tastes good."

The following day, he told his mate about his discovery. "It tastes great," said the mechanic. "I think I'll try a little more today."

The next day, the mechanic told his mate he'd drunk a pint of the stuff. His friend was worried but didn't say anything until the next day, when the mechanic revealed he'd drunk two pints.

"Don't you know that brake fluid is toxic? It's really bad for you," said his mate.

"I know what I'm doing," snapped the mechanic. "I can stop any time I want to."

A man goes to the doctor complaining of a terrible bad breath.

"I've tried everything, doctor," he says, nearly in tears. "I changed toothpaste ten times, tried mints, mouthwash, you name it. I can't get rid of this terrible odour."

The nods and asks the guy to get undressed. After a thorough examination, he allows him to put his clothes back on.

"You seem to have a rash around your anus. We will have to treat this first. In the meantime, try not to chew your fingernails."

A wife and her husband were having a dinner party for some important guests. The wife was very excited about this and wanted everything to be perfect. At the very last minute, she realized that she didn't have any snails for the dinner party, so she asked her husband to run down to the beach with the bucket to gather some snails.

Very grudgingly he agreed. He took the bucket, walked out the door, down the steps and out to the park. As he was collecting the snails, he noticed a beautiful woman strolling alongside the path. He kept thinking to himself, "Wouldn't it be great if she would even just come down and talk to me?" He went back to gathering the snails. All of a sudden he looked up and the beautiful woman was standing right over him. They started talking and she invited him back to her place. They ended up spending the night together.

At seven o'clock the next morning he woke up and exclaimed, "Oh no! My wife's dinner party!" He gathered all his clothes, put them on real fast, grabbed his bucket and ran out the door.

He ran from the park all the way to his first floor apartment. He was in such a hurry that when he got to the top of the stairs, he dropped the bucket of snails. There were snails all down the stairs. The door opened just then, with a very angry wife standing in the doorway, wondering where he's been all this time.

He looked at the snails all down the steps, then he looked at her, then back at the snails and said, "Come on guys, we're almost there!"

A man goes to his doctor for a complete check-up. Afterwards, the doctor comes out with the results. "I'm afraid I have some bad news," says the doctor. "You don't have much time."

"Oh, no; that's terrible. How long have I got?" the man asks.

"Ten," says the doctor.

"Ten what? Months? Weeks?"

"Nine..." continues the doctor.

The Chief Rabbi challenges the Pope to a game of golf.

The Pope then meets with the College of Cardinals to discuss the proposal. "Your Holiness," says one of the Cardinals, "I am afraid that this would tarnish our image in the world. You're terrible at golf."

"Don't we have a Cardinal to represent me?" says the Pope.

"There is a man named Jack Nicklaus, an American golfer, who is a devout Catholic. We can arrange to make him a Cardinal, and then ask him to play as your personal representative," says the Cardinal.

Of course, Nicklaus is honoured, and he agrees to play as a representative of the Pope.

The day after the match, Nicklaus reports to the Vatican to inform the Pope of the result. "I have some good news and some bad news, Your Holiness," says Nicklaus.

"Tell me the good news, Cardinal Nicklaus," says the Pope.

"Well, Your Holiness, I don't like to brag, but even though I have played some terrific rounds of golf in my life, this was the best I have ever played, by far. I must have been inspired from above."

"How can there be bad news, then?" the Pope asks.

"I lost by three strokes to Rabbi Woods," replies Nicklaus.

A husband and wife went to see a European 'art' movie at their local cinema. It's pretty strong stuff and involves a lot of graphic sex – all in the name of art of course. The husband thinks it's great but the wife is a bit disturbed by the content, particularly by a scene of people masturbating which left nothing to the imagination. As the couple are having a drink afterwards, the wife says to her husband, "You know dear, I find it very difficult to deal with masturbation in the movies," to which the husband replies, "Oh, sorry love, I'll stop doing it then!"

One of the main host computers of a very busy internal network went down, bringing down with it half the intranet of the building which depended on it. The network in-house engineer soon gave up and told his boss to call for a specialist.

The specialist arrived, had a talk with the engineer, then took one look at the computer and nodded thoughtfully. He then opened his briefcase, produced a small rubber hammer and, his ear stuck to the computer case, hit a spot softly, after which the system did a kind of 'Wooosh' noise and restarted straight away.

Two days later the office manager received a bill from the consultant for £2,000.

Immediately he called the engineer's agency and exclaimed, 'Two thousand pounds for fixing that computer? You were only here five minutes! I want the bill itemized!'

The next day the new bill arrived. It read, 'Tapping computer with hammer: £1'

'Knowing where to tap: £1,999'.

A man walks into a pub with a small doll in his hand and says to the barmaid, "What's this?"

He then pokes the doll in the stomach and a man in the corner of the pub screams. Without saying a word, the man then leaves.

The next day, the man walks back in the pub at the same time, and says to the same barmaid, "What's this?"

He pokes the doll in the stomach as before and, once again, a man in the corner screams.

As the man is about to leave again, the barmaid shouts, "I don't know; what is it?"

"Déja voodoo," replies the man.

Australian Etiquette Guide

General rules:
1. Never take a beer to a job interview.
2. Don't burn rubber while travelling in a funeral procession.
3. It's tacky to take an esky to church.
4. Even if you're certain you're included in the will, it's rude to take the trailer to the funeral home.

Dining:
1. When decanting wine from the box, tilt the paper cup and pour slowly so as not to 'bruise' the wine.
2. A centrepiece for the table should never be anything prepared by a taxidermist.

Personal hygiene:
1. While ears need to be cleaned regularly, this should be done in private, using one's OWN car keys.
2. Dirt and grease under the fingernails is a no-no, as they detract from a woman's jewellery and alter the taste of finger foods.

Dating (outside the family):
1. Always offer to bait your date's hook, especially on the first date.
2. Establish with her parents what time she's expected back. Some will say "10pm", others might say "Monday." If the latter is the answer, it's the man's responsibility to get her to school on time.

Theatre etiquette:
1. Crying babies should be taken to the lobby and picked up after the movie has ended.
2. Refrain from talking to characters on the screen. Tests have proven they can't hear you.

Weddings:

1. Livestock is a poor choice for a wedding gift.
2. For the groom, at least, rent a tux. A tracksuit with a cummerbund and a clean football jumper can create a tacky appearance.
3. Though uncomfortable, say "yes" to socks and shoes for the occasion.

Driving:

1. Dim your headlights for approaching vehicles, even if the gun's loaded and the kangaroo is in sight.
2. Never tow another car using panty hose and duct tape.
3. When sending your wife down the road with a petrol can, it's impolite to ask her to bring back beer, too.

An Essex girl was driving down the A13 when her car phone rang.

It was her boyfriend, urgently warning her, "Treacle, I just heard on the news that there's a car going the wrong way on the A13. Please be careful!"

"It's not just one car!" said the Essex girl. "There's hundreds of them!"

A man walks into a pub holding a turtle. The turtle has two bandaged legs, a black eye and his shell is held together with duct tape. The landlord asks, "What's wrong with your turtle?" "Nothing," the man responds. "This turtle's very fast. Have your dog stand at the end of the bar. Then go and stand at the other end of the room and call him. Before that mutt reaches you, my turtle will be there." So the landlord, wanting to see this, sets his dog at one side of the room. Then he goes to the other side and calls him. Suddenly, the guy picks up his bandaged turtle and throws it across the room, narrowly missing the landlord and smashing it into the wall. "Told you!"

Two mice walk into a bar for a few ales when a giraffe walks in.

"Look at that. She's a beauty," says one mouse.

"Well, why not try your luck?" his friend suggests.

So the mouse goes over to the giraffe and starts talking to her, and within five minutes they're out the door and gone into the night.

Next day, the second mouse is in the bar drinking away, when his friend staggers in. The mouse is absolutely stuffed, worn out, ruined, an ex-mouse.

The mouse helps his pal up on to a stool, pours a drink down his throat and asks: "What the hell happened to you? I saw you leave with the giraffe: what happened after that? Was she all right?"

The first mouse says: "Yeah, she was really something else. We went out to dinner, had a couple of glasses of wine and she invited me back to her place to spend the night. And oh, man! I've never had a night like it!"

"But how come you look like you're so exhausted?"

"Well', says the mouse, "between the kissing and the screwing, I must have run a thousand miles!"

A retired corporate executive decides to take a holiday. He books himself on a Caribbean cruise and proceeds to have the time of his life – that is, until the ship sinks. He finds himself on an island with no other people, no supplies, nothing. After about four months, he is lying on the beach when the most gorgeous woman he has ever seen rows up to the shore.

In disbelief, he asks, "Where did you come from? How did you get here?"

She replies, "I rowed from the other side of the island. I landed here when my cruise ship sank."

"Amazing," he notes. "You were really lucky to have a row boat wash up with you."

"Oh, this thing?" explains the woman. "I made the boat out

of raw material I found on the island. The oars were whittled from gum tree branches. I wove the bottom from palm branches, and the sides and stern came from a eucalyptus tree."

"But, where did you get the tools?" asks the amazed castaway.

"Oh, that was no problem," replies the woman. "On the south side of the island, a very unusual stratum of alluvial rock is exposed. I found if I fired it to a certain temperature in my kiln, it melted like iron. I used that for tools and used the tools to make the hardware." The guy is stunned.

"Let's row over to my place," she says. After a few minutes of rowing, she docks the boat at a small wharf. As the man looks to shore, he nearly falls off the boat. Before him is a stone walk leading to an exquisite bungalow painted in blue and white. Trying to hide his continued amazement, the man accepts a drink, and they sit down on her sofa to talk.

"I'm going to slip into something more comfortable," says the woman. She soon returns wearing nothing but vines, strategically positioned. She beckons for him to sit down next to her.

"Tell me," she begins suggestively, "We've been out here for many months. You've been lonely. There's something I'm sure you've been longing for..." She stares into his eyes.

He can't believe what he's hearing. "You mean," he swallows excitedly and tears start to well in his eyes, "you've built a kebab shop?"

One day at a bus stop there's a girl wearing a skin-tight miniskirt.

Just as she's about to get on the bus she realizes that her skirt is so tight she can't lift her foot high enough to reach the first step.

Thinking it will give her enough slack to raise her leg, she reaches back and unzips her skirt a little. However, she can't reach the step, so she reaches back once again to unzip it a little more, but still she can't reach the step. So, with her skirt zipper halfway down, she reaches back and unzips her skirt all the way. Thinking that she can get on the step now, she lifts up her leg, only to realize it's still impossible.

Seeing how embarrassed the girl is, the man standing behind her puts his hands around her waist and lifts her up on to the first step of the bus. The girl turns around furiously and screams, "How dare you touch me that way? I don't even know you!"

Shocked, the man says, "Well, after you reached around and unzipped my fly three times, I figured that we were friends."

A family was given some venison by a friend. The wife cooked up the deer steaks and served them to the husband and children.

The husband thought it would be fun to have his son guess what it was that they were eating.

"Is it beef?" little Eddie asked.

"No. I'll give you a clue," the dad said. "It's what your mum sometimes calls me."

"Is it useless, pathetic loser?" said Eddie.

A policeman in a small town stopped a motorist who was speeding down the High Street. "But officer," the man began, "I can explain."

"Quiet!" snapped the officer. "I'm going to let you spend the night in jail until the sergeant gets back."

"But officer, I just wanted to say..."

"I said be quiet! You're going to jail!"

A few hours later the officer looked in on his prisoner and said, "Lucky for you, the sarge is at his daughter's wedding so he'll be in a good mood when he gets back."

"Don't count on it," answered the bloke in the cell. "I'm the groom."

A man and his wife walk into a dentist's office. The man says to the dentist, "Doc, I'm in one hell of a hurry! I have two mates sitting out in my car waiting for us to go and play golf, so forget about the anaesthetic and just pull the tooth and be done with it. We have a 10am tee time at the best golf course in town and it's 9:30 already. I don't have time to wait for the anaesthetic to work!"

The dentist thinks to himself, "My goodness; this is a brave man asking to have his tooth pulled without using anything to kill the pain." So the dentist asks him, "Which tooth is it, sir?"

The man turns to his wife and says, "Open your mouth and show him, dear."

Sherlock Holmes and Dr. Watson were on a camping trip. They had a bottle of wine and went to bed. A couple hours later Holmes woke up and said: " Watson look up and tell me what you see."

Watson was silent a minute then said... " uh, I see millions and millions of stars."

Holmes replied "... and what does that tell you Watson?"

Watson said, "Well, astrologically I see Leo is in Saturn. Astronomically I see that there are millions of galaxies and potentially billions of planets. Meteorologically I predict it will be a beautiful day tomorrow. Theologically I see God is all powerful and we are small and insignificant."

Holmes after a few moments of disgusted silence said, "Watson, you fool! Some scoundrel has stolen our tent."

A man walks into a pub, orders a beer and begins punching his hand with his finger as if he was dialling a phone.

"What are you doing, mate?" asks the very curious landlord.

"I've had a phone installed in my hand because I was tired of carrying one around," the man answers. "Try it!"

The man dials a number and puts his hand up to the landlord's ear. The owner of the pub across the street picks up and the landlord can't believe it.

"Amazing, eh?" says the man. "Now, where's the gents?"

The landlord tells him, but when the man doesn't come back for over an hour, the landlord goes looking for him. He finds him in the gents, spread-eagled against the wall with his trousers around his ankles and a roll of toilet paper coming out of his underpants.

"My God!" the landlord yells. "Were you mugged?"

The man turns to him and says, "No, I'm fine. Just waiting for a fax."

A motorist screeches to a halt on a garage forecourt, looking for the man who sold him his car.

"Oi!" he shouts at a salesman. "I want a bloody word with you."

"What's the matter, sir?" says the salesman. "Everything OK with your car?"

"No, everything is not OK with my car. I bought this heap on the understanding that it was going to give me good performance and it'll only get to 110 uphill. It's ridiculous."

Taken aback, the salesman says, "Well, excuse me, sir, but I must point out that 110 uphill is very impressive for a car in this class."

"Impressive?" the man yells. "Not when I live at 136 it's not!"

A man walks into a bar with a really trendy new shirt on. The bartender is a woman and she says, "Hey, nice shirt. Really suits you. Where d'you get it?" "Oh, René Kent," comes the reply and the woman is impressed.

Shortly, a man walks into the bar with a really trendy, new pair of trousers on. The bartender says, "Hey, nice trousers. Really suit you. Where d'you get them?" "Oh, René Kent," comes the reply and the woman is impressed. Then another man walks into the bar with a really trendy, new pair of shoes on. The bartender says, "Hey, nice shoes. Really suit you. Where d'you get them?" "Oh, René Kent," comes the reply and the woman is impressed. After a while the door to the bar suddenly bangs open and a man dressed only in his underpants runs in. "Who the hell do you think you are?" asks the bartender. "I'm René Kent!" comes the strained reply.

Little Johnny keeps asking his Dad for a television in his bedroom, to which his Dad keeps saying 'No', but after prolonged nagging, the dad agrees.

Several nights later Johnny comes downstairs and asks, "Dad, what's Love Juice?" Dad is horrified, and after looking at Mum, who's also gobsmacked, proceeds to give his son the dreaded sex talk.

Johnny now sits on sofa with his mouth open in amazement. Dad asks, "So, what is it you've been watching then, son?" Johnny replies, "Wimbledon."

In Jerusalem, a female CNN journalist hears about a very old Jewish man who has been going to the Wailing Wall to pray, twice a day, every day for years. So she goes to check it out. She walks to the Wailing Wall and there he is walking slowly up to the holy site. She watches him pray and after about 45 minutes, when he turns to leave, she approaches him for an interview.

"I'm Rebecca Smith from CNN. Sir, how long have you been coming to the Wailing Wall and praying?" she begins.

"For about 60 years," says the old fella.

"60 years! That's amazing! What do you pray for?"

"I pray for peace between the Muslims and the Jews. I pray for all the hatred to stop and I pray for all our children to grow up in safety and friendship," says the wizened old gent.

"How do you feel after doing this for 60 years?"

"Like I'm talking to a brick wall."

A woman goes to see her GP about something that has been troubling her for some time.

"Doctor, I keep thinking I'm a cartoon character," she says. "One day it's Mickey Mouse, the next it's Donald Duck. This morning I woke up and I was convinced I was Bambi."

"Well," replies the Doc. "It just sounds to me like you're having Disney spells."

An American decided to write a book about famous churches around the world. For his first chapter he decided to write about famous English and Scottish cathedrals. So he bought a plane ticket and made the trip to London, thinking that he would work his way northwards. On his first day, he was inside a church taking photographs when he noticed a golden telephone mounted on the wall with a sign that read '£10,000 per call'.

The American, being intrigued, asked a priest who was strolling by what the telephone was used for. The priest replied that it was a direct line to heaven and that for £10,000 you could talk to God.

The American thanked the priest and went along his way. Next stop was in Salisbury. There, at a very large cathedral, he saw the same golden telephone with the same sign under it. He wondered if this was the same kind of telephone he saw in London and he asked a nearby nun what its purpose was. She told him that it was a direct line to heaven and that for £10,000 he could talk to God. "O.K., thank you," said the American.

He then travelled to Bath, Nottingham, Coventry and Manchester and in every church he saw the same golden telephone with the same "£10,000 per call" sign under it.

With his first chapter going well, he left England and travelled north to Scotland and again at his first stop at St. Giles Cathedral in Edinburgh, there was the same golden telephone, but this time the sign under it read "10p per call."

The American was surprised so he asked the minister about the sign. "Vicar, I've travelled all over England and I've seen this same golden telephone in many cathedrals and churches. I'm told that it is a direct line to heaven, but in all the cities in England the price was £10,000 per call. Why is it so cheap here?" The minister smiled and answered,

"You're in Scotland now my son... it's a local call".

It took Bob a little while to accept the fact that his penis seemed to grow. Of course he was delighted, as was his wife, but it soon grew to an impressive twenty inches and Bob decided it was time to go and see a GP. After an initial examination, the physician explained to the couple that, though rare, Bob's condition could be cured through corrective surgery. "We just have to operate – a simple thing, really – and all will be fine again."

"And how long will Bob be on crutches?" the wife asked anxiously. "Crutches? Why would he need crutches?" the surprised doctor asked. "Well," said the wife suspiciously, "You are planning to lengthen his legs, aren't you?"

A married couple were in a terrible accident where the woman's face was severely burned. The doctor told the husband that they couldn't graft any skin from her body because she was too skinny.

The husband nicely offered to donate some of his own skin. However, the only skin on his body that the doctor felt was suitable would have to come from his buttocks. The husband and wife agreed that they would tell no one about where the skin came from and requested that the doctor also honour their secret. After all, this was a very delicate matter.

After the surgery was completed, everyone was astounded at the woman's new beauty. She looked even more beautiful than she ever had before! All her friends and relatives just went on and on about her youthful beauty!

One day, she was alone with her husband and she was overcome with emotion at his sacrifice. She said, "Dear, I just want to thank you for everything you did for me. There is no way I could never repay you."

"My darling," he replied, "I get all the thanks I need every time I see your mother kiss you on the cheek."

Two young travellers are braving their way across Mexico behind the wheel of an old van, when they come across a group of bandits standing behind a roadblock.

The head honcho walks around to the door, sticks a gun into their faces and says, "Start masturbating, gringos!"

Shocked but fearing for their lives, the pair duly oblige – and, despite the stress, manage to perform. As soon as they've finished the bandit chief leans in and demands "Again!"

They manage a repeat performance, but are then told to continue until, tired and sore, the pair are physically incapable of another erection.

"Good work," smiles the toothless Mexican as a dark figure emerges from the trees. "Now drive my sister into town."

An agent finds out that his top actress client has been moonlighting as an escort. Having long lusted after her, he asks if he can have sex with her later that night. She agrees, but says, "You'll have to pay like everyone else."

The agent agrees and meets the actress at her house that night. After turning out all the lights, they have sex. The actress falls asleep, but ten minutes later, she is awoken and the scene repeats itself. This goes on for the next few hours.

Eventually, the actress screams out, "This is amazing! I never knew agents were so virile."

A voice from the dark replies, "Lady, I'm not your agent. He's at the door selling tickets."

It was Frank's first time at bear-hunting. After some time in the mountains, he spotted a small brown bear and shot it. Just then there was a tap on his shoulder. He turned around to see a big black bear. The bear said: "You've got two choices. I either maul you to death or we have sex." Frank decided to bend over.

Even though he felt sore for two weeks, Frank soon recovered and vowed revenge. He headed out on another trip where he found the black bear and shot it. There was another tap on his shoulder. This time a huge grizzly bear stood right next to him. The grizzly said: "What a huge mistake, Frank. You've got two choices. Either I maul you to death or we'll have rough sex." Again, Frank thought it was better to comply.

Although he survived, it took several months before Frank finally recovered. Outraged, he headed back to the mountains, managed to track down the grizzly and shot it. He felt sweet revenge, but then there was a tap on his shoulder. He turned round to find a giant polar bear standing there. The polar bear said: "Admit it, Frank. You don't come here for the hunting, do you?"

Mary Clancy goes up to Father O'Grady after his Sunday morning service, and she's in tears.

He says, "So what's bothering you, Mary my dear?"

She says, "Oh, Father, I've got terrible news. My husband passed away last night."

The priest says, "Oh, Mary, that's terrible. Tell me, Mary, did he have any last requests?"

She says, "That he did, Father."

The priest says, "What did he ask, Mary?"

She says, "He said, 'Please Mary, put down that damn gun...'"

47

What will history remember Bill Clinton as?
The President after Bush.

What's a bloke's idea of doing housework?
Lifting his leg so you can hoover.

What's the biggest crime committed by transvestites?
Male fraud.

What do you call a hippy's wife?
Mississippi.

How do you make a bear cross?
Nail two of them together.

A husband and wife visit a counsellor after 15 years of marriage.
The counsellor asks them what the problem is and the wife starts ranting, listing every problem they've had during their marriage. She goes on and on and on; suddenly the counsellor gets up, walks around the desk and kisses her passionately. The woman shuts up immediately and sits in a daze. The counsellor turns to the husband and says, "This is what your wife needs at least three times a week. Can you do this?"

The husband thinks for a moment and replies, "Well, I can drop her off here on Mondays and Wednesdays, but on Fridays, I'm out drinking."

These individual quotes were reportedly taken from actual employee performance evaluations. You may want to consider using them for someone you work with...

- Since my last report, this employee has reached rock bottom and has started to dig.

- His men would follow him anywhere, but only out of morbid curiosity.

- I would not allow this employee to breed.

- This employee is really not so much a has-been as a definitely won't be.

- Works well when under constant supervision and cornered like a rat in a trap.

- When she opens her mouth, it seems that it is only to change feet.

- He would be out of his depth in a parking lot puddle.

- This young lady has delusions of adequacy.

- He sets low personal standards and then consistently fails to achieve them.

- This employee is depriving a village somewhere of an idiot.

- This employee should go far, and the sooner he starts, the better.

- Got a full six-pack, but lacks the plastic thing to hold it all together.

- A gross ignoramus – 144 times worse than an ordinary ignoramus.

- He doesn't have ulcers, but he's a carrier.

- I would like to go hunting with him sometime.

- He's been working with glue too much.

- He would argue with a signpost.

- He brings a lot of joy whenever he leaves the room.

- If his IQ ever reaches 50, he should sell.

- If you see two people talking and one looks bored, he's the other one.

- A photographic memory but with the lens cover glued on.

- A prime candidate for natural deselection.

- Donated his brain to science before he was done using it.

- Gates are down, the lights are flashing, but the train isn't coming.

- Has two brains: one is lost and the other is out looking for it.

- If he were any more stupid, he'd have to be watered twice a week.

- If you give him a penny for his thoughts, you'd get change.

- If you stand close enough to him, you can hear the oceans.

- It's hard to believe that he beat out 1,000,000 other sperm.

- One neuron short of a synapse.

- Some drink from the fountain of knowledge; he only gargled.

- The wheel is turning, but the hamster is dead.

A young naval student is asked by an old sea captain: "What would you do if a sudden storm sprang up on the starboard?"

"Throw out an anchor, sir," the student replies promptly.

"And what would you do if a storm sprang up aft?"

"Throw out another anchor, sir," comes back the student.

"And if another terrific storm sprang up forward, what would you do?" says the captain.

"Throw out another anchor," replies the student.

"Hold on," says the captain, "Where are you getting all your anchors from?"

"Same place you're getting your storms, sir."

A man walks into an antiques shop. After a while, he chooses a brass rat and brings it to the counter.

"That will be £10 for the brass rat and £1,000 for the story behind it," said the owner.

"Thanks, but I'll pay the £10 and pass on the story," replies the man.

So the man buys the brass rat and leaves the shop. As he walks down the street, he notices all sorts of rats following him. The further he walks, the more rats follow. He walks down to the pier and still more rats come out and follow him. So, he decides to walk out into the water and all the rats drown. Afterwards, he goes back to the shop.

"Ah-ha, you're back!" says the owner. "You've come back for the story, right?"

"Nope," says the man. "You got any brass lawyers?"

What's the similarity between students and sperm?
Only one in a million turns out useful.

Amazingly, a 65-year-old woman has a baby. All her relatives come to visit and meet the newest member of their family. They all ask if they can see the baby, but the mother keeps saying, "Not yet."

Finally, a cousin asks, "When can we see the baby?"

"When it cries," says the elderly mother.

"But why do we have to wait until the baby cries?" the cousin asks impatiently.

"Because I've forgotten where I've put it."

A psychology tutor is giving her class an oral test on mental health. Singling out a student, she grills him on manic depression: "How would you diagnose a patient who walks back and forth screaming at the top of his lungs one minute, then sits in a chair weeping uncontrollably the next?"

The young man thinks for a moment, then offers his answer: "Premiership manager?"

Sean Connery gets a call from his agent one day. The agent says, "Sean, I've got you a job, starts tomorrow, early. You'll have to be there for ten-ish."

"Tennish?" says Sean, "But I don't even have a racket."

A man walks into the office of an eminent psychiatrist and sits down to explain his problem.

"Yes, well, you see, I've got this problem," the man says. "I keep hallucinating that I'm a dog. A large, white, hairy dog. It's crazy. I don't know what to do!"

"Ah, a common canine complex," said the doctor soothingly. "It's all right: we can cure this together if we work hard and concentrate. Come over here, lie down on the couch and tell me more about it."

"Oh no, Doctor. I'm not allowed on the furniture," the man says, horrified.

One Christmas season a long time ago, Santa was getting ready for his annual trip...but there were problems everywhere. Four of his elves got sick and the trainee elves did not produce the toys as fast as the regular ones so Santa was beginning to feel the pressure of being behind schedule. Then Mrs. Claus told Santa that her mom was coming to visit. This stressed Santa even more.

When he went to harness the reindeer, he found that three of them were about to give birth and two had jumped the fence and were out, heaven knows where. More stress. Then when he began to load the sleigh one of the boards cracked and the toy bag fell to the ground and scattered the toys.

Frustrated, Santa went into the house for a cup of coffee and a shot of whiskey. When he went to the cupboard, he discovered that the elves had hid the liquor and there was nothing to drink. In his frustration, he accidentally dropped the coffeepot and it broke into hundreds of little pieces all over the kitchen floor. He went to get the broom and found that mice had eaten the straw it was made from.

Just then the doorbell rang and Santa cursed on his way to the door. He opened the door and there was a little angel with a great big Christmas tree. The angel said, very cheerfully, "Merry Christmas, Santa. Isn't it just a lovely day? I have a beautiful tree for you. Isn't it just a lovely tree? Where would you like me to stick it?"

Thus began the tradition of the little angel on top of the Christmas tree.

A man and his wife are having an argument about who should brew the coffee each morning. The wife says, "You should do it, because you get up first." The husband says, "You're in charge of cooking around here and I can just wait for my coffee." Wife replies, "No, you should do it, and besides, it's in the Bible that the man should do the coffee." Husband replies, "I can't believe that. Show me." So she fetches the Bible, opens the New Testament and shows him at the top of several pages that it does indeed say... "HEBREWS".

A blonde, a brunette and a redhead all work at the same office for a female boss who always goes home early. "Hey, girls," says the brunette, "let's go home early tomorrow. She'll never know."

So the next day, they all leave right after the boss does. The brunette gets some extra gardening done, the redhead goes to a bar and the blonde goes home to find her husband having sex with the female boss!

She quietly sneaks out of the house and returns at her normal time.

"That was fun, says the brunette. "We should do it again sometime."

"No way," says the blonde. "I almost got caught."

'Squawks' are problems noted by the U.S. Air Force pilots and left for maintenance crews to fix before the next flight. Here are some actual complaints logged by Air Force pilots and the replies from the maintenance crew.

(C) = complaint; (S) = solution

(C) Left inside main tyre almost needs replacement;
    (S) Almost replaced left inside main tyre

(C) Test flight OK, except auto land very rough;
    (S) Auto land not installed on this aircraft

(C) No. 2 propeller seeping prop fluid;
    (S) No. 2 propeller seepage normal – No. 1, 3 and 4 propellers lack normal seepage

(C) Something loose in cockpit;
    (S) Something tightened in cockpit

(C) Evidence of leak in right main landing gear;
    (S) Evidence removed

(C) DME volume unbelievably loud;
    (S) Volume set to believable level

(C) Dead bugs on windshield; (S) Live bugs been ordered

(C) Autopilot in altitude hold mode produces a 200 fpm descent; (S) Cannot reproduce the problem on ground

(C) IFF inoperative;
    (S) IFF always inoperative in OFF mode

(C) Friction locks cause throttle levers to stick;
    (S) That is what they are there for

(C) No. 3 engine missing;
    (S) Engine found on right wing after brief search

(C) Aircraft handles funny;
    (S) Warned aircraft to "fly properly and be serious"

(C) Target radar hums;
    (S) Reprogrammed target radar with proper words

What do you call a lawyer with an IQ of 50?
    Your Honour.

An old couple are sitting in church. After listening to the priest's sermon the old lady says to her husband, "I've just done a silent fart; what should I do?"

The old man replies: "Turn your bloody hearing aid up!"

Three Essex girls are flying back from an exotic holiday when their plane crashes into the sea. The three survive and are washed up on a deserted island. They've been stranded for days when they find a magic lamp. They rub it and eventually a genie pops out. "Since I can only grant three wishes," he says, "you may each have one."

Number one says, "I've been stuck here for days. I miss my family, my husband, and my life. I just want to go home."

She disappears in a flash and is returned to her family.

Number two then says, "I've been stuck here for days as well. I miss my local boozer and Friday night kebabs. I want to go home too."

She vanishes as well, and finds herself back down the pub.

Suddenly, number three starts crying uncontrollably.

The genie asks, "My dear, what's the matter?"

She whimpers, "I'm lonely. I wish my mates were still here."
What is meaner than a pitbull with an STI?

Whatever gave it the STI in the first place

On trial in a rural American town, an English man thinks he has no chance of getting off a murder charge, despite his innocence. So, shortly before the jury retires, he bribes one of the jurors to find him guilty of the lesser crime of manslaughter.

The jury is out for over three days before eventually returning a verdict of manslaughter.

The relieved defendant collars the bribed juror and says: "Thanks. However did you manage it?"

"It wasn't easy," admits the juror. "All the others wanted to acquit you."

A university student delivers a pizza to an old man's house.

"I suppose you want a tip?" says the old man.

"That would be great," says the student, "but the other guy who does deliveries told me not to expect too much; he said if I got 50p, I'd be lucky."

The old man looks hurt. 'Well, to prove him wrong, here's £5. What are you studying?'

"Applied psychology," replies the student.

"My husband and I have been trying anal sex recently," the woman says, somewhat red-cheeked, to her GP. "I mean, is this OK?"

"Do you enjoy it?" the doctor asks.

"As a matter of fact, we do," she replies.

"Does it hurt you?"

"No, it's fine," she replies.

"Well, I don't see why you shouldn't carry on, as long as you're careful not to get pregnant."

"Pregnant?" the woman says, astonished. "I can get pregnant this way?"

"Well, of course: where do you think lawyers come from?" the doctor replies.

What do the Inland Revenue, an ostrich and a pelican all have in common?

They can all stick their bills up their arses.

What's the difference between a bad golfer and a bad skydiver?

The golfer goes "Thump..." "DAMN!"

Q: What is the difference between medium and rare?

A: Six inches is medium, eight inches is rare.

What's six inches long, three inches wide and drives women wild?
  A £50 note.

Why did the village idiot keep removing and then replacing the lid from a competition bottle of Coke?
  It read, "Sorry, please try again" under the lid.

A man walks into a record shop and asks, "What have you got by The Doors?"
  The owner replies, "A mop and a fire extinguisher".

What's the best way to stop aunts and grandmothers cackling, "You're next!" at family weddings?
  Start telling your aunts and grandmothers, "You're next!" at family funerals.

Saint George went to a transvestite party and said:
  "How do you like me with my drag on?"

Q: What's the difference between a girlfriend and a wife?
A: 45 pounds.
Q: What's the difference between a boyfriend and a husband?
A: 45 minutes.

Two American women, one from the north and one from the deep south, are seated next to one another on a plane.
  "Where you flyin' to?" asks the redneck, to which the northern woman turns up her nose.
  "Don't you know you should never end a sentence with a preposition?" she says.
  The southern woman thinks about this for a second. "OK, where you flyin' to, bitch?"

A man was passing a country estate and saw a sign on the gate. It read: "Please ring bell for the caretaker." He rang the bell and an old man appeared.

"Are you the caretaker?" the fellow asked.

"Yes, I am," replied the old man. "What do you want?"

"I'd just like to know why you can't ring the bell yourself."

A couple of OAPs – a man and a woman – are sitting outside their old folks' home talking of the old days. All of a sudden an ice cream van pulls up at the gate with the tune playing. The woman says, "I'd love an ice cream, you know," to which the man replies, "Would you like me to get you one?" "Don't bother," the old dear says, "by the time you get to the van you'll never remember what I wanted anyway." "Don't be silly," says the man, "I won't forget. Now, come on: what do you want?" "Well, OK, then," says the woman, "I'll have a double-scoop of strawberry with chocolate sauce, nuts and a flake on top." "A double-scoop of strawberry with chocolate sauce, nuts and a flake on top coming right up," says the man and off he goes. Five minutes later he comes back carrying four hot dogs and two large Cokes. "Oh, my God," says the woman, "I knew I shouldn't have trusted you – where's the gravy?"

Albert Einstein arrives at a party and introduces himself to the first person he sees and asks, "What is your IQ?" to which the man answers: "241.""That is wonderful!," cries Albert in delight. "We shall talk about the Grand Unified Theory." The next person Albert introduces himself is a woman and he asks her: "What is your IQ?" To which the lady answers, "144."

"That is great!" responds Albert, very pleased with this party indeed. "We can discuss politics and current affairs. We will have much to discuss!" Albert goes to another person and asks, "What is your IQ?" to which the man answers, "51." Albert responds, "Spurs doing well this season aren't they?"

A boy went up to his father and asked, "What is the difference between potentially and realistically?"

The father pondered for a while, then answered, "Go and ask your mother if she would sleep with Brad Pitt for a million pounds. Also, ask your sister if she would sleep with Zac Efron for a million pounds. Come back and tell me what you have learned."

So the boy went to his mother and asked, "Would you sleep with Brad Pitt for a million pounds?"

The mother replied, "Of course I would. I wouldn't pass up an opportunity like that."

The boy then went to his sister and said, "Would you sleep with Zac Efron for a million pounds?"

She replied, "Oh my god yes! I would be insane to pass up that opportunity."

The boy then thought about it for a couple of days and went back to his father.

His father asked, "Did you find out the difference between potentially and realistically?"

The boy replied, "Yes, potentially we're sitting on two million pounds, but realistically we're living with two slappers."

The phone at the local hospital rings and the duty medic picks it up to hear a man jabbering on the other end.

"My wife's contractions are only two minutes apart!" he says.

"Is this her first child?" the doctor asks.

"No, you idiot" the man shouts "This is her husband!"

A middle-aged woman has a heart attack and is taken to the hospital. While on the operating table she has a near-death experience. Seeing God, she asks: "Is my time up?"

God says, "No, you have another 43 years, two months and eight days to live."

Upon recovery, the woman decides to stay in the hospital and have a facelift, liposuction and a tummy tuck.

While crossing the street on her way home, she's killed by an ambulance. Arriving in front of God, she demands, "I thought you said I had another 40 years?"

God replies, "I didn't recognise you."

The new vicar's wife had a baby and he appealed to the congregation for a salary increase to cover the new addition to his family.

The congregation agreed that it was only fair, and approved it.

When the next child arrived, the vicar appealed and again the congregation approved the increase.

Several years and five children later, the congregation was getting hacked off with the increasing expenses. This turned into a rather loud meeting one night at the vicarage.

Finally, the vicar stood up and shouted, "Having children is an Act of God!"

An old fisherman in the back stood up and shouted back, "So are rain and snow, but we wear rubbers for them!"

A woman goes into a dentist's office, and after her examination, the dentist says to her, "I'm sorry to tell you this, but I'm going to have to drill that tooth."

Horrified, the woman replies, "Oh, no! I'd rather have a baby." The dentist replies, "Make up your mind; I have to adjust the chair."

It's a stockbroker's first day in prison and on meeting his psychotic-looking cellmate, the nutter notices how scared the stockbroker looks and decides to put him at ease.

"I'm in for a white-collar crime, too."

"Oh, really?" says the stockbroker, sighing with relief.

"Yes," says the cellmate, "I killed a vicar."

A blonde was having a great time at a party and was soon spotted by a guy who swiftly led her upstairs. He started to undress her, then, surprised, saw that she was wearing shower caps on her tits.

"Hey, what's with the shower caps?" the guy asked her.

"What shower caps?" she answered, "These are booby condoms!"

An Aussie lass goes to her gynaecologist and tells the doctor that no matter how hard she and her husband have tried, she just can't get pregnant.

The doctor says, "OK; take off your clothes and lay down on the table."

The girl sighs and says, "Fair dos mate, but I was really hoping to have my husband's baby."

An old man turns to his wife and asks if she's ever cheated on him. "I must confess," she says, "I've been unfaithful to you twice."

"What!?" he screams. "When?"

"The first time was when we were denied a mortgage," she explains, "and I went to persuade the banker to give us the loan."

"What about the second time?" says the man.

"Remember when you ran for mayor," the wife begins, "and you were behind by 300 votes?"

A non-too-bright zebra escaped from a zoo and ended up in a field full of cows.

He walked up to one and said: 'Hi there. What do you do around here then?'

"I eat grass all day and get milked morning and night," replied the cow.

"Oh," the zebra said. He walked idly about and met another cow.

"Hi there! Say, what do you do around here then?" he asked again.

"I eat grass all day and get milked morning and night," replied the cow.

The zebra nodded, pleased by the quietness and the sense of purpose of the cows' life, then walked over to a bull. "Hello," he said. "What do you do around here?"

The bull looked him up and down and said: "Get those pyjamas off and I'll show you."

A woman's husband has been slipping in and out of a coma for several months, yet she stays lovingly by his bedside every day. Finally, he comes to and motions for her to come near.

"You, my love," he says, "have been with me through all the bad times. When I was fired, you were there for me. When the business failed, you were there. When I got shot, you were by my side. When we lost the house, you stood by me throughout. When my health started failing, you were still by my side. You know what?"

"What dear?" she asks gently.

"I think you bring me bad luck."

Three women die together in an accident and go to Heaven. When they get there, St Peter says, "We only have one rule here in Heaven; don't step on the ducks."

Sure enough, there are ducks everywhere in heaven. It is almost impossible not to step on a duck and although they try their best to avoid them, the first woman accidentally steps on one. Along comes St Peter with the ugliest man she ever saw.

St Peter chains them together and says, "Your punishment for stepping on a duck is to spend eternity chained to this ugly man."

The next day, the second woman steps on a duck and along comes St Peter. With him is another extremely ugly man. He chains them together with the same admonition as he gave the first woman.

The third woman, having observed all this, is very, very careful where she steps. She manages to go months without stepping on any ducks, but one day St Peter comes up to her with the most handsome man she's ever seen and, silently, he chains them together. The happy woman says, "Wonder what I did to deserve being chained to you for all of eternity?"

The guy says, "I don't know about you, but I stepped on a duck."

A guy walks into his local with a giraffe and a monkey. All three of them get utterly shitfaced. The man and the monkey manage to prop each other up and make it to the door but the giraffe is too big for them to help and he collapses on the floor. As the man opens the door the barman shouts across the bar, "Oi, mate, you can't leave that lyin' there!" and the man shouts back, "That's no lion – it's a giraffe and I can't move him!"

A guy goes into a girl's house and she shows him into the living room. She excuses herself to go to the kitchen to make some drinks. As he's standing there alone, he notices a vase on the mantelpiece.

He picks it up and as he's looking at it, she walks back in. He says, "What's this?"

"Oh, my father's ashes are in there," she replies.

Turning red, he apologizes.

She continues, "Yeah; he's too lazy to go to get an ashtray."

A woman had been married three times and pretended she was still a virgin.

Somebody asked her how that could be possible.

"Well," she said. "The first time I married an octogenarian and he died before we could consummate the marriage.

"The second time I married a naval officer and war broke out on our wedding day.

"The third time I married a Microsoft Windows programmer and he just sat on the edge of the bed and kept telling me how good it was going to be."

A guy walks into a watchmaker's shop and asks the man behind the counter for a potato clock.

"A potato clock?" says the watchmaker, "I've never heard of a potato clock. Why do you want one?"

The customer sighs. "Well, you see," he says, "I went for a job interview yesterday and was offered the job. So I asked the boss what time I should start, and he said nine o'clock."

"So?" asks the kindly old shopkeeper.

"Well," replies the man, "he said to do that, I'll need to get a potato clock."

A man calls home to his wife and says, "Honey, I've been asked to go fishing with my boss and several of his friends. We'll be gone for a week. This is a good opportunity for me to get that promotion I've been wanting. We're leaving from the office and I'll swing by the house to pick my things up. Oh – please pack my new blue silk pyjamas."

The wife thinks this sounds a little suspicious but being a good wife she does exactly what her husband asked. The following weekend he comes home a little tired but otherwise looking good.

The wife welcomes him home and asks if he caught many fish.

He says, "Loads! But why didn't you pack my new blue silk pyjamas like I asked you to do?"

The wife replies, "I did. They were in your tackle box..."

A missionary has spent years teaching agriculture and 'civilization' to some people in a distant land. One day, he wants to start teaching them English. So he takes the tribal chief and points at a tree.

"Tree," says the missionary.

"Tree," mimics the chief.

The holy man then points to a rock.

"Rock," he says.

"Rock," copies the chief.

All of a sudden, they come upon two people having sex in the bushes. Embarrassed, the missionary blurts out that they are 'riding a bike'. Then the chief pulls out his blowpipe and shoots the two people.

"What are you doing?" yells the missionary. "I've spent all this time civilizing you, and you do this!"

"My bike," says the chief.

An office manager arrives at his department and sees an employee sitting behind his desk, totally stressed out.

He gives him a spot of advice: "I went home every afternoon for two weeks and had myself pampered by my wife. It was fantastic, and it really helped me; maybe you should give it a try, too."

Two weeks later, when the manager arrives at his department, he sees the same man happy and full of energy at his desk. The faxes are piling up, and the computer is running at full speed.

"Excellent," says the manager, "I see you followed my advice."

"I did," answers the employee. "It was great! By the way, I didn't know you had such a nice house!"

A man walks into a dentist's office and says, "I think I'm a moth."

The dentist replies, "You shouldn't be here. You should be seeing a psychiatrist."

The man replies, "I am seeing a psychiatrist."

The dentist says, "Well, then, what are you doing here?"

The man says, "Your light was on."

One winter morning an old couple, Norman and Sarah, are listening to the radio over breakfast. The announcer says, "We're going to have eight to ten inches of snow today. You must park your car on the even-numbered side of the street, so the snow ploughs can get through."

Norman's wife goes out and moves her car.

A week later while they are eating breakfast, the radio announcer says, "We're expecting ten to twelve inches of snow today. You must park your car on the odd-numbered side of the street, so the snow ploughs can get through."

Norman's wife dutifully goes out and moves her car again.

The next week again they're having breakfast, when the radio announcer says: "We're expecting twelve to fourteen inches of snow today. You must park..." Then the power goes out. Norman's wife is very upset, and with a worried look on her face she says, "Honey, I don't know what to do. Which side of the street do I need to park on so the snow plough can get through?"

With love and understanding in his voice, Norman says, "Why don't you just leave it in the garage this time, dear?"

A young man's mother is now retired and living in Miami Beach. He doesn't see her that often. His father is no longer around and he is worried that his mum is lonely. For her birthday, he purchases a rare parrot, trained to speak seven languages. He has a courier deliver the bird to his dear old mother. A few days later, he calls to see that she got the bird. "Mum, what do you think of the parrot?"

"It was a little tough, actually. I should have cooked it longer," says the old dear.

"You ate the bird? Mum, that bird was really expensive. It spoke seven languages!" says the horrified son.

"Oh, excuse me! If the bird was so damn smart, why didn't it say something when I put it in the oven?"

A man crawls out of the desert and into a small village, which has some market stalls in the street.

He crawls up to the first one. "Water, water! Give me water!"

"I'm sorry," says the first stallholder, "I only sell custard."

The man crawls up to the second stall. "Water, water! Give me water!" he cries.

"I'm sorry," says the second stallholder, "I only sell cream and sponge."

The man then crawls up to a third stall. "Water, water! Give me water!" he cries.

"I'm sorry," says the third stallholder, "I only sell hundreds and thousands."

"I can't believe no one has any water," says the parched man.

"I know," says the stallholder, "it is a trifle bazaar."

A man goes into a lawyer's office and says, "I heard people have sued tobacco companies for giving them lung cancer."

The lawyer says, "Yes, that's perfectly true."

The man says, "Well, I'm interested in sueing someone, too."

The lawyer says, "OK. Who are you talking about?"

The man replies, "I'd like to sue all the breweries for the ugly women I've slept with."

An Amish woman is driving her horse and buggy down the road when she gets pulled over.

"You have a broken reflector on your buggy," the policeman says, "but more important, one of your reins is looped around your horse's balls. That's cruelty to animals. Have your husband take care of that right away!"

Later that day, the woman tells her husband, "A policeman pulled me over today for two reasons. First, he said the reflector was broken."

"Well, that's easily fixed," says her husband. "What else?"

"I'm not sure: something about the emergency brake."

What's the difference between a bad lawyer and a good lawyer?

A bad lawyer can let a case drag on for months. A good lawyer can make it last for years.

A honeymooning couple buy a talking parrot and take it to their room, but the groom becomes annoyed when it keeps a running commentary on his lovemaking. Finally, he throws a towel over the cage and threatens to give the bird to the zoo if it doesn't keep quiet.

Early the next morning, the couple have trouble closing a suitcase.

"You get on top and I'll try," the groom instructs. But that doesn't work. The new bride figures they need more weight on top of the suitcase to shut it.

"You try getting on top," she says.

Still no success. Finally, the groom says, "Look, let's both get on top."

At this point the parrot uses his beak to pull the towel off and says, "Zoo or no zoo, I have to see this!"

A girl walks into her local pharmacy and asks if the store sells large-sized condoms.

"Yes we do," he says. "We have them in large and extra-large sizes. Would you like to buy a packet?"

"No," she replies. "But do you mind if I wait around until somebody does?"

A man is confused about sex and the sabbath. He just cannot work out whether having sex on the sabbath is a sin or not because he doesn't know whether it is work or play. He goes to see his local priest and asks him what his opinion is on this question.

The priest gets his bible down and flicks through it, reading a passage here and a passage there.

Eventually he tells the man, "Well my son, after consulting the good book I have decided that sex is closest to work and that therefore you should not practice it on the sabbath."

The man thanks the priest but, as that wasn't really the answer he was looking for, he decides to go and see the local minister, who is married and may see things a bit more his way. He asks the minister the question and, to his disappointment, the minister gives him the same answer as the priest, "No sex on the sabbath."

The man decides to go and see holy man of a different faith – the local Rabbi. The Rabbi is asked the question and he ponders it over. Eventually he says, "Well my son, I have come to the conclusion that sex is definitely play so therefore you can have sex on the sabbath."

The man says "That's great Rabbi, but how do you come to that conclusion when so many others disagree?"

The Rabbi thinks a little and then says quietly, "If sex were work, my wife would get the maid to do it!"

It's a beautiful day in County Kerry and people all over the county are sitting outside the pubs enjoying stout by the pint. In a cosy pub one man turns to his friend and says, "You see that man over there?" His friend nods. "Have you noticed that he's the spitting image of me? It's bloody uncanny, that's what it is, to be sure. I'm going to go over there and ask him a few questions: after all, 'tis not every day that you get to meet someone who could be your exact double, now is it?" And off he goes to see the man he is talking about. He taps him on the shoulder and says, "Excuse me, I couldn't help noticing from over there that you look almost exactly the same as me. I was thinking what an incredible coincidence that was!" "Me too, me too," replies the man, "I noticed you earlier and I was just about to come over and talk when I saw you coming over anyway. 'Tis an incredible thing to be sure. So whereabouts are you from?" he asks. "Well, I'm from Galway, originally," says the first man. "No: that's incredible!" says the second, "Me too! It's just unbelievable. What street did you live in?" "Why, I lived in Moher Street for 20 years, so I did," comes the reply from the first man. "No! I can't believe it – I did too," says the second. "And what number in that street was it?" he asks. "Why, I lived in number 20," comes the reply. "Unbelievable," comes the reply, "that's the number I lived in. And what were your parents' names?" "Ruari and Siobhan" comes the reply. "This really is uncanny," the first man says, "those are the exact names of my parents too!" At this point the two men continue talking and the new bar staff turn up for their shift. The new guy asks, "Anything happening?" and the guy about to go replies, "No, not really; just the Rix twins drunk again!"

The room was full of pregnant women and their partners. The Lamaze class was in full swing. The instructor was teaching the women how to breathe properly, and informing the men how to give the necessary assurances at this stage of the plan.

"Ladies, exercise is good for you," announced the teacher. "Walking is especially beneficial. And, gentlemen, it wouldn't hurt you to take the time to go walking with your partner."

The room was very quiet. Finally, a man in the middle of the group raised his hand.

"Yes?" asked the instructor.

"Is it all right if she carries a golf bag while we walk?"

A frog goes into a London bank and approaches the teller. He can see from her nameplate that the teller's name is Patricia Whack. He says, "Ms. Whack, I'd like to get a loan to buy a boat and go on a long vacation."

Patti looks at the frog in disbelief and asks how much he wants to borrow. The frog says £30,000. The teller asks his name and the frog says that his name is Kermit Jagger and that it's OK, he knows the bank manager. Patti explains that £30,000 is a substantial amount of money and that he will need to secure the loan. She asks if he has anything he can use as collateral. The frog says, "Sure. I have this," and he produces a tiny pink porcelain elephant, about half an inch tall. It's bright pink and perfectly formed, but of no obvious visible value.

Very confused, Patti explains that she'll have to consult with the manager and disappears into a back office. She finds the manager and reports: "There's a frog called Kermit Jagger out there who claims to know you, and he wants to borrow £30,000. He wants to use this as collateral," she says, holding up the tiny pink elephant. "I mean, what the heck is this?"

The bank manager looks back at her and says: "It's a knick-knack, Patti Whack. Give the frog a loan. His old man's a Rolling Stone!"

In the middle of a very dark and stormy night, a man is alone, hitchhiking on the side of the road. Suddenly, in the distance, he sees the headlights of a car coming towards him, which slowed to a standstill right by him. Without hesitation, the man hurriedly gets into the car and closes the door only to realize there is no one behind the wheel.

All of a sudden the car begins to move. Scared, the passenger starts to pray and when the car starts to slow down on a hill he makes a break for it, grabs the door handle, rolls out of the car and sprints to the nearest town.

He runs into a crowded pub, asks for two shots of whisky and begins to tell everybody about the horrible experience he just went through. Everyone in the pub is stunned and there is still a creepy atmosphere about half an hour later when two guys walk into the pub.

They look at one another in amazement and one says to the other, "Look Mick, that's the idiot that jumped in the car when we were pushing it!"

A man was driving home one evening and realized that it was his daughter's birthday and he hadn't bought her a present. He drove to the shopping centre and ran to the toy shop and he asked the manager: "How much is that new Barbie in the window?"

The Manager replied: "Which one? We have 'Barbie goes to the gym' for £19.95, 'Barbie goes to the Ball' for £19.95, 'Barbie goes shopping' for £19.95, 'Barbie goes to the beach' for £19.95, 'Barbie goes to the Nightclub' for £19.95 and 'Divorced Barbie' for £399.99."

"Why is the Divorced Barbie £399.99, when all the others are £19.95?" the dad asked.

"Divorced Barbie comes with Ken's car, Ken's House, Ken's boat, Ken's dog, Ken's cat And Ken's furniture," replied the shop manager.

A man walks into a chemist and asks for a bottle of Viagra. The pharmacist eyes him suspiciously. "Do you have a prescription for that?" he asks.

"No," says the man, "but will this picture of my wife do?"

A man turns to his new girlfriend and says, "Since I first laid eyes upon your beautiful body, my darling, I've wanted to make love to you really, really badly."

The girlfriend responds, "Well, you succeeded."

A young ventriloquist is touring the clubs and one night does a show in a pub in Shropshire. With his puppet on his knee, he's going through his usual dumb blonde routine when a blonde woman stands on her chair and starts shouting angrily:

'I've heard enough of your stupid blonde jokes. What makes you think you can stereotype women that way? What does the colour of a person's hair have to do with her worth as a human being? It's guys like you who keep women like me from being respected at work and in the community and from reaching our full potential, because you and your kind continue to perpetuate discrimination against not only blondes, but women in general!' The ventriloquist, embarrassed, begins to apologize, but the blonde yells, 'You stay out of this, buster! I'm talking to that little jerk on your knee!'

A woman walks into a gun shop and asks the salesman if he can help her pick out a rifle.

"It's for my husband," she explains.

"Did he tell you what calibre to get?" asks the salesman.

"Are you kidding? He doesn't even know I'm going to shoot him."

A nine-year-old boy walks into a bar and demands the barmaid give him a Scotch on the rocks.

"Hey, do you want to get me into trouble?" the barmaid asks.

"Maybe later," says the kid, "but for now I'll just have my drink."

A fire starts inside a chemical plant and the alarm goes out to fire stations miles around. After crews have been fighting the fire for more than an hour, the chemical company president approaches the fire chief and says, 'All our secret formulae are in the vault. They must be saved. I'll give £100,000 to the firemen who bring them out safely.' Suddenly, another engine comes roaring down the road and drives straight into the middle of the inferno. The other men watch, unbelieving, as the firemen hop off their engine and heroically extinguish the fire, saving the secret formulae. The company president walks over to reward the volunteers and asks them, 'What do you fellas plan to do with the money?' The driver looks him right in the eye and answers, 'Well, the first thing we're going to do is fix the brakes.'

Ladies' man Shane Warne is at an Ashes press conference. An Aussie journalist asks, "What would you do if you only had 30 minutes to live, Shane?"

"Ah, mate," he says, "I'd shag the first thing that moved."

The journalist then asks the same question of Freddie Flintoff: "What would you do if you only had 30 minutes to live?"

Freddie eyes Warnie suspiciously and says, "I'd sit very, very still."

A drunk gets on a bus late at night and sits next to an old woman. The old woman looks him up and down and says, "You know what, my boy, you're going straight to hell." "Oh shit," says the drunk, "I'm on the wrong bus!"

A Scotsman walked into a chemist's shop and asked to speak to a male pharmacist. The woman behind the counter explained that she was the pharmacist, that she and her sister owned the business, and they didn't have any male employees.

"But I have an embarrassing male problem," said the Scot.

"You can tell me about it – I am a qualified medical professional," encouraged the pharmacist.

"Well then," he said, raising his kilt to reveal an enormous, erect penis. "This has been like this for three days now, and I've tried everything to make it go down. What can you give me for it?"

Flustered, the pharmacist said she'd consult with her sister, and shot into the back room. She came back two minutes later and said, 'We've discussed it, and the best we can do is £2,000 a month, a company car and a one-third share of the business.'

A policeman got out of his car and the lad who was stopped for speeding rolled down his window. "I've been waiting for you all day," the policeman said.

"Yeah," replied the lad. "Well, I got here as fast as I could."

A man goes to see a doctor and tells him he hasn't been feeling very well lately. The doctor examines him for a few minutes and then takes three jars of big coloured pills from a medicine cabinet.

"Here is your treatment: you are going to take this green pill in the morning, with a big glass of water, then the yellow pill after lunch, with a big glass of water and finally this red pill, again with a big glass of water. As you can see, these pills are pretty big, you might actually need two glasses of water at night."

The patient stares at the huge pills, horrified. "Jeez, doc; that's a lot of pills... Er...what exactly is my problem?"

"You're not drinking enough water," the doctor replied.

Two brooms were hanging in the closet and after a while, they got to know each other so well, they decided to get married. One broom was, of course, the bride broom...and the other the groom broom. The bride broom looked very beautiful in her white dress. The groom broom was handsome and suave in his tuxedo. The wedding was lovely. Afterward, at the wedding dinner, the bride broom leaned over and said to the groom broom, "I think I am going to have a little whisk broom!"

"Impossible!" said the groom broom, "we haven't even swept together!"

A man was walking on the sidewalk and noticed up ahead that little Johnny was wearing a red fire man's hat and sitting in a red wagon. It appeared that the wagon was being pulled slowly by a large labrador retriever.

When he got closer to the lad, he noticed that Johnny had a rope tied around the dog's testicles, which probably accounted for why the dog was walking so gingerly.

Smiling, he spoke to the little boy, 'That's really a nice fire engine you have there son, but I'll bet the dog would pull you faster if you tied that rope around his neck.'

"Yeah,' Johnny replied, 'but then I wouldn't have a siren."

Every single one of these is completely and utterly true:

1) Triangular sandwiches taste better than square ones.

2) At the end of every party there is always a girl crying.

3) One of the most awkward things that can happen in a pub is when your pint to toilet cycle gets synchronised with a complete stranger.

4) You've never quite sure whether it's ok to eat green crisps.

5) Everyone who grew up in the 80s has entered the digits 55378008 into a calculator.

6) Reading when you're drunk is horrible.

7) Sharpening a pencil with a knife makes you feel really manly.

8) Your never quite sure whether it's against the law or not to have a fire in your back garden.

9) Nobody ever dares make cup a soup in a bowl.

10) You never know where to look when eating a banana.

11) Its impossible to describe the smell of a wet cat.

12) Prodding a fire with a stick makes you feel manly.

13) Rummaging in an overgrown garden will always turn up a bouncy ball.

14) You always feel a bit scared when stroking horses.

15) Everyone always remembers the day a dog ran into your school.

16) The most embarrassing thing you can do as schoolchild is

to call your teacher mum or dad.

17) The smaller the monkey the more it looks like it would kill you at the first given opportunity.

18) Some days you see lots of people on crutches.

19) Every bloke has at some stage while taking a pee flushed half way through and then raced against the flush.

20) Old women with mobile phones look wrong!

21) Its impossible to look cool whilst picking up a Frisbee.

22) Driving through a tunnel makes you feel excited.

23) You never ever run out of salt.

24) Old ladies can eat more than you think.

25) You can't respect a man who carries a dog.

26) There's no panic like the panic you momentarily feel when you've got your hand or head stuck in something.

27) No one knows the origins of their metal coat hangers.

28) Despite constant warning, you have never met anybody who has had their arm broken by a swan.

29) The most painful household incident is wearing socks and stepping on an upturned plug.

30) People who don't drive slam car doors too hard.

31) You've turned into your dad the day you put aside a thin piece of wood specifically to stir paint with.

32) Everyone had an uncle who tried to steal their nose.

33) Bricks are horrible to carry.

34) In every plate of chips there is a bad chip.
A blonde, a brunette and a redhead are having a breaststroke swimming competition across the English Channel. The brunette finishes first, then the redhead second but the blonde never finished. When the lifeboat found her, way behind, she said, "I don't want to be a tattletale or anything, but the other two – you know? They used their arms."

The Ultimate Computer had finally been built and, after making sure that the intensive indoor tests all proved 100 per cent positive, the Ultimate Computer was presented to the CEO.

The engineer stepped forward to give his prepared demo. "This," he said, "is the Ultimate Computer. It will give an intelligent answer to any question you may care to ask it."

The CEO, amused, asked: "Where is my father?"

After an infinitesimal pause, the super computer answer comes through: "Your father is fishing off the coast of Florida."

The COE's face falls. "Actually, my father is dead. He died five years ago," he says, in a tone suggesting he is not amused any more.

The engineer gulps and mutters: "You should rephrase the question – make it more precise. That might produce a correct answer this time."

The CEO frowns and says: "All right. Where is my mother's husband?"

There is a small pause again and the printer spits out the answer to the second question:

"Your mother's husband is dead. However, your father is still fishing off the coast of Florida."

A guy is driving down the road at 100mph singing, "Twenty-one today, twenty-one today!" Soon, a cop pulls him over and says, "Because it's your birthday, I'll let you off." Despite the cop's warning, the guy screeches off and is soon doing a ton down the road again. The cop, in hot pursuit, then sees the man mow down a traffic warden. Suddenly, the man starts singing, "Twenty-two today, twenty-two today!"

A couple was celebrating their golden wedding anniversary. Their domestic tranquillity had long been the talk of the town and a local newspaper reporter was inquiring as to the secret of their long and happy marriage.

"Well, it dates back to our honeymoon," explained the man. "We visited the Grand Canyon and took a trip down to the bottom of the canyon by pack mule. We hadn't gone too far when my wife's mule stumbled. My wife quietly said, "That's once." "We proceeded a little further and the mule stumbled again. Once more my wife quietly said, "That's twice."

"'We hadn't gone a half-mile when the mule stumbled the third time. My wife quietly removed a revolver from her purse and shot the mule dead. I started an angry protest over her treatment of the mule, when she looked at me, and quietly said, "That's once."

"We lived happily ever after."

Two seagulls were flying over the beach at a seaside resort one boiling hot August Bank Holiday afternoon. Every way they looked, there were so many people there wasn't a speck of sand to be seen.

"Ah," said one to the other contemptuously, "takes all the skill out of it, doesn't it?"

Three Rabbis were playing golf one day. Another fellow, who had no golfing partner, asked if he could join in to make up a foursome. The Rabbis were more than willing and they all had a jolly good round of golf. At the end of the game the man had lost miserably, and his score was a good thirty shots more than all the Rabbis. He found this confusing, because he's quite a keen weekend golfer, and the Rabbis are men of the cloth. So he asks, 'how come you guys are all such good golfers?' and one of the Rabbis replies, 'well son, when you lead a good, religious and pure life, as part of a temple, your rewards are many. Being good at Golf is just one of our rewards.' So the man goes home and has a think, and decides what the hey, I don't have much going on in my life anyway, I may as well go for it and try to improve my golf. So, he finds a temple near where he lives, he joins it and attends classes three times a week.

One year later the four of them all play golf again but it is the same story: the man loses miserably again. 'So what's that all about?' he asks the Rabbis again, 'I joined a temple, I go three times a week, and I lead a good, pure life.'

One of the Rabbis replies, 'which temple did you join?' and the man says, 'Shalom Shalom on 4th Avenue.' The Rabbi replies, 'Oh no! That one's for tennis!'

What do you call two Mexicans playing basketball?
Juan on Juan

A sloaney Londoner is getting old so she decides to make her will and to include her final requests. She is talking to her priest and she tells him that when she has been cremated she would like to have her remains scattered in Harvey Nics, dear. 'But why's that?' asks the priest and the woman replies, 'I want to be sure that my daughters will visit me at least once a week!'

A young man moved into a new apartment on his own and went to the lobby to put his name on his mailbox.

While there, an attractive young lady wearing a robe came out of the apartment next to the mailboxes. The young lad smiled at the woman and she started a conversation with him. As they talked, her robe slipped open and it was obvious that she had nothing else on. The poor lad broke into a sweat trying to maintain eye contact.

After a few minutes, she placed her hand on his arm and said, "I hear someone coming, let's go to my apartment." He followed her into her apartment; she closed the door and leaned against it, allowing her robe to fall off completely. Now naked, she purred at him, "What would you say is my best feature?"

Flustered and embarrassed, he finally squeaked, "It's got to be your ears!"

Astounded, and a little hurt she asked, "My ears? Look at these breasts; they are full and 100% natural! I work out every day! My butt is firm and solid! Look at my skin, no blemishes anywhere! How can you think that the best part of my body is my ears?"

Clearing his throat, he stammered, "Outside, when you said you heard someone coming? That was me."

A drunken bum is sitting on a barstool when a really high-class bird sits down next to him. He immediately turns around and says to her, "Hey, darlin": how's about you and me getting together for a bit of how's your father? I've got a couple of euro and you look like you could do with a little cash!' The woman looks at him coldly before replying, "What makes you think I charge by the inch?"

An Aussie walks into a library and asks the librarian, "Excuse me, mate, can I have a burger and large fries, please?"

Tutting, the librarian replies: "Excuse me, sir; this is a library."

The Aussie leans over the counter. "I'm sorry, mate," he whispers. "Can I have a burger and large fries, please?"

A blonde, a brunette and a redhead are on a walk in the mountains when they find a bridge over a deep ridge. They are half-way across when a fairy appears out of nowhere.

"Welcome to the fairy bridge," she says. "If you want to pass, you need to jump over and shout the name of an animal: then you will be transformed into this animal and land harmlessly."

The brunette goes first and, as she jumps over the edge of the bridge, she shouts "Lion!" and sure enough, whoosh! she gets transformed into a great lion which gently descends to the ground and disappears into the trees.

When it is her turn, the redhead swings her legs over the edge of the bridge and shouts "Eagle!" and whoosh! she is transformed into a magnificent eagle which soars to the heavens.

The blonde finds this pretty neat but, just as she jumps over the bridge, she realizes she hasn't thought about what animal she wanted to be.

"Crap," she says.

What do men and money in the bank have in common?
  Both lose interest after withdrawal.

A plumber attended to a leaking tap at a stately home. After a two-minute job, he demanded £75. "Christ, even I don't charge this much and I'm a surgeon!" said the owner. The plumber replied, "You're right – that's why I switched from surgery to plumbing."

One day, a diver is enjoying the aquatic world 20 feet below the sea's surface when he notices a bloke at the same depth, but with no scuba gear whatsoever. The diver goes down another 20 feet and, after a few minutes, the bloke joins him. The diver goes down 25 feet more and minutes later the same bloke joins him again. This confuses the diver, so he takes out a waterproof chalkboard set and writes, "How the hell are you able to stay this deep under water without breathing apparatus?"
  The other guy grabs the board, erases what the diver has written, and scribbles, "I'm drowning, you bloody moron!"

Why are pirates called pirates?
They just arrrr!

There's a bar where all the regulars are really into bodybuilding. The owner is a bodybuilder and he only employs bodybuilders as bar staff. The walls are covered in bodybuilder photos and they are always having bodybuilder competitions. On the wall behind the bar is a sign that says 'Win £1,000: Beat The Bartender.' Written below it are the rules to the competition. The bartenders are so strong that, after any one of them as squeezed a lemon with his bare hands, nobody can ever squeeze anything else out of it: anyone who can will win the prize. The space around the bar is filled with photos of people who tried to win the competition but failed. One day a skinny little man walks into the bar and announces that he'd like to try for the prize. It is a Saturday night, the bar is packed and everybody starts to laugh. The guy's head is about the size of the bartender's hand and nobody believes he has a chance.

The bartender picks up a lemon and starts to squeeze it. Juice comes gushing out quickly but after a few seconds it stops as the man squeezes everything out: juice, pips, pith and even squashed rind. The bartender then hands the lemon to the tiny old man. The man puts his hand around the wizened, almost unrecognizable, lemon and proceeds to squeeze. To the astonishment of everyone present, juice begins to drip from the fruit and before long seven, eight, nine, and then ten full drops have been squeezed! Everyone starts to cheer and the bartender coughs up the money. "That's amazing – really amazing," says the bartender. "Are you a secret bodybuilder? Are you a martial arts expert? How did you do it?" "Easy enough," says the man, "I work for the Inland Revenue."

Man walks into the pub and the barman says, "Say, mate, aren't you Dave Redman from down the road?" "No, mate, sorry," says the man. "Ah right," said the barman, "you must have a double." "Cheers – JD on the rocks!" replied the man.

The flower vendor is an old hand at unloading his last few bunches each day. Appealing to a businessman on his way home, the vendor says, "How about a nice bunch of roses to surprise your wife?"

"Haven't got a wife," the businessman responds.

"Then how about some carnations for your girlfriend?" the vendor proposes without missing a beat.

"Haven't got a girlfriend."

The vendor breaks into a big smile. "Oh, then you'll want all the flowers I've got left. You have a lot to celebrate!"

A Scotsman, an Englishman and an Aussie are having a drink in America.

"Y'know," says the Scotsman, "I still prefer the pubs back home. In Glasgow there's a little bar called McTavish's. Now the landlord there goes out of his way for the locals so much that when you buy four drinks, he'll buy the fifth one for you."

"Well", says the Englishman, "at my local, the Red Lion, the barman there will buy you your third drink after you buy the first two."

"Ahhhhh, that's nothing", says the Aussie. "Back home in Sydney there's Bruce's Bar. Now, the moment you set foot in the place they'll buy you a drink, then another, all the drinks you like. Then, when you've had enough drinks, they'll take you upstairs and see that you get laid, and it's all on the house."

The Englishman and Scotsman immediately scorn the Aussie's claims. But the Aussie swears every word is true.

"Well," says the Englishman "has this actually happened to you?"

"Not me personally, no," says the Aussie. "But it did happen to my sister."

A blonde, a brunette and a redhead are running away from the cops when they providentially stumble upon an old barn to hide in. They find three big sacks on the floor of the barn and promptly jump in them. About a minute later, a police car comes to a screaming halt by the barn door and a policeman steps out. He enters the barn and spots the suspicious-looking sacks. He kicks the first one.

"Meow," says the redhead.

"It must be a cat," says the policeman, and he kicks the second sack.

'Woof,' says the brunette.

"Must be a dog," mutters the policeman, and he kicks the third sack.

"Potatoes," says the blonde.

Jesus and Satan are having an ongoing argument about who's better on their computer. Finally, God says, "I am going to set up a test which will take two hours and I will judge who does the better job."

So Satan and Jesus sit down at the keyboards and type away. They do everything their PCs can handle. But, ten minutes before the time's up, lightning suddenly flashes across the sky, and the electricity goes off.

Satan stares at his blank screen and screams in every curse word known in the underworld. Jesus just sighs. The electricity finally flickers back on, and each of them reboots.

Satan starts searching, frantically screaming, "It's gone! It's all gone! I lost everything when the power went out!"

Meanwhile, Jesus quietly starts printing out all his files from the past two hours. Satan sees this and becomes even more irate. "Wait! He cheated! How did he do it!?"

God shrugs and says, "Jesus saves."

"We specialise in hygiene," said the sign at the bread shop and the customer was delighted when he saw the baker use tongs to pick up his rolls and put them in a bag.

"Untouched by human hands!" said the baker.

"Very good," said the customer as he immediately started to eat one of the rolls, "but tell me: what's that piece of string hanging out of your flies?"

"Hygiene," said the baker. "When I have a pee, I pull it out with the string."

"How do you put it back?" asked the customer.

"With the tongs, of course," replied the baker.

A famous Welsh footballer died and upon arriving at the Pearly Gates was asked by the angel waiting for him, "Do you know of any reason why you should not enter the kingdom of heaven?" "Well," said the footballer, "Once I was playing for Wales against England and I used my hand to push the ball past an English defender. The ref never saw it and I went on to score."

"Ah, that's OK," said the angel. "We can let you in."

"Oh great!" replied the footballer. "That's been on my mind for ages. Thanks, St Peter!"

"That's OK," said the angel. "Oh, and by the way boyo, St Peter's off today – I'm St David."

An old woman visits her doctor to ask his help in reviving her husband's libido.

"What about trying Viagra?" asks the doctor.

"Not a chance", she says. "He won't even take an aspirin."

"Not a problem", replies the doctor. "Drop it into his coffee. He won't even taste it. Give it a try and call me in a week to let me know how things went".

It wasn't a week later that she ends up calling the doctor.

"It was horrid: just terrible, doctor," cries the old dear.

"Really? What happened?" asks the doctor.

"Well, I did as you advised and slipped it in his coffee and the effect was almost immediate! He jumped straight up, with a twinkle in his eye, and ripped my clothes to tatters and took me then and there."

"Why so terrible?" asks the doctor, "Was the sex that bad?"

"Oh, no, doctor," says the old lady. "It was the best sex I've had in 25 years! But I'll never be able to show my face in Starbucks again."

A teacher asks her class, "If there are five birds sitting on a fence and you shoot one of them, how many would be left?" She calls on Billy who replies, "None – they'd all fly away on the first gunshot."

The teacher says, "The correct answer is four, but I like your thinking."

Then little Billy says, "I have a question for you, miss. There are three women sitting on a bench having an ice cream. One is delicately licking the sides, the second is gobbling down the top and sucking the cone, while the third is nibbling on the top, which one is married?"

"Erm, the one that's gobbled down the top?" asks the teacher, blushing. To which Billy replies, "The correct answer is the one with the ring on, but I like your thinking."

A man goes to the dentist and asks how much it is for a tooth extraction. "£85 for an extraction, sir," was the dentist's reply. "Have you not got anything cheaper?" replied the man, getting agitated. "But that's the normal charge for an extraction, sir," said the dentist. "What if I don't use any anaesthetic?" asked the man hopefully. "Well, it's highly unusual, sir, but if that's what you want, I suppose I can do it for £60," said the dentist. "Hmm, what about if you used one of your dental trainees and still without any anaesthetic?" asked the man. "Well, it's possible, but it'll be a lot more painful. If that was the case we could bring the price down to, say, £30," said the dentist. "What if you use it as part of a student training session?" the man asked. "Hmm, well, OK... it'll be good for the students, I suppose. I'll charge you only £5 in that case," said the dentist. "OK, now you're talking. It's a deal!" said the man. "Can you confirm an appointment next Tuesday for the wife?"

Sarah hated Sunday school and always daydreamed. At school the teacher asks Sarah, "Who made the earth?" Will, who sits behind her, pokes her with a ruler to wake her up. "God Almighty!" she shouts. "Correct," says the teacher. "Who is the saviour of the earth?" asks the teacher. Will poked her again. "Jesus Christ!" she shouts. "Correct. And what did Eve say to Adam after their tenth child?" Will prangs her again and she shouts, "If you poke me with that one more time I'll snap it in half!"

A primary teacher starts a new job at the Watford Learning Centre and, trying to make a good impression on her first day, explains to her class that she is a Watford fan. She asks her students to raise their hands if they, too, are Watford fans. Everyone in the class raises their hand except one little girl.

The teacher looks at the girl with surprise and says: "Mary, why didn't you raise your hand?"

"Because I'm not a Watford fan," the little girl replies.

The teacher, still shocked, asks: "Well, if you're not a Watford fan, what team do you support?"

"I'm West Ham, and proud of it," Mary replies.

The teacher could not believe her ears. "Mary, you live in Watford. Why are you a West Ham fan?"

"Because my mum and dad both come from Barking, and they're both West Ham fans. So, I'm a West Ham fan, too."

"Well," says the teacher, in an obviously annoyed tone, "that's no reason for you to be a West Ham fan too. You don't have to be just like your parents all of the time. What if your mum was a prostitute and your dad was a drug addict and car thief, what would you be then?"

"In that case," Mary smiles, "I'd be a Chelsea supporter."

A Chinese man had three daughters, he asked his eldest daughter what kind of man she would like to marry.

"I would like to marry a man with three dragons on his chest", said the eldest daughter.

He then asked his second daughter who she would like to marry.

"I would like to marry a man with two dragons on his chest," said the second daughter.

He finally asked his youngest daughter who she would like to marry.

The youngest daughter replies, "I would like to marry a man with one draggin' on the ground."

A wife, frustrated by her husband's bone-idleness around the house in the DIY department, sees cause for concern one day when the toilet clogs up. She decides to ask if he'd mind seeing to it, and is greeted with a gruff, "What; do I look like a toilet cleaner?"

The next day the waste disposal unit seizes up. Summoning all her courage she says, "Sorry to bother you, dear. The waste disposal's broken – would you try to fix it for me?"

"What; do I look like a plumber? Get me a beer and sod off!" is the reply.

To cap it all, the next day the washing machine goes on the blink and, taking her life in her hands, the wife addresses the sofa-bound slob: "Darling, I know you're busy, but the washing machine's packed up."

"What; do I look like a bloody washing machine repairman?" her old man says.

Finally fed-up, she calls out three different repairmen to come and fix her appliances.

That evening, she informs her husband of this. He frowns angrily and asks, "So how much will it cost?"

"Well, they said I could pay them either by baking a cake or screwing them all," she says.

"What type of cake did they want?" he growls.

"What; do I look like Delia Smith?" she replies.

Newsflash... Hot off the wire from the Australian Medical Association: Australian Medical Association researchers have made a remarkable discovery. It seems that some patients needing blood transfusions may benefit from receiving chicken blood rather than human blood. It tends to make the men cocky and the women lay better.

A duck walks into a pub and asks the barman: "Got any bread?"

"No."

"Got any bread?"

"No."

"Got any bread?"

"No, we have no bread."

"Got any bread?"

"No, we haven't got any bread."

"Got any bread?"

"No, are you deaf, we haven't got any sodding bread. Ask me again and I'll nail your damn beak to the bar you irritating bloody bird!"

"Got any nails?"

"No."

"Got any bread?"

A man goes to his doctor and asks if there's a way to make his undersized penis any bigger. The doctor says there is a revolutionary surgery where a baby elephant trunk is grafted on to the end of his member. At just £3,000 for the operation the man agrees and six weeks later he's ready to try out his newly enlarged member.

While he is having dinner with his new date he feels an unusual stirring in his trousers and thinks tonight could be the night. They continue chatting over dinner when suddenly his penis flies out of his zipper, steals a bun from the table and disappears insides his trousers once more.

"Wow! Can you do that again?" asks his date, clearly impressed.

"My dick can," the man replies, "but I don't think my arse can take another bread roll."

The CIA had an opening for an assassin. After all the interviews and tests, three candidates were left – two men and a woman. For the final test, CIA agents took one man to a door and gave him a gun. "We must know that you'll follow instructions, no matter what. Inside this room is your wife. Kill her." The man said, "I could never do that." The agent said, "Then you're not the man for this job." The same thing happened with the second man. Finally, the woman was given the same instructions to kill her husband. She took the gun and went into the room. Shots were heard. Then screaming and banging on the walls. Then silence. Then the woman came out, wiping sweat from her brow. "This gun was loaded with blanks," she said. "I had to beat him to death with the chair."

A customer at Morris' Gourmet Grocery marvelled at the proprietor's quick wit and intelligence.

"Tell me, Morris; what makes you so smart?"

"I wouldn't share my secret with just anyone," Morris replies, lowering his voice so the other shoppers won't hear, "but, since you're a good and faithful customer, I'll let you in on it. Fish heads: you eat enough of them, you'll be positively brilliant."

"You sell them here?" the customer asks.

'Only £4 apiece,' says Morris.

The customer buys three. A week later, he's back in the store complaining that the fish heads were disgusting and he isn't any smarter.

"You didn't eat enough," says Morris.

The customer goes home with 20 more fish heads. Two weeks later, he's back and this time he's really angry.

'Hey, Morris,' he says, 'You're selling me fish heads for £4 apiece when I just found out I can buy the whole fish for £2. You're ripping me off!'

"You see?" says Morris. "You're smarter already."

A photographer for a national magazine is assigned to get photos of a great forest fire. Smoke at the scene is too thick to get any good shots, so he frantically calls his office to hire a plane.

"It will be waiting for you at the airport!" he is assured by his editor. As soon as he gets to the small, rural airport, sure enough, a plane is warming up near the runway. He jumps in with his equipment and yells, "Let's go! Let's go!" The pilot swings the plane into the wind and soon they are airborne.

"Fly over the north side of the fire," says the photographer, "and make three or four low-level passes."

"Why?" asks the pilot.

"Because I'm going to take pictures! I'm a photographer, and photographers take pictures!" says the photographer with great exasperation.

After a long gulp, the pilot says, "You mean you're not the instructor?"

What do you call a Scottish cloakroom attendant?

Angus McCoatup.

All of Jake's friends always got mad at him because no matter how bad a situation was he would always say, "It could be worse".

Finally his friends decided to make up something that he couldn't say, "It could be worse" about. When they were playing golf one day Steve said to Jake, "Did you hear what happened to Fred?"

"No," said Jake.

"Fred came home Thursday and found his wife in bed with another man, killed them both and then turned the gun on himself."

"It could be worse," said Jake, predictably.

"How could it be any worse than that?" Steve asked.

"Well", Jake said, "If it had happened a day earlier, I'd be dead."

Five Germans in an Audi Quattro arrive at the Italian border. The Italian Customs agent stops them: "It'sa illegala to putta five people in a Quattro."

"Wat do you mean it'z illegal?" asks the German driver.

"Quattro meansa four," replies the Italian official.

"Quattro is just ze name of ze automobile," the German says in disbelief. "Look at ze papers: this car is designed to kerry five."

"You can'ta pulla thata one on me!" replies the Italian. "Quattro meansa four. You hava five people ina your car and you are breakinga tha law!"

The German driver is angry. "You idiot! Call ze supervisor over, I want to speak to somevone with more intelligence!"

"Sorry," says the Italian. "He'sa busy with two guys in a Fiat Uno."

The owner of a family-run bakery was being questioned by the Inland Revenue about his tax return, having reported a net profit of £45,000 for the year.

"Why don't you people leave me alone?" the baker said. "I work like a dog, everyone in my family helps out and the place is only closed three days a year. And you want to know how I made £45,000?"

"It's not your income that bothers us," the taxman said. "It's these deductions. You listed six trips to Bermuda for you and your wife."

"Oh, that?" the owner said smiling. "I forgot to tell you – we also deliver."

The teacher had given her class an assignment. She'd asked her pupils to get their parents to tell them a story that had a moral at the end of it. "So what have you got for me, Johnny?" she asks one pupil sitting at the back of the class.

"Well," replies Johnny. "My mum told a story about my dad. Dad was a pilot in Desert Storm, and his plane got hit. He had to bail out over enemy territory, and all he had was a small flask of whiskey, a pistol and a survival knife. He drank the whiskey on the way down, so it wouldn't fall into enemy hands, and then his parachute landed right in the middle of 20 enemy troops. He shot 15 of them with the gun, until he ran out of bullets, killed four more with the knife, until the blade broke, and then he killed the last one with his bare hands."

"Good heavens!" said the horrified teacher. "What kind of moral did your mum teach you from that horrible story?" The boy replied: "Stay the hell away from dad when he's been drinking."

Bill Gates dies and goes to heaven. At the door, Saint Peter fits him with a £5,000 suit for everything he's achieved on earth. Later, as Bill's walking around heaven, he sees a man with a much more expensive- looking suit than his. The computer genius is extremely angry with this so he goes to Saint Peter and says, 'This man has a more expensive suit than me. Who is he?'

Saint Peter says, "Ah; that's the captain of the Titanic."

Bill is furious at this and argues, "But I created the Windows operating system and I get less than him?"

Saint Peter replies, "The Titanic only crashed once!"

How do you know that a blonde's been using a word processor?

There's Tippex all over the screen.

Irish engineers Paddy and Shamus are standing at the base of a flagpole, looking up.

A blonde woman walks by and asks, "What are you doing?"

"We're supposed to find the height of the flagpole," says Shamus, "but we don't have a ladder."

The blonde takes a wrench from her purse, loosens a few bolts, and lays the pole down. Next she pulls a tape measure from her pocket, takes a measurement and announces, "Five metres." She then walks away.

Paddy shakes his head and laughs. "Ain't that just like a blonde, Shamus? We ask for the height and she gives us the length!"

The Seven Dwarves were invited to an audience with the Pope, so off they go to the Vatican. After the greeting, they push Dopey to the front, saying: "Go on, Dopey: ask him: ask him!" So Dopey says to the Pope: "Do they have any nuns in Alaska?" and the Pope answers, "Of course they do, Dopey: there are nuns in every state in the USA." The dwarves push Dopey forward again: "Ask him the other one: ask him the other one." So Dopey asks "Do they have any black nuns in Alaska?" The Pope has a think and answers, "Yes, Dopey: they do have black nuns in Alaska." So the dwarves push Dopey forward again, saying, "Ask him the other one: ask him the other one." So Dopey says, "Are there any black dwarf nuns in Alaska?" At the end of his tether, the Pope replies: "Come on now, Dopey, don't be silly: there are no black dwarf nuns in Alaska." To which all the dwarves begin a chant: "Dopey fucked a penguin, Dopey fucked a penguin."

Once upon a time a long way away there was a kingdom with a king who had a daughter. He wanted her to marry a brave man who would desire her and make her happy. So he devised a test: if any man could swim across his huge lake of crocodiles they could have the choice of a castle, untold riches or his daughter's hand in marriage. People gathered from miles around and many volunteered to try. "I can do it," a man cried, jumped in the water and was instantly swallowed up by the crocodiles. "I can do better than that," said another, who jumped in and was instantly swallowed up by the crocodiles. Next, there was a loud splash and a man began to swim. He made it all the way and was greeted by the king. "Would you like the castle, the cash or the fair princess, brave sir?" he asked. "None of them," the man replied, "I want the fucker who pushed me in in the first place!"

A man is talking in his favourite bar with his favourite friends on a Sunday night. He says, "So, check this out – last night when I was down here with you lot, a bloody burglar broke into my house." "Well out of order," says his mate, "Did he get anything." says another. "Yup," says the man, "a smack in the face, a kick up the arse, a plank in the bollocks and a dinner-plate over his head – the missus thought it was me coming home pissed again!"

A man is sitting in a rough bar drinking. He orders a fresh pint but suddenly is overcome with the urge to go to the toilet. He doesn't trust anyone in the crummy bar but he has to go, so he scribbles on a cigarette paper, "I spat in this: don't drink it!" and he gums the paper to the side of his pint glass. He goes off to the toilet and comes back a couple of minutes later to find another cigarette paper stuck to his glass. On it is written, "So did we!"

An F-16 was flying escort with a B-52 and the pilot was generally making a nuisance of himself by flying rolls and other silly show-off manoeuvres around the lumbering old bomber.

Fed up with the smaller plane's antics, the pilot of the B-52 announced on the radio to the F-16:

"Anything you can do, I can do better."

Not to be outdone, the fighter pilot announced that he would rise to the challenge.

"OK, then. Try this."

The B-52, however, continued its flight, straight and level, apparently not having changed anything.

Perplexed, the fighter pilot asked, "So? What did you do?"

"We just shut down two engines."

A little boy and his younger brother were bored one day so decided to do interesting, grown-up stuff like swearing. The older boy says to his brother, "I know: next time we're downstairs with mum, I'll say "Hell" and you can say "Ass" – how's about that?' The younger boy nods his agreement and they troop off downstairs to have their breakfast. As they walk into the kitchen their mother says to the older child, 'And what would you like for your breakfast, dear?' to which he replies, 'Well, Hell, mum, I'd like some cornflakes please.' Upon hearing such profanity, the mother whacks the child really hard around the back of the head. The boy starts crying and runs off upstairs. The mother turns to the younger boy and looks him square in the face. 'And what would you like for your breakfast, young man?' she says. 'I don't really know, mum,' he starts to say, 'but you can bet your ass it won't be cornflakes!'

A huge muscular man walks into a bar and orders a beer. The bartender can't help but stare at the guy because in contrast to his large muscles, the man has a head that is the size of an orange. The bartender hands him the beer and says, "You know, I'm not gay but I want to compliment you on your physique, it's really phenomenal! But I have a question, why is your head so small?"

The big guy nods slowly. He's obviously fielded this question many times.

"One day," he begins, "I was hunting and got lost in the woods. I heard someone crying for help. I followed the cries and they led me to a frog that was sitting next to a stream."

'Kiss me, kiss me and I will turn into a genie and grant you three wishes.' the frog says."

"I looked around to see if I was alone and gave the frog a kiss. WHOOSH! The frog turned into a beautiful, voluptuous woman. She said, 'Thank you. As a reward, you now have three wishes'. I looked down at my scrawny 115 pound body and said, 'I want a body like Arnold Schwarzenegger!'"

"She nodded, snapped her fingers and WHOOSH! there I was so big that I ripped out of my clothes and was standing there naked! She then asked: 'What is your second wish?'"

"I looked hungrily at her beautiful body and replied, 'I want to make sensuous love with you by the stream.' She nodded, laid down and beckoned me. We made love right there by the stream for hours! God, I was a love machine."

"Afterwards, as we lay next to each other, sweating from our glorious lovemaking she whispered in my ear, "You know you have one more wish, what will it be?"

"I looked at her and replied: 'how about a little head?'"

A man goes into the barbers. The barber asks, "Do you want a crew cut?" The man replies, "No thanks, it's just for me."

Two men are drinking together in the bar on the top floor of the Empire State Building. The first one says to the second, "You know what? I bet you a hundred bucks I can jump out of that window and not hurt myself." "Bullshit – you're on," says the second man and the first man walks over to the window, opens it and jumps out. Two seconds later – whoosh! – and he is thrown back in. The second guy thinks that this is incredible but thinks it must be a fluke, so he offers double or nothing if the first guy can somehow do it again. The first guy takes him up on the bet and walks over to the window, opens it and jumps out again. Two seconds later – whoosh! – and he is thrown back in again. The second guy is amazed again, but now he figures that there must be one of those freak gusts of wind that you get around tall buildings. So, he says to the first guy, "How about this, then: double or quits again, but this time I jump out of the window?" "You're on", says the first guy and the second guy walks up to the window, opens it and jumps out. Five seconds later – whoosh! splat! – he is squashed flat and dead on the sidewalk, 70 floors below. The barman pours another drink and says to the remaining man, "You can be a real wanker when you've been drinking, Superman!"

There are two old drunks in a bar. The first one says, "Ya know, when I was 30 and got a hard-on, I couldn't bend it with either of my hands. By the time I was 40, I could bend it about 10 degrees if I tried really hard. By the time I was 50, I could bend it about 20 degrees, no problem. I'm gonna be 60 next week, and now I can almost bend it in half with just one hand."

"So," says the second drunk, "what's your point?"

"Well," says the first, "I'm just wondering how much stronger I'm gonna get!"

Once upon a time, there was a beautiful, independent princess who was very self-assured. One day she was walking in the forest when she chanced upon a frog sitting on a rock in a stream. To her amazement, the frog begins to talk to her: "Fair princess, I am a handsome prince, trapped by a witch in the foul, slimy body of this poor frog. Won't you kiss me once to break the spell and we can live happily ever after in my castle with my mother and my father and my knights and you can bear my children and look after them and prepare my meals and clean my sheets and all will be well!"

That night, as the beautiful, independent princess ate her frog's legs, she thought to herself and laughed out loud: "Not this time!"

How do you know a blonde has been sending e-mail?
There's an envelope in the CD drive.

Why do women love men who have been circumcised?
They can't resist something with 20 per cent off!

What's the last thing a drummer says before leaving a band?
"Why don't we try one of my songs?"

Two tall trees, a birch and a beech, are growing in the woods. A small tree begins to grow between them. One tree says to the other: "Is that a son of a beech or a son of a birch?" The other says he cannot tell. Just then a woodpecker lands in the sapling. The tall tree asks: "Woodpecker, you're a tree expert. Can you tell if that's a son of a beech or a son of a birch?" The woodpecker takes a taste of the small tree. He replies: "It is neither a son of a beech nor a son of a birch. That, my friends, is the best piece of ash I have ever put my pecker in."

A little girl walks into her parents' bathroom and notices for the first time her father's nakedness. Immediately, she is curious: he has equipment that she doesn't have.

She asks, "What are those round things hanging there, daddy?"

Proudly, he replies, "Those, sweetheart, are God's Apples of Life. Without them we wouldn't be here."

Puzzled, she seeks her mummy out and tells her what daddy has said. After she tells her mum, her mummy asks: "Did he say anything about the dead branch they're hanging from?"

A woman goes to see her priest because she has a problem with the couple of female parrots that she owns – they just will not behave themselves. All they can say is, 'Hello, we are prostitutes. Do you wanna have a good time?' The father agrees that that's a terrible situation but he realizes very quickly that he has a simple solution. He asks the woman to bring her two parrots over to his house, because he too has two parrots – his are male – and he has bought them up to read the Bible and to pray and all that sort of 'good' stuff. He figures that his good parrots will be a very good influence on her 'bad' parrots and that all will live happily together eventually.

The next day, the woman brings her two female parrots over to the priest's house. She sees the priest's two parrots in their cage. They are praying, burning incense and fiddling with their rosary beads, all in a very devout manner. The woman puts her parrots down next to the priest's parrots and hers pipe up, 'Hello, we are prostitutes. Do you wanna have a good time?' Upon hearing this, one of the priest's parrots turns to the other one and says, 'put the good book away my man, our prayers have been answered!'

A man is walking along a remote beach on the South coast of England. After about twenty minutes he hears a deep, booming voice say, "DIG!" He looks up, down, left, right, but he cannot see where the voice could possibly could have come from, so he carries on. "I SAID DIG!" says the same deep, booming voice. The man figures that the sensible thing to do under these circumstances is to do as he's told, so he starts digging in the sand at the point where he first heard the voice. After about ten minutes he digs up a little metal box, about one foot square. On the front of it is an old rusted padlock. He hears a deep, booming voice say, "OPEN!" so he pulls and pushes and tweaks and bends until the padlock breaks. Inside, the box is full of gold coins. The deep, booming voice says, "TO THE CASINO!" so the man packs up the box, puts it in his car and drives to the nearest casino. He's had a right result so far, he reckons, so he may as well carry it on. He changes the coins for a big stack of chips and starts to wander round the casino when the deep, booming voice says, "ROULETTE!" so he goes to the roulette table. There are a few people playing but he has no problem getting in on the game. Just then, the deep, booming voice says, "TWENTY-SEVEN" so he puts a couple of chips on that number. "ALL OF IT", the deep, booming voice says so the man loads all the rest of the chips onto twenty-seven. The croupier spins the wheel and rolls the ball. The crowd gathered round the table is silent as the ball spins. And spins. And spins. Eventually, it stops on... number twenty-six. And the deep, booming voice says, "SHIT!"

What does a redneck always say just before he dies?
  "Hey, watch this."

One night, a man rolls over in bed and gives his wife a big, knowing grin. Immediately realizing his intentions she says, "Not tonight darling. I have an appointment with the gynaecologist tomorrow morning and I want to stay fresh and clean."

Dejected and disappointed, the man rolls over and tries to get to sleep. A few minutes later he rolls over and prods his wife again.

"Tell me; do you have a dental appointment tomorrow, too?"

Little Tommy is sitting on a park bench stuffing a bag of pick-and-mix into his mouth when an old lady comes over to tell him off. "Son, don't you know that eating all those sweets will rot your teeth and make you sick?"

"My grandfather lived to be 105 years old!" replies Tommy.

"Did he always eat a whole bag of sweets in one go?" the old lady retorts.

"No", answers Tommy, "but he did mind his own business."

Three dustmen are doing their last round before Christmas. The first goes to a house, knocks and finds himself being invited in by a stunning blonde, who takes him upstairs and gives him a good seeing-to.

Afterwards, he rushes out and brags to his two pals about it, so the second decides to try his luck. Sure enough, the same thing happens to him.

Finally, the dustcart driver, reckoning he's on to a sure thing, gets out and knocks on the door. The woman answers, smiles and gives him a fiver.

Severely disappointed, the man asks: "How come I just get money, when you gave my pals a proper Christmas bonus?" "Well," the woman replies, "when I asked my husband about tipping you all, he said 'Give the driver £5 and screw the other two.'"

During WW II an American soldier has been on the front line in Europe for three months, when he is finally given a week of R & R. He catches a supply boat to a base in the south of England, and then catches a train to London. The train is extremely crowded and he can't find a seat. He is dead on his feet and walks the length of the train looking for any place to sit down. Finally he finds a compartment with seats facing each other; there is room for two people on each seat. On one side sits a proper-looking, older British lady with a small dog sitting in the empty seat beside her.

"Could I please sit in that seat?" asks the Yank.

The lady is insulted. "You bloody Americans are so rude," she says. "Can't you see my dog is sitting there?"

"Lady, I love dogs," says the American. "I have a couple at home – so I would be glad to hold your dog if I could sit down."

The lady replies, "You Americans are not only rude; you are arrogant too."

He leans against the wall for a time, but is so tired he finally says, "Lady, I've been on the front line in Europe for three months with not a decent rest for all that time. Could I please sit there and hold your dog?"

The lady replies, "You Americans are not only rude and arrogant; you are also obnoxious!"

With that comment, the soldier calmly steps in, picks up the dog, throws it out the window, and sits down. The lady is speechless.

An elderly, neatly-dressed Englishman sitting across on the other seat suddenly says, "Young man, I do not know if all you Americans fit the lady's description of you or not: but I do know that you Americans do a lot of things wrong. You drive on the wrong side of the road, you hold your fork with the wrong hand, and now you have just thrown the wrong bitch out of the window."

An artist asks a gallery-owner if there's been any interest in his paintings recently.

"I have good news and bad news," the gallery owner tells him. "The good news is a gentleman inquired about your work and wondered if it would appreciate in value after your death. When I told him it would, he bought all 15 of your paintings."

"That's great," the artist says. "What's the bad news?"

"He was your doctor."

Marty was doing some river fishing. A big one bit, and when he fished it out he had a big surprise: it was a goldfish. "Oi, fisherman," said the fish, "if you set me free I'll give you whatever you want. I'm a magic fish and I'll grant you three wishes." "Sounds good to me," thought Marty. "I've got it made now." "OK, then," said Marty. 'My first wish is to have a truck full of money'. 'At your command', said the goldfish. A top-of-the-range truck filled to the brim with cash appeared on the road next to the river; the key appeared in Marty's hand. "My second wish is to have a different top model to sleep with every night of every year." "At your command," said the goldfish, and a diary appeared in Marty's hand with a full schedule of women filled in. "My third wish is for my cock to touch the floor," said Marty. "At your command," said the goldfish, and he cut Marty's legs off.

One morning at breakfast, Chuck walks up behind his wife and pinches her arse. "You know, Daisy, if you firmed this up we'd be able to get rid of your girdle," he says. Now Daisy is most insulted by this, of course, but she decides to let it go – it's only breakfast time, after all.

The next day, Chuck walks up behind his wife and pinches her breast. "You know, Daisy, if you firmed this up we'd be able to get rid of your bra," he says. Daisy can't bite her lip another time, so she turns around and grasps his cock firmly, saying, "You know, Chuck, if you firmed this up we'd be able to get rid of the postman, the gardener, the pool man and your brother!"

A farmer is helping a cow give birth when he notices his four-year-old son standing wide-eyed at the fence, witnessing the entire thing.

"Dammit," the man says to himself. "Now I'm going to have to explain about the birds and the bees." Not wanting to jump the gun, the man decides to wait and see if his son asks any questions.

After everything is finished, he walks over to his lad and asks, "Well, son, do you have any questions?"

"Just one," the child says. "How fast was the calf going when it hit that cow?"

There were these two priests who rode bicycles to their parish church every week. One day one of the priests shows up to 'work' without his bicycle. The other priest says to him, "Where's your bike gone Father Michael?" to which Father Michael replies, "I'm not really sure, but I think it's been stolen!" The other priest tells him that, at the next sermon he gives, to read out the ten commandments, and by the time he gets to 'Thou Shalt Not Steal' someone will own up to stealing the bicycle from him.

The next time the two priests see each other they are both on bicycles again. The other priest asks Father Michael, "So you made the thief own up then did you father?" and Father Michael says, "Well not really, I took your advice sure enough and I was reading out the Ten Commandments. I got to 'Thou Shalt Not Commit Adultery, when I all of a sudden remembered where I'd left my bike!"

Two men standing in a bar have been drinking all day long. Both are heavily inebriated. The first man goes a bit green, then throws up all over himself. 'Oh no, the wife's going to kill me; I promised I wouldn't drink today.' His friend stops him short: 'Don't you worry about a thing, pal. Place a ten-pound note in your jacket pocket and tell the missus some other guy hurled on you. Then the man put that money in your pocket to pay for the cleaning bill.' The guy agrees and spends the rest of the day downing beers. On arriving home, his wife sees the mess he's in straight away and she asks: 'Have you been drinking?' 'No, I certainly have not. Some other guy threw up on me and gave me a tenner for my troubles. Check in my jacket pocket if you don't believe me.' She checks. 'But there's £20 in here.' 'Oh yeah, didn't I say? He shat my pants as well..."

How are tornadoes and marriage alike?

They both begin with a lot of blowing and sucking, and in the end you lose your house.

A man staggers into hospital with two black eyes and a golf club tightly wrapped round his throat. The doctor on duty asks him what happened.

"Well, doc, it was like this," the man says. "I was out for a quiet round of golf with the missus and she shanked her ball something terrible. It landed in a field full of cows, so we both went to look for it. I was having a good look round but couldn't find it. Anyway, I noticed a white thing in the arse of one of the cows so I walked over, lifted up its tail and there was my wife's golf ball, rammed right up there. That's when I made my only mistake."

"And what was that, then?" asked the doc.

"Well, I turned to get my wife's attention, lifted the cow's tail and shouted, 'Hey! This looks like yours!'"

A blonde is looking at a bulletin board at her workplace and sees an ad which says, 'Luxury Ocean Cruise Only £5'.

She copies the details, goes to the address and hands the ad and a fiver to the secretary. The secretary points to a burly guy sitting in a battered sofa, reading a newspaper.

The guy stands up and knocks the blonde unconscious. When she wakes up, she's tied to a log and floating down the river. She starts to think maybe this wasn't such a good idea after all.

Then she sees one of her colleagues (who is also blonde) floating right next to her.

Sighing, she says, "So do you think they're going to serve us some food on this trip?"

"They didn't last year," the other blonde replies.

A very successful lawyer parks his brand-new BMW in front of the office, ready to show it off to his colleagues. As he gets out, a truck comes along, too close to the kerb, and completely tears off the Beemer's driver's door.

The lawyer immediately grabs his mobile, dials 999, and in about five minutes a police car turns up. Before the cop has a chance to ask any questions, the lawyer starts screaming hysterically. The BMW, which he'd just picked up the day before, is now completely ruined and will never be the same, no matter how the body shop tries to make it new again.

After the lawyer finally winds down from his rant, the cop shakes his head in disgust. "I can't believe how materialistic you lawyers are," he says. "You're so focused on your possessions that you neglect the most important things in life."

"How can you say such a thing?" asks the lawyer.

The cop replies, "You sick sod; don't you even realize that your left arm's missing? It got ripped off when the truck hit you!"

"My God!" screams the lawyer. "Where's my Rolex?"

A mild-mannered man was tired of being bossed around by his wife, so he went to a psychiatrist. The psychiatrist said he needed to build his self-esteem and gave him a book on assertiveness, which he read on the way home.

Rendered bold by what he had read, the man stormed into the house and walked up to his wife. Pointing a finger in her face, he said, "From now on, I want you to know that I am the man of this house and my word is law! I want you to prepare me a gourmet meal tonight and when I'm finished eating my meal, I expect a sumptuous dessert afterward. Then, after dinner, you're going to draw me my bath so I can relax. And when I'm finished with my bath, guess who's going to dress me and comb my hair?"

"The funeral director!" said his wife.

A mafia godfather finds out that his bookkeeper has swindled him out of ten million dollars. This bookkeeper is deaf, so the godfather brings along his attorney, who knows sign language.

The godfather asks the bookkeeper, "Where's the ten million you embezzled from me?"

The attorney, using sign language, asks the bookkeeper where the money is hidden.

The bookkeeper signs, "I don't know what you're talking about."

The attorney tells the godfather: "He says he doesn't know what you're talking about."

At this point, the godfather pulls out a 9mm pistol, puts it to the bookkeeper's temple, cocks it and says, "Ask him again!"

"He'll kill you if you don't talk," signs the attorney.

The bookkeeper signs back: "OK. You win! The money is buried in my cousin Enzo's back yard."

The godfather asks the attorney, "Well, what'd he say?"

The attorney replies, "He says you don't have the balls..."

Late one night a mugger jumps the Chancellor of the Exchequer on his way back to 11 Downing Street. "Give me your money," the mugger demands.

Indignant, the politician replies, "You can't do this – I'm the Chancellor of the Exchequer!"

"In that case," replies the robber, "give me MY money."

Did you hear about the dyslexic pimp?
He bought a warehouse.

What do you call an artist with brown fingers?
Picasso.

A man goes to confession. In the booth he says, "Forgive me father for I have sinned. I... almost... had an affair with a woman."

"Almost? What do you mean almost?" says the priest, not really understanding what the man is going on about.

"Well father," the man continues, 'we got undressed and rubbed against one another, but then we both thought better of it and so we stopped."

"Very good,' says the priest, "but rubbing up against it is just the same as putting it in. You must not go near that woman again. You must say five Hail Marys and you must put £50 in the donation box by the door."

The man thanks the priest and walks to the door of the church. He stops by the donation box, pauses and then starts to leave. The priest runs up to him and says, "Oi, I saw that, you didn't put anything in the donation box did you?"

"Well no I didn't father," the man says, "I rubbed up against it, and as you say, that's the same as putting it in!"

A man finds a genie in a bottle, and is offered three wishes. First he asks for a fast sports car. Suddenly, a Ferrari appears before him. Next, he asks for a big house. Suddenly, he's sitting in a huge mansion. Finally, he asks to be made irresistible to women. Suddenly, he turns into a box of luxury chocolates.

How do you know if you've caught bird flu?
You're suddenly unable to park and all you can talk about is shoes.

Did you hear about the Welsh Mafia boss?
He'll make you an offer you can't understand.

Paddy and Mick worked together, and were both laid off, so they went to the benefits office. When asked his profession Paddy answered "Panty Stitcher. I sew the elastic onto ladies cotton panties and thongs."

The clerk looked up panty stitcher. Finding it classified as unskilled labour she gave him £45 a week unemployment benefit.

Mick was asked his occupation. 'Diesel fitter' he replied. Since diesel fitter was a skilled job, the clerk gave Mick £90 a week, When Paddy found out he was furious. He stormed back in to find out why his friend was collecting double his pay.

The clerk explained: "Panty stitchers are unskilled and diesel fitters are skilled labour."

"What skill?" yelled Paddy. "I sew the elastic on the panties and thongs. Mick puts them on his head and says "Yep, Diesel fitter."

A computer once beat me at chess, but it was no match for me at kick-boxing.

"Dad, what's a transvestite?"
"I don't know, but ask your mother, he'll know!"

A policeman walks over to a parked car and asks the driver if the car is licensed.
"Of course it is," replies the driver.
"Great, I'll have a pint then."

What do you call a dog with brass balls and no hind legs?
Sparky.

One night a burglar is trying to break into a house. He's sneaking across the lawn when he hears a voice say, "Jesus is watching you!"

The burglar jumps, turns around and looks up and down the garden. Not seeing anything, he begins creeping across the lawn again.

From the dark, "Jesus is watching you!" can be heard once more. Now the burglar is really freaked out and starts to look around again.

Eventually, he sees a parrot in a cage by the side of the house. The burglar goes up to the parrot and says, "Did you say that?" To which the parrot answers, "Yes, I did."

So the burglar says, "What's your name?"

The parrot stares at him. "Clarence," he says.

"What kind of stupid idiot would name his parrot Clarence?" says the burglar, laughing. The parrot remains quiet for a moment and then replies, "The same stupid idiot that named his Rottweiler Jesus."

An extremely drunk man looking for a brothel stumbles blindly into a chiropodist's office instead. He weaves over to the receptionist. Without looking up, she waves him over to the examination bed.

"Stick it through that curtain," she says. Looking forward to something kinky, the drunk whips out his penis and sticks it through the crack in the curtains.

"That's not a foot!" screams the receptionist.

"Christ!" replies the drunk. "I didn't know you had a minimum."

Three Aussies were working on a high-rise building project –
Steve, Bruce and Bluey. Steve falls off and is killed instantly.
As the ambulance takes the body away, Bruce says, "Someone
should go and tell his wife."

Bluey says, "OK; I'm pretty good at that sensitive stuff, so
let me do it."

Two hours later, he comes back carrying a crate of beer.

Bruce says, "Where did you get that from, Bluey?"

"Steve's wife gave it to me," Bluey replies.

"That's unbelievable," says Bruce. "You told the lady her
husband was dead and she gave you the beer?"

"Well, not exactly," Bluey says. "When she answered the
door, I said to her, 'You must be Steve's widow.' She said, 'I'm
not a widow.' And I said, 'I'll bet you a crate of beer you are.'"

Last night police were called to a branch of Pizza Hut after the
body of a member of staff was found covered in mushrooms,
onions, ham and cheese. The police spokesman said that
there was a strong possibility that the man had topped
himself.

Bruce is driving over the Sydney Harbour Bridge one day when
he sees his girlfriend, Sheila, about to throw herself off. Bruce
slams on the brakes and yells, "Sheila, what the hell d'ya
think you're doing?"

Sheila turns around with a tear in her eye and says, "G'day,
Bruce; ya got me pregnant and so now I'm gonna kill meself."

Bruce gets a lump in his throat when he hears this.
"Strewth, Sheila; not only are you a great shag, but you're a
real sport, too!"

A soldier, not noted as being very bright, was sitting at the table, looking at a mug upside-down. A sergeant came to sit next to him with his lunch and the soldier told him:

'I can't drink from this mug. It has no opening.'

The sergeant examined the mug and says:

'You're right. And besides, it has no bottom either.'

How are politicians like nappies?

You have to change them frequently, and for the same reason.

Three blondes go to a funfair and buy a raffle ticket. As it is for charity, everyone wins a small prize. The first blonde wins a case of spaghetti sauce. The second wins a small Stilton cheese. The third wins a toilet brush.

The following day, they meet at the first blonde's place and she says:

"Wasn't that great? I love spaghetti!"

"And I adore cheese," comment the second blonde, then asks the third: "How's the toilet brush?"

"Not so good, I'm afraid," she answers. "In fact, I think I'll go back to paper."

Why do police have trouble solving murders by rednecks?

Because they all have the same DNA.

What should you do if you're attacked by a gang of clowns?

Go for the juggler.

How is it one careless match can start a forest fire, but it takes a whole box to start a campfire?

A blind man enters a Ladies Bar by mistake. He finds his way to a bar stool and orders a drink. After sitting there for a while, he yells to the bartender, "Hey, you wanna hear a blonde joke?"

The bar immediately falls absolutely quiet.

In a very deep, husky voice, the woman next to him says, "Before you tell that joke, sir, you should know five important things: one, the bartender is a blonde woman. Second, the bouncer is a blonde woman. Third, I'm a blonde woman with a black belt in karate. Fourth, the woman sitting next to me is also a blonde and a professional weightlifter. Fifth, the blonde lady to your right is a professional wrestler. Now think about it seriously, Mister. Do you still wanna tell that joke?"

The blind man thinks for a second, shakes his head and declares, "Nah. Not if I'm gonna have to explain it five times."

Some friends of a guy called Shakey call the police anonymously and report their mate to be hiding drugs in his firewood. Within hours, the drug squad descend on Shakey's house, go out to the shed and take an axe to every piece of firewood without finding any drugs. After the disgruntled cops leave, the phone rings at Shakey's house. It's his mates:

"Hey, Shakes. Did the cops come?"

"Yeah!"

"Did they chop up your firewood?"

"Yep."

"Happy birthday, mate."

An Englishman, an Irishman, a Scotsman, a Catholic, a Jew and a blind man walk into a pub. The landlord says: "Is this some kind of joke?"

A man goes on holiday to the Caribbean, quickly falls asleep on the sand and ends up with a terrible sunburn. Wincing in pain as even a slight wind touches his scorched skin, the man hobbles off to the local doctor for help. The doctor takes one look at the man's legs and says, "I don't have anything to treat sunburn that bad. Try taking these Viagra pills."

"I've got sunburn!" cries the man. "What the hell's Viagra going to do?"

"Well, nothing for the sunburn," the doctor replies. "But it will help keep the sheets off your legs tonight."

After his business goes bust, a redneck called Scooter finds himself in dire financial trouble, and resorts to prayer. "God, please help me," he wails. "I've lost my business, and if I don't get some money, I'm going to lose my car as well. Please let me win the lottery."

Saturday night comes, and Scooter watches aghast as someone else wins. Again, he begins to pray:

"God, please let me win the lottery! I've lost my business, my car, and I'm going to lose my house."

Next Saturday night comes, and Scooter still has no luck. Once again, he prays. "God, why haven't you helped me?" he cries. "I've lost my business, my house, my car, and my children are starving! I've always been a good servant to you; please let me win the lottery just this once!"

Suddenly, there is a blinding flash of light as the heavens open, and Scooter is confronted with the glowing, ethereal vision of God himself.

"Scooter," he booms. "Meet me half-way on this. Buy a ticket."

How many drinkers does it take to change a lightbulb?
Never mind. We'll drink in the dark.

A woman has twins and, because she can't take care of them properly, gives them up for adoption. One of them goes to a family in Egypt and is named Ahmal. The other goes to a family in Spain; they name him Juan. Years later, Juan sends a picture of himself to his birth mother. Upon receiving the picture, she goes to see her GP and says:

"I feel so bad! I want to see my children again! Look, Juan sent me a picture!" She hands the picture over to the doctor.

"I want a picture of his brother, too!" she wails.

Her doctor answers: "Come on, they're twins! If you've seen Juan, you've seen Ahmal."

A woman's dishwasher breaks down, so she calls a repairman. Since she has to go to work the next day, she tells the repairman, "I'll leave the key under the mat. Fix the dishwasher, leave the bill on the counter, and I'll send you a cheque in the post. Oh, by the way; don't worry about my bulldog. He won't bother you. But, whatever you do, do not, under any circumstances, talk to my parrot! I repeat, do not talk to my parrot!"

When the repairman arrives at the woman's apartment the following day, he discovers the biggest, meanest-looking bulldog he has ever seen. But, just as the woman warns, the dog just lays there on the carpet watching the repairman go about his work. The parrot, however, is driving the man nuts the whole time with his incessant yelling, cursing and name-calling.

Finally the repairman can contain himself no longer and yells, "Shut up, you stupid ugly bird!"

The parrot replies, "Get him, Spike."

A very attractive blonde arrives at a casino and bets £20,000 on a single roll of the dice.

"I hope you don't mind," she says, "but I feel much luckier when I'm completely naked."

With that, she strips off, bends over the table slowly and rolls the dice. Then she yells out, "Yes! I've won! I've won!" She jumps up and down, hugs each of the dealers, scoops up all the chips on the table along with her clothes, and then quickly departs.

The dealers stare at each other utterly dumbfounded.

Finally, one of them asks, "So, what did she roll?"

"No idea," replies the other. "I thought you were watching."

A man tells his doctor he's unable to do all the things round the house that he used to. After an examination, he says, "Tell me in plain English what's wrong with me, Doc."

"Well, in layman's terms, you're lazy," says the doctor.

"OK. Now give me a medical term, so I can tell my wife."A little girl asks her mother, "Mum, can I take the dog for a walk around the park?"

Mum replies, "No, because the dog's on heat."

"What does that mean?" asks the child.

"Go and ask your father. I think he's in the garage."

The little girl goes to the garage and asks, "Dad, may I take Susie for a walk around the block? I asked Mum, but she said that Susie was on heat, and to come and talk to you."

The dad thinks for a second. He then takes a rag, soaks it with petrol and scrubs the dog's rear end with it. "OK," he says, "you can go now, but keep Susie on the leash."

The little girl leaves. She returns a few minutes later with no dog on the leash.

"Hey, where's Susie?" the dad says.

"She'll be here in a minute," the little girl says. "She ran out of petrol and another dog's pushing her home."

In The Beginning was The Plan...

And then came the Assumptions

And the Assumptions were without form

And the Plan was completely without substance

And the darkness was upon the face of the workers

And they spoke among themselves, saying... "It is a crock of shit, and it stinketh."

And the workers went unto their Supervisors and sayeth, "It is a pile of dung and none may abide the odour thereof."

And the Supervisors went unto their Managers and sayeth unto them, "It is a container of excrement and it is very strong, such that none may abide by it."

And the Managers went unto their Directors and sayeth, "It is a vessel of fertiliser, and none may abide its strength."

And the Directors spoke amongst themselves, saying one to another, "It contains that which aids plant growth, and it is very strong."

And the Directors went unto the Vice Presidents and sayeth unto them, "It promotes growth and is very powerful."

And the Vice Presidents went unto the President and sayeth unto him, "This new Plan will actively promote the growth and efficiency of this Company, and in these areas in particular."

And the President looked upon the Plan, and saw that it was good, and the Plan became Policy.

A young lady entered the doctor's office carrying an infant. "Doctor," she explained, "the baby seems to be ailing. Instead of gaining weight, he lost three ounces this week."

The doctor examined the child and then started to squeeze the lady's breasts. Too stunned to react, she lets him unbutton her blouse, deftly removing the bra and stroking her right nipple, emitting a thoughtful "Mmmm..."

"Young lady," he announced, "No wonder the baby is losing weight, you haven't got any milk!"

"Of course not!" she shrieked. "It's not mine, it's my sister's!"

Four people were travelling in the same carriage on a French train. There was an old, distinguished lady wearing a fur coat and a haughty expression; what was probably her granddaughter, a stunning 20-year-old of Playboy calibre; a highly decorated General; and a soldier fresh from boot camp.

They spend the time chatting about trivial things, and then entered a very long tunnel. While in the tunnel, the sound of a kiss was distinctly heard, followed by the unmistakable sound of a hand slapping a cheek. Silence followed, as all were lost in their respective thoughts:

The old lady was thinking: "Isn't it wonderful that, in this day and age there are still young people ready to defend young women's honour!"

The young woman was thinking: "How strange that he would want to kiss this old hag beside me, when I am available!"

The General was thinking, rubbing his stinging cheek: "I am outraged that any woman could think I would try to sneak a kiss in the dark."

The soldier had a big grin on his face and was thinking: "Isn't it great that someone can kiss the back of their own hand, then smack a General in the face and get away with it?"

A rich lawyer is approached by a charity for a donation. The man from the charity is concerned that the lawyer makes over £1,000,000 a year but doesn't give a penny to good causes.

"First of all," says the lawyer, "my mother is sick and dying in the hospital, and it's not covered by insurance. Second, I have five kids through three divorced marriages. Third, my sister's husband suddenly died and she has no one to support her four children."

"I'm terribly sorry," says the charity man. "I feel bad about asking for money."

The lawyer responds, "Yeah; well, if I'm not giving them anything, why should you get any?"

A man walks through a big shopping centre with his teenage son.

The boy tosses a 50p up in the air and catches it between his teeth to impress his dad, but he fails to clamp down with his teeth and ends up choking on the money. As the boy coughs and wheezes the father panics and shouts, "Help! Is there a doctor in the house? My son's choking!"

Not too far from the action, a man sitting in a cafe reading a paper hears the father's cries and patiently puts down his coffee and folds his paper. He then walks over to the boy, grabs him by the balls and squeezes the hell out of them.

The startled lad immediately coughs up the 50p and the man catches it in his hand and walks away.

The amazed father runs over and says, "Thank you, sir; you saved my son's life. Are you a doctor?"

"No," the man replies, "I work for HM Revenue and Customs."

After Quasimodo's death, the bishop of Notre Dame sent word that a new bell ringer was needed. The bishop decided that he would conduct the interviews personally and went up into the belfry to begin the screening process.

After observing several applicants demonstrate their skills, he decided to call it a day when a lone, armless man approached him and announced that he was here to apply for the job. The bishop was incredulous. "You have no arms!" he said.

"No matter", said the man, "Observe!" He then began striking the bells with his face, producing a beautiful melody.

The bishop listened in astonishment, convinced that he had finally found a suitable replacement for Quasimodo. Suddenly, rushing forward to strike a bell, the armless man tripped and plunged headlong out of the belfry window to his death in the street below. The stunned bishop rushed to his side. When he reached to street, a crowd had gathered around the fallen figure, drawn by the beautiful music they had heard only moments before. As they silently parted to let the bishop through, one of them asked: "Bishop, who was this man?"

"I don't know his name", the bishop sadly replied, "but his face rings a bell."

The following day the bishop had to continue his interviews for a bell ringer. The first man to approach him said: "Your Excellency, I am the brother of the poor, armless wretch who fell to his death from this belfry yesterday. I pray that you honor his life by allowing me to replace him in this duty."

The bishop agreed to give the man an audition, and as the armless man's brother stooped to pick up a mallet to strike the first bell, he groaned, clutched at his chest and died on the spot.

Two monks, hearing the bishop's cries of grief at this second tragedy, rushed up the stairs to his side. "What has happened?" the first asked breathlessly. "Who is this man?"

"I don't know his name", sighed the distraught bishop, "but he's a dead ringer for his brother."

How many psychiatrists does it take to change a light bulb?
   Only one, but it really has to want to change.

Two Eskimos sitting in a kayak were chilly, but when they lit a fire in the craft it sank – proving once and for all that you can't have your kayak and heat it.

A man goes into a fish and chip shop and says "Can I have fish and chips twice, please?"
   The shop owner says, "I heard you the first time."

A blonde is arrested at the airport check-in for having a bomb in her bag and is being grilled by the custom officer:
   "How come you have a bomb in your bag?" he barks.
   "It's just because I'm afraid of flying," the blonde wails.
   'You are afraid of flying, therefore you carry a bomb with you?'
   "Oh, I'm just afraid someone will bring a bomb on the plane."
   The custom officer shakes his head to try and clear his thoughts and asks again, in an incredulous tone:
   "If you're afraid of someone carrying a bomb with them on a plane, why do YOU carry one?"
   "It's simple," replies the blonde. "figured the odds against two people carrying a bomb with them would be much higher, so the plane would be far safer."

An elderly Floridian calls 911 on her cell phone to report that her car has been broken into. She is hysterical as she explains her situation to the dispatcher:

"They've stolen the stereo, the steering wheel, the brake pedal and even the accelerator!" she cries.

The dispatcher says, "Stay calm. An officer is on the way."

A few minutes later, the officer radios in. "Disregard," he says. "She got in the back seat by mistake."

A drunken man staggers into a Catholic church, sits down in the confessional and says nothing. The bewildered priest coughs to attract his attention, but still the man says nothing.

The priest then knocks on the wall three times in a final attempt to get the man to confess. Finally, the drunk replies, "No use knockin', mate; there's no paper in this one either."

One day, a French spy received a coded message from a British MI6 agent. It read: S370HSSV-0773H.

The spy was stumped, so he sent it to his similarly clueless boss, who forwarded it to Russia.

The Russians couldn't solve it either, so they asked the Germans.

The Germans, having received this same message during WWII from the Brits, suggested turning it upside down.

A man goes to hospital for a circumcision operation and he wakes up in the morning surrounded by hospital staff. He wonders what the hell is going on and then he feels an enormous piece of padding between his legs.

The head surgeon says to him, "Look here, sir; we're all really, really sorry, but I'm afraid we made a mistake and got a bit carried away with the chopping. We've ended up giving you a complete sex change operation."

The man screams and shouts and cries his eyes out. "Oh, my God," he says eventually, "there's so much I'll never be able to do again. I will never, ever be able to experience an erection."

The head surgeon strokes him on the head and says, "Of course you will, of course you will. It just won't be yours, that's all!"

A man inserted an advertisement in the classifieds:

"Wife wanted."

The next day he received a hundred letters. They all said the same thing: "You can have mine."

Did you hear about the man who collected five thousand door knockers?

He won a no-bell prize.

After a briefing on land mines, the captain asked for questions.

An intrepid solder raised his hand and asked "If we do happen to step on a mine, Sir, what do we do?"

"Normal procedure, soldier, is to jump 200 feet in the air and scatter oneself over a wide area."

A language instructor was explaining to her class that in French, nouns, unlike their English counterparts, are grammatically designated as masculine or feminine. For instance, "house" in French, is feminine (une maison) while "pencil" is masculine (un crayon).

One student then asked her what gender the word computer (ordinateur) was. She didn't know, so she decided to split the class into two, for fun, so that they could argue for it. Both groups were required to give four reasons for their recommendation.

The men's group decided that computers should definitely be of the feminine gender (une ordinateur), because:

1. No one but their creator understands their internal logic and even then only partially.
2. The native language they use to communicate with other computers is incomprehensible to everyone else.
3. Even the smallest mistakes are stored in long-term memory for possible later retrieval.
4. As soon as you make a commitment to one, you find yourself spending half your pay check on accessories for it.

The women's group, however, concluded that computers should be masculine (un ordinateur), because:

1. In order to do anything with them, you have to turn them on.
2. They have a lot of data but still can't think for themselves.
3. They are supposed to help you solve problems, but half the time they ARE the problem.
4. As soon as you commit to one, you realize that if you'd waited a little longer, you could have gotten a better model.

A young man enters the doctor's office complaining of being run-down.

'Well, what can I say?' says the doctor. 'Book a few days off and rest – take a vacation, even: spend the weekend at home and sleep.'

'I can't do that, doctor,' the young man replies, shaking his head. 'I work in the stock market; it's a very profitable line of work and I'll lose a lot of money if I take time off.'

'In this case, change your lifestyle, don't go clubbing and so on: cut down on sex, for instance.'

'What? I'm a young man, in my prime, and you want me to give up sex?'

'Well, you could get married,' the doctor mused. 'That way you could taper off gradually.'

Little Johnny is sitting in a biology class, and the teacher says that an interesting phenomenon of nature is that only humans stutter; no other animal in the world does this. Johnny's hand shoots up.

"Not correct, Miss!" he says.

"Please explain, Johnny," replies the teacher.

"Well, Miss, the other day I was playing with my cat. The neighbours' pitbull came around the corner, and my cat went 'ffffffffff! ffffffffffff! ffffffffff!', and before he could say 'f*ck off!', the dog ate him!"

After his first day at school, Timmy comes home full of questions for his parents. Unfortunately some of them are not really what his parents hoped he'd be learning at school. So Timmy goes up to his mother and says, "Mummy, what's a pussy? Everyone says that word in the playground and I don't know what it means."

Timmy's mother picks up an illustrated dictionary and flicks to the page with a cat on it. She shows him the picture. Then Timmy says, "Mummy, what's a bitch? Everyone says that word in the playground and I don't know what it means."

Timmy's mother picks up the dictionary and flicks to the page with a dog on it, and shows Timmy the female.

Timmy is still curious so he goes to find his father. He says, "Daddy, what's a pussy? Everyone says that word in the playground and I'm still not sure what it means."

Timmy's dad figures it is time to teach the boy a thing or two, so he picks up a jazzmag, draws a circle around the pussy that's on the page and shows the picture to the boy. "That's a pussy," he says.

Then Timmy says, "Daddy, what's a bitch? Everyone says that word in the playground and I'm still not sure what it means."

Timmy's father replies, 'Everything outside the circle!'

A woman golfer comes running into the clubhouse in pain.

"Christ, what happened?" says the club pro.

"I got stung by a bee between the first and second holes," she replies.

"Hmmm," the pro murmurs. "Sounds like your stance was a little wide."

What do blondes and doorknobs have in common?
Everyone gets a turn.

Have you heard about the new super-sensitive condom?

It hangs around after the man leaves and gives the woman a hug.

A man buys a 12 pack of condoms with his girlfriend and gets down to business straight away. A few days later, the two are at it again, and the woman realizes that there are only three condoms left. A little confused, she confronts the man as to where the other condoms have gone. "I was masturbating," he replies. The girlfriend looks confused and says, "I've never heard of that." The next day she asks a male friend if he does the same, to which he replies, "Yeah, of course." The woman shrieks back, "Really? You've masturbated with a condom?" The man looks surprised and says, "Oh no, sorry. I thought you said have I ever cheated on my girlfriend."

On his first night in prison, a convict is glumly eating his dinner when another inmate jumps to his feet, shouts, "Thirty-seven!" and all the other inmates laugh hysterically. Another shouts back, "Four hundred and twenty!" and gets the same reaction.

"What's going on?" says the new inmate to his cellmate.

"It's like this," says the convict. "We only have one joke book in this prison and everyone knows all the jokes off by heart, so instead of telling the whole joke, we just stand up and shout out a page number."

A few days later, the new convict decides that it's time to join in, so he stands up and shouts, "Fourteen!"

Total silence ensues. Turning to his cellmate, he asks, "What went wrong?"

The convict replies, "It's the way you tell 'em."

A drunken bum has collapsed on the corner of the street. A policeman comes up to him and asks him what he's up to. "Well," the bum says, "apparently the world rotates on a 24-hour cycle, so I'm waiting for my house to come by. I don't think it'll be long, because I saw my neighbour not so long ago!"

Dad was happy typing away on his computer and didn't notice his six-year-old daughter sneaking up behind him. Then she turned and ran into the kitchen, squealing to the rest of the family, "I know Daddy's password! I know Daddy's password!"
"What is it?" her sister asked eagerly.
Proudly she replied, "Asterisk, asterisk, asterisk, asterisk!"

An old nun who lives in a convent next to a construction site notices the bad language of the workers, and decides to spend some time with them to correct their ways.
She decides she'll take her lunch, sit with the workers and talk with them, so she puts her sandwich in a brown bag and walks over to the spot where the men are eating. She walks up to the group and with a big smile says: "Do you men know Jesus Christ?"
They shake their heads and look at each other. One of the workers looks up into the steelwork and yells, "Anybody up there know Jesus Christ?"
One of the steelworkers shouts, "Why?"
The worker yells back, "His wife's here with his lunch."

What's the title of the next *Da Vinci Code* film sequel?
I Know What You Did Last Supper

A young man stops at an ice cream van and asks the blonde serving:

"What flavours do you have?"

"Vanilla, chocolate, strawberry..." then she sneezes violently and her throat makes a rasping voice.

"You have laryngitis?" he enquires in a sympathetic voice.

"No, only vanilla, chocolate and strawberry."

A man calls a local hospital.

"Hello. Could you connect me to the person who gives information about patients? I'd like to find out if a patient is getting better, doing as expected or getting worse," he says.

The voice on the other end says, "What is the patient's name and room number?"

"Brian Johnson, room 302," says the man.

"I'll connect you with the nursing station," says the receptionist.

After a brief pause, the man hears: "3-A Nursing Station. How can I help you?"

"I'd like to know the condition of Brian Johnson in room 302," says the man.

"Just a moment. Let me look at his records... Mr Johnson is doing very well. In fact, he's had two full meals, his blood pressure is fine, he's to be taken off the heart monitor in a couple of hours and, if he continues this improvement, Dr. Cohen is going to send him home Tuesday at noon."

The man says, "What a relief! Oh, that's fantastic... that's wonderful news!"

The nurse says, "Are you are a family member or a close friend?"

"Neither! I'm Brian Johnson in 302! Nobody here tells me anything."

Why was the leper caught speeding?

He couldn't take his foot off the accelerator.

A British doctor says, "Medicine in my country is so advanced that we can take a brain out of one man, put it in another and have him looking for work in six weeks.

A German doctor says, "That's nothing. We can take a brain out of one person, put it in another and have him preparing for war in four weeks."

The American doctor, not to be outdone, says, "You guys are way behind. We just took a man with no brain, put him in the White House and now half the country is looking for work, and the other half is preparing for war."

A private who was going to be court-martialled asked the lawyer representing him for advice on what to wear. 'Wear your shabbiest uniform. Let them think you are sorry and repentant,' the lawyer replied. Then he asked a friend the same question, but got the opposite advice. 'Don't let them intimidate you. Wear your best uniform, with all the decorations and awards you got.'

Confused, the man went to his chaplain, told him of the conflicting advice and requested some resolution of the dilemma. 'Let me tell you a story,' replied the chaplain.

'A woman, about to be married, asked her mother what to wear on her wedding night. "Wear a heavy, long, flannel nightgown that goes right up to your neck." But when she asked her best friend, she got conflicting advice. Wear your most sexy negligee, with a V-neck right down to your navel.'

The private protested: 'What does all this have to do with me getting court-martialled?'

The priest replied, 'No matter what you wear, you are going to get screwed.'

What does a pimp put on his CV as a job title?
  Holesaler.

How do you know if a stoner's crashed into your house?
  He's still there.

While flying to South Africa, a plane crashes in desolate mountain terrain. The only survivor is an elderly lady who manages to stumble out of the wreckage. After crawling, hungry and exhausted, for several miles she finds shelter in a cave. After some time a Red Cross search party arrives, and begins crossing the mountain range looking for survivors. After a few hours they spot the cave entrance. "Is anyone alive in there?" shouts the group leader.
  "Who's that?" shouts the old lady.
  "Red Cross!" answers the leader.
  "Jesus, you guys get everywhere!" shouts the old dear. "I've already donated."

A man comes home from work one day to find his wife sitting outside with her bags packed, He asks her what she is doing and she replies "I'm going to Las Vegas."
  The man asks why she's decided to leave and she says "I found out that I can make a lot of money doing what I give you for free. In Vegas you get paid $400 for giving someone oral sex."
  The man ponders his wife's reply, goes into the house, packs his own bags and joins her outside.
  "And where do you think you're going?" She asks.
  "I'm going to Las Vegas as well."
  "Why?"
  "I want to see how you're going to live on $400 a year."

While out for a drive, an elderly couple stop at a service station for lunch. Back on the road afterwards, the elderly woman realizes that she's left her glasses in the service station.

By then, they've travelled quite a distance and have to go even further before they can find a place to turn around.

The old fella moans and complains all the way back to the restaurant. He called his wife every name he can think of and when they finally arrive back at the service station, and the woman gets out of the car to retrieve her glasses, the man yells to her, "And while you're in there, you might as well get my wallet, too!"

Why do men name their penis?

We don't want a total stranger making 90 per cent of our decisions.

How many Frenchmen does it take to defend Paris?

It's never been tried.

A mother walked into the bathroom one day and was shocked to find her son scrubbing away furiously at his cock using a toothbrush and toothpaste. "Oh, my God: what on earth's going on?" she said.

"Don't try and stop me, Mum," the boy said. "I'm doing this three times a day because if you think I'm going to end up with a cavity that looks as bad as my sister's you've got another think coming!"

An Australian man was having coffee and croissants with butter and jam in a cafe when an American tourist, chewing gum, sat down next to him. The Australian politely ignored the American, who, nevertheless, started up a conversation.

The American snapped his gum and said, "You Australian folk eat the whole bread?" The Australian frowned, annoyed with being bothered during his breakfast and replied, "Of course."

The American blew a huge bubble. "We don't. In the States, we only eat what's inside. The crusts we collect in a container, recycle them, transform them into croissants and sell them to Australia."

The American had a smirk on his face. The Australian listened in silence. The American persisted. "D'ya eat jam with the bread?"

Sighing, the Australian replied, "Of course."

Cracking his gum between his teeth, the American said, "We don't. In the States, we eat fresh fruit for breakfast, then we put all the peels, seeds and leftovers in containers, recycle them, transform them into jam and sell it to Australia." The Australian then asked, "Do you have sex in the States?"

The American smiled and said, "Why of course we do."

The Australian leaned closer to him and asked, "And what do you do with the condoms once you've used them?"

"We throw them away, of course."

"We don't. In Australia, we put them in a container, recycle them, melt them down into chewing gum and sell them to the United States. Why do you think it's called Wrigley's?"

A guy is shipwrecked on a celebrity cruise and wakes up stranded on a desert island with Kelly Brook. Anyway, after a few weeks they are having passionate sex. This is all fine and dandy for a bit, but the guy starts getting a bit depressed. Kelly comes up to him on the beach one day and asks, "What's the matter?"

"Well, it's wonderful," says the guy. "I'm on a tropical island with a beautiful woman, but... I miss my mates and going to the pub with them."

So Kelly replies, "Well, I'm an actress. Maybe if I get dressed in some of those male clothes which were left behind in the trunks, I can pretend to be one of your mates down the pub."

It sounded a bit weird but he thought he'd give it a try, so Kelly gets into the male clothing and they sit down next to each other. Then the guy goes, "Hey Joe, you'll never guess who I've been shagging."

Two brothers, Brian and Phil, make a deal that whichever one dies first will contact the living one from the afterlife. Brian dies a few years later. Phil doesn't hear from him for about a year and ruefully figures that there is no afterlife.

Then one day he gets a call. It's Brian. "So there is an afterlife! What's it like?" asks Phil.

"Well," begins Brian. "I sleep really late. I get up, have a big breakfast, then I have sex – lots of sex. Then I go back to sleep, but I get up for lunch, have a big lunch and have some more sex – lots more sex. Then I take a nap: then a huge dinner and loads more sex. Then I go to sleep and wake up the next day."

"Oh, my God," says Phil. "Heaven sounds amazing!"

"I'm not in heaven," says Brian. "I'm a lion in Windsor Safari Park."

A computer programmer was out walking one day when a frog called out to him and said: "If you kiss me, I'll turn into a beautiful princess."

Delighted with his find, he bent over, picked up the frog and put it in his pocket.

The frog spoke up again and said: "If you kiss me and turn me back into a beautiful princess, I will stay with you for one week." The computer programmer took the frog out of his pocket, smiled at it and returned it to his pocket.

The frog then cried out: "If you kiss me and turn me back into a princess, I'll stay with you for one week and do ANYTHING you want."

Again the computer programmer took the frog out, smiled at it and put it back into his pocket. Finally, the frog asked:

"What's the matter with you? I've told you I'm a beautiful princess, that I'll stay with you for a week and do anything you want. Why won't you kiss me?"

The computer programmer said: "Look, I'm a computer programmer. I don't have time for a girlfriend: but a talking frog – now that's cool."

I went to the butchers the other day and I bet him fifty quid that he couldn't reach the meat off the top shelf. He declined, saying that the steaks were too high.

Two cannibals are eating a clown.

One says to the other: "Does this taste funny to you?"

Mark returned from a doctor's visit one day and told his wife Alma that the doctor said he only had 24 hours to live. Wiping away her tears, he asked her to make love with him.

Of course she agreed and they made passionate love.

Six hours later, Mark went to her again and said, "Honey, now I only have 18 hours left to live. Maybe we could make love again?"

Alma agrees and again they make love. Later, Mark is getting into bed when he realized he now had only eight hours of life left. He touched Alma's shoulder and said, "Honey? Please? Just one more time before I die."

She agreed, then rolled over and fell asleep. Mark, however, heard the clock ticking in his head and he tossed and turned until he was down to only four more hours.

He tapped his wife on the shoulder to wake her up. "Honey, I only have four hours left! Could we...?"

His wife sat up abruptly, turned to him and said, "Listen Mark, I have to get up in the morning! You don't!"

A man who hates his wife's cat decides to get rid of it by driving it to the next town and leaving it there. But when he gets home, the cat's already back. The next day, he drops the cat off even further away, but the same thing happens. Finally, the man dumps the cat hundreds of miles away.

Hours later, the man calls home to his wife: "Honey, is the cat there?"

"Yes," she says.

"Can you put him on? I'm lost."

Japan has banned all animal transport after discovering some nibbled beds in Tokyo.
They think it could be a case of Futon Mouse.

Three blondes witness a violent crime. Two days later, they are summoned by the police to identify a suspect. In order to check they are reliable witnesses, the inspector says he will show them a mug-shot for thirty seconds, then ask each one for a description. He shows the mug-shot to the first blonde for thirty seconds, then covers it and asks her if she thinks she would recognize the face.

"Yes, easy," she replies. "The guy in the picture has only one eye."

The inspector blinks in confusion, then says, "He's got only one eye because it's a profile shot!"

Shaking his head, he repeats the procedure for the second blonde and again asks if she would recognize him.

"Easy! He only has one ear," she answers.

"Come on, what's the matter with you two? It's a profile shot! You're seeing this man from the side!" shouts the inspector.

Expecting the worst, he repeats the procedure with the third blonde, then says, "Would you recognize the suspect from this picture if you saw him in real life? And think before you give me a stupid answer."

The third blonde looks hard at the photo, and remains silent for a minute, then says, "Yeah, it's easy: he's wearing contact lenses."

This takes the inspector by surprise. He picks up the photo and looks really hard at it but can't tell if the suspect wears contact lenses or not. With a suspicious look at the third blonde, he checks the full report on the suspect. Sure enough, when the mug-shot was taken, he was wearing contact lenses!

Baffled, the inspector goes back to the third blonde and asks her, "How could you tell he was wearing contact lenses?"

"Well," she says, "he can't wear regular glasses with only one eye and one ear, now, can he?"

Two old men are arguing about whose dog is smarter.

"My dog's practically a genius," the first fella boasts. "Every morning he waits patiently for the newspaper to be delivered and then brings it in to me."

"I know," the second fella replies.

"What do you mean?" the first man asks. "How do you know?"

The second man answers, "My dog told me about it."

A man visits his GP with a delicate matter: "I was thinking about getting a vasectomy."

"Well, that's a big decision," says the doctor. "Have you talked it over with your family?"

"Oh, yes," says the man. "They're in favour of it, 15 to seven."

Morris, an 82-year-old man, went to the doctor to get a physical.

A few days later, the doctor saw Morris walking down the street with a gorgeous young woman on his arm.

A couple of days later, the doctor spoke to Morris and said, "You're really doing great, aren't you?"

Morris replied, "Just doing what you said, Doc: 'Get a hot mamma and be cheerful.'"

The doctor said, "I said, 'You've got a heart murmur; be careful.'"

Two prostitutes after the Christmas holidays. "What did you ask Santa Claus to give you?" asks one. "Hundred quid, as usual," replies the other.

A koala bear escapes from the zoo, decides to get himself a night out on the town and chances upon a prostitute. He spends the entire night with her, but every time they have sex he stops to eat a sandwich.

The prostitute is a little surprised but figures, "Hey, I'm having sex with a koala bear, so what the heck?"

In the morning the bear gets up, has a shower and is starting to walk out of the door when the prostitute calls him back.

"Aren't you forgetting something, honey?" she asks.

The bear turns around, looks at her and shrugs his shoulders. She realizes he doesn't understand so she beckons him back and gets a dictionary. In it, she looks up the word 'prostitute' and the definition is, 'Someone who has sex and gets paid for it.'

The koala understands, but picks up the dictionary and flicks to the 'koala' definition. It says simply, 'Eats shoots and leaves.'

Two Mexicans have been lost in the desert for weeks. At death's door, they see a tree in the distance. As they get nearer, they see that it's draped with rasher upon rasher of bacon: smoked bacon, crispy bacon, juicy bacon, all sorts of bacon.

"Hey, Pepe," says the first Mexican, "ees a bacon tree! We're saved!"

So Pepe goes on ahead and runs up to the tree. As he gets to within five feet of it, he's gunned down in a hail of bullets.

His friend drops down on the sand and yells across to the dying man: "Pepe! Pepe! Que pasa, hombre?"

With his last breath Pepe calls out, "Ugh, run, amigo, run – ees not a bacon tree, ees a ham bush."

What do you do with a three-legged dog?

Take it for a drag.

A man walking along a beach is deep in prayer. Suddenly, the sky clouds over, and in a booming voice the Lord says, "Because you have been so faithful to me, I will grant you one wish."

The man says, "Build a bridge from my home in Manchester to the Greek islands, so whenever I want a holiday I can just drive there."

The Lord says, "Your request is very selfish. Think of the supports required to reach the bottom of the sea: the concrete and steel it would take: the destruction to the environment and the havoc caused to shipping lanes. Your bridge will nearly exhaust all of the world's natural resources. Take a little more time and think of something else."

The man says: "OK Lord, you're right, I'm sorry I was thoughtless. I wish I could understand my wife: how she feels inside: why she cries."

The Lord replies, "So, do you want two lanes or four on that bridge, then?"

A man is walking through the Sahara desert, desperate for water, when he sees something far off in the distance. Hoping to find water, he walks towards the image, only to find a little old man sitting at a card table with a bunch of neckties laid out on it. The man asks, "Please, I'm dying of thirst; can I have some water?"

The man replies, "I don't have any water, but why don't you buy a tie? Here's one that goes nicely with your ripped clothes."

The young guy shouts, "I don't want a tie, you idiot, I need water!"

"OK, don't buy a tie. But to show you what a nice guy I am, I'll tell you that over that hill there, about four miles, is a nice restaurant. Walk that way; they'll give you all the water you want."

The man thanks him and walks away towards the hill and eventually disappears. Three hours later he comes crawling back to where the man is sitting behind his card table. He says, "I told you: about four miles over that hill. Couldn't you find it?"

The young fella rasps, "I found it all right. They wouldn't let me in without a tie."

Christopher invites his nosy mother over for dinner. She's been encouraging him to find a wife for years, and when she arrives she notices that the live-in housekeeper is a very attractive woman who gets on very well with her son. She can't help wondering if maybe there's something going on – they get on so well – but her son denies everything: "Mother, I assure you that my relationship with my housekeeper is strictly professional."

A few days later, the housekeeper tells Christopher that ever since his mother came over for dinner she has been unable to find the silver tray brandy is always served on. A curious affair indeed, thinks Christopher: I wonder what my mother is up to now. So he writes his mother a letter:

Dear Mother,
Regarding my silver tray, I'm obviously not saying that you did take it, and I'm not saying that you did not take it, but the fact remains that I have been unable to find it since you came over for dinner.
  Love,
  Christopher.

A couple of days later, Christopher receives a reply:

Dear Christopher,
Regarding your housekeeper, I'm obviously not saying that you do sleep with her, and I'm not saying that you do not sleep with her, but the fact remains that if she was sleeping in her own bed she would have found the silver tray by now!
  Love,
  Mother.

Four brothers grow up to become wealthy doctors and lawyers. At a meal, they're discussing what gifts they're about to give their elderly mother for her birthday. The first brother pipes up, "I've had a big house built for her."

Another sibling chips in with, 'Well I've had a £100,000 cinema installed in that house for her.'

"That's nothing," offers the third brother. "I had my car dealer deliver her a brand-new Ferrari Enzo."

The remaining brother finally speaks up: 'You know how mum loved reading the Bible, but she can't read so well these days? Well, I met this priest who has a parrot that recites the entire book! It took 12 years to teach him – and I've had to pledge to contribute £100,000 to the church – but I've got him! Mum just has to name the chapter and verse and the parrot will recite it.' The brothers are impressed.

Post-birthday, mum pens some thank-you notes. "David, the house you built is so huge! I live in only one room, but I have to clean the whole place! Not great, but thanks anyway, son." To her second eldest she writes: "Michael, that cinema holds 50 people... but all my friends are dead! I'll never use it. Thank you for the gesture all the same." "Peter," she writes to her third eldest, "I'm too old to drive, so I never use the Enzo. The thought was kind. Thanks."

Finally, the youngest boy receives his letter: "Dearest Richard! You were the only son to have the good sense to put a little thought into your gift. The chicken was absolutely delicious!"

A blonde finds her way to her doctor and tells him that she's really worried because every part of her body hurts.

'Show me where', says the doctor, concerned.

The blonde touches her own arm and screams, 'Ouch!'. Next she touches her leg, her nose, her elbow and every time she howls in pain.

She looks at her doctor and says, 'See? I told you: it hurts everywhere!'

The doctor pokes her in the chest and says, 'Don't worry; it's not serious. You've just got a broken index finger.'

Tom, an 80-year-old farmer, is at the doctor's telling him how he's going to marry a mail-order bride.

"How old is the new bride to be?" asks the Doc.

"She'll be twenty-one in November." Tom proudly proclaims.

Being the wise man that he is, the doctor realizes that the sexual appetite of a young woman won't be satisfied by an 80-year-old man, and wanting his old patient's remaining years to be happy the doctor tactfully suggests that Tom should consider getting a hired hand to help him out on the farm, knowing nature will take its own course.

About four months later, the doctor runs into Tom on the street.

"How's the new wife?" asks the doctor.

Tom proudly says, "She's pregnant."

The doctor, happy that his sage advice has worked out, continues, "And how's the hired hand?"

Without hesitating, Tom replies, "She's pregnant too!"

What do you call a man who doesn't cheat on his wife when he's away on business?

An astronaut.

How many kids with Attention Deficit Hyperactivity Disorder does it take to change a lightbulb?

Wanna ride bikes?

Why do cows have bells?

Because their horns don't work

A blonde wanted to get her pet dog in a smooth-haired dog contest and decided to help her dog a little by going to the chemist for some hair-removal lotion.

The assistant hands her a bottle of special shampoo and says, "Remember to keep your arms in the air for at least three minutes."

"Er, it's not for my armpits," the blonde replies blushing slightly, "it's for my Chihuahua."

"In that case, don't ride a bike for three days," the assistant says.

A drunken bum has too much to drink one night in his local. He can hardly stand up but he knows that he absolutely has to take a piss. He staggers over to the toilets, getting his cock out as he does so. He crashes through the door, cock in hand, only to bump into two women because he's stumbled into the ladies instead. One of the women screams and shouts, 'This is for ladies, my good man!' and the bum replies, as he fumbles to put away his cock, 'So is this, lady!

An old man, a boy and a donkey were going to town. The boy rode on the donkey and the old man walked. As they went along, they passed some people who remarked it was a shame the old man was walking and the boy was riding. The man and the boy thought maybe the critics were right, so they changed positions.

Later, they passed some people who remarked it was a shame the old man was making the little boy walk.

They then decided they both would walk!

Soon they passed some more people who thought they were stupid to walk when they had a decent donkey to ride, so they both rode the donkey.

Then they passed some people who shamed them by saying how awful it was to put such a load on a poor donkey. The boy and man said they were probably right, so they decided to carry the donkey. As they crossed the bridge, they lost their grip on the animal and it fell into the river and drowned.

The moral of the story?

If you try to please everyone, you might as well kiss your ass good-bye.

What did the sign on the brothel door say?

We're closed. Beat it.

A blonde and a brunette are out driving. As they've had a few beers, the brunette tells the blonde to look out for cops. They drive for a while, and then the blonde taps the brunette on the shoulder and says:

"Hold on, there's a cop car behind us"

"Shit!' says the brunette. 'Are their lights on?"

The blonde has to think for a moment, then says, 'Er... Yes. No. Yes. No. Yes. No...'

Why does a chicken coop have two doors?

If it had four, it would be a chicken sedan.

A man walks into a pub, sits down, orders three pints of lager, drinks them and then leaves. This continues daily for several weeks.

Curious, the pub landlord approaches him one day: "Why do you always order three pints of lager?" he asks.

"Well," says the man, "my two brothers and I always used to have a pint each and since they've both passed on, I've continued to order the three beers in their honour."

The landlord is taken aback by such nobility and welcomes the man whenever he then visits the pub. But two weeks later, the man strolls in and orders not his usual three pints, but only two. Surprised, the landlord asks what the problem is.

"Oh, no problem at all," smiles the man, "I've just decided to stop drinking."

Two military policemen were chasing a fleeing draftee who ran into the courtyard of a convent where a nun was seated on a bench reading a book.

"Sister, please hide me! I don't want to be drafted!"

"OK. Hide under my skirt."

The two policemen finally entered the convent and asked the nun if she had seen anyone.

"I am sorry, officers; I didn't," she replied.

After they left, she told the young boy that the coast was clear.

"Thank you, sister!" the boy says, very relieved. Then he felt he'd better give her some kind of compliment as a way to show his appreciation of her sacrifice.

"Say," he starts, "you have nice legs for a nun!'"

"Don't get any ideas," the nun growls. "If you reach up a little farther you'll find a set of balls! I'm not going to be drafted either!"

A woman accompanied her husband to the doctor's office. After his check-up, the doctor called the wife into his office alone.

He said, "Your husband is suffering from a very severe disease, combined with horrible stress. If you don't do the following, your husband will surely die. Each morning, fix him a healthy breakfast. Be pleasant, and make sure he is in a good mood. For lunch, make him a nutritious meal. Don't burden him with chores, as he will have had a hard day. Don't discuss your problems with him, it will only make his stress worse. And most importantly... make love with your husband several times a week. If you can do this for the next ten months to a year, I think your husband will regain his health completely."

On the way home, the husband asked his wife, "What did the doctor say?"

"You're going to die," she replied.

Why did Euro Disney have to close down?

Health and Safety found a five-foot mouse in the restaurant.

Four surgeons took a coffee break and discussed their work. The first said, "I think accountants are the easiest to operate on. You open them up and everything inside is numbered."

The second said, "Librarians are easier. You open them up and everything is alphabeticized."

The third said, "I like to operate on electricians. You open them up and everything inside is colour-coded."

The fourth one said, "I like to operate on lawyers. They're heartless, spineless, gutless and their heads and their arses are interchangeable."

A man is sitting at a bar enjoying a drink when an exceptionally gorgeous young woman walks in. The man can't take his eyes off her. Noticing his overly attentive stare, she walks directly over to him and before he can even apologise for gawping, she makes him an offer: 'I'll do absolutely anything you want me to, no matter how kinky it is, for £100. However, there is one condition..."

Naturally, the man asks what the condition is. "Well," says the woman, "you have to tell me what you want me to do in three words."

The man considers the proposition for a moment, takes out his wallet and slowly counts out five £20 notes. He presses each note into the young woman's hand, looks excitedly into her eyes and finally says: "Paint my house."

A man is invited to a fancy dress party, but is reluctant to go because he is bald and has a wooden leg. He writes a letter to a fancy dress shop telling them of his problem and, sure enough, a few days later a package arrives that contains a pirate outfit. Attached is a note that reads, "We hope this is suitable – we thought the bandana would cover your bald head and with a wooden leg you would really look the part."

The man is furious and writes a really rude letter of complaint.

About a week later another parcel arrives. Inside is a monk's outfit with another note, "Sorry for any offence caused – we hope this is better, as the long cassock will hide your leg and with your bald head you will look just the part."

Once again, the man is furious and this time writes the shop an even ruder letter of complaint.

Then another package arrives. Inside is a jar of treacle and another note: "Take the jar of treacle, pour it over your head, shove your wooden leg up your arse and go as a toffee apple."

What's the difference between an Argentine football fan and a bad cup of coffee?

Nothing; they're both bitter.

Did you hear about the New Zealand farmer who thought he had an STD?

It turns out that he was just allergic to wool.

Johnny was in class when the teacher farted. Embarrassed, she said, "Johnny, stop that!"

To which Johnny replied, "Which way did it go, miss?"

A Polish man goes to have his eyes tested. He walks in, and the ophthalmologist points to a card on the far wall with the letters "CZWXNQSTACZ" on it.

"Can you read that?" the ophthalmologist asks. "Read it?" the Polish man replies, "I slept with his sister."

One night a policewoman pulls over a drunk driver. She asks him to step out of his car and says, "Anything you say can and will be held against you."

The drunk thinks about this for a moment and says, "Breasts. "

An Essex girl walks into the local dry cleaners. She places a garment on the counter "I'll be back tomorrow afternoon to pick up my dress." she says.

"Come again?" says the clerk, cupping his ear.
"No" she replies. "This time it's mayonnaise."

An attractive woman from New York is driving through a remote part of Texas when her car breaks down. A few minutes later, a cowboy on horseback wearing leather chaps comes along.

"Howdy, ma'am. I'm Pete; can I give you a ride into town?"

The woman accepts, climbs up behind him on the horse and they ride off.

Every few minutes, the cowboy lets out a whoop so loud that it echoes from the surrounding hills. When they arrive in town, he lets her off at a service station and yells one final "Yahoo!" before riding off.

"What did you do to get Pete so excited?" the service-station attendant asks.

"Nothing," she says, "I just sat behind him on the horse, put my arms around his waist and held on to his saddle horn so I wouldn't fall off."

"Lady," the attendant says, "apart from those chaps, Pete rides bareback."

What does an Aussie use for protection during sex?

A bus shelter.

Two rats in a sewer talking to each other. One says to the other, "I'm sick of eating shit."

The other rat says, "It's ok, I've spoken to the lads, we're on the piss tomorrow."

An American tourist in Dublin decides to duck out of his tour group and explore the city on his own. He wanders around, taking in the sights and occasionally stopping at a quaint pub to soak up the local culture, chat with the lads and have a pint of Guinness. After a while, he finds himself in a very high-class area: big, stately residences, no pubs, no shops, no restaurants and, worst of all, no public toilets. He really needs to go after all those pints of Guinness and manages to find a narrow side-street – the perfect solution to his problem. As he's unzipping, he's tapped on the shoulder by a policeman, who says, "I say, sir, you simply cannot do that here, you know."

"I'm very sorry, officer," replies the American, "but I really, really have to go and I just can't find a public toilet."

"Ah, yes," says the policeman. "Just follow me."

He leads him to a back delivery alley, then along a wall to a gate, which he opens. "In there," points the policeman. "Whizz away, sir. Anywhere you want." The fellow enters and finds himself in the most beautiful garden he has ever seen: manicured grass lawns, statues, fountains, sculptured hedges and huge beds of gorgeous flowers, all in perfect bloom. Since he has the policeman's blessing, he unburdens himself and is greatly relieved. As he goes back through the gate, he says to the policeman, "That was really decent of you; is that what you call the famed Irish hospitality?"

"No, sir," replies the cop. "That's what we call the British Embassy."

Who has the easiest job in the English cricket squad?
  The guy who removes the red ball marks from the bats.

What is the height of optimism?
  An English batsman applying sunscreen.

What's a blonde's favourite nursery rhyme?
  Humpme Dumpme

What's round and snarling?
  A vicious circle.

A young man joins a big corporate empire as a trainee. On his
very first day of work, he dials the canteen and shouts into
the phone, "Get me a coffee, quickly!"
  The voice from the other side responds, "You fool, you've
dialled the wrong extension. Do you know who you're talking
to?"
  The trainee goes white and says, "No, who is it?"
  The voice on the end of the line continues, "It's the
company CEO."
  The trainee thinks for a moment and shouts back, "And do
you know who you're talking to, you fool?"
  "No," replies the CEO indignantly.
  "Good," says the trainee, and slams down the phone.

An Asian man walks into the currency exchange in New York
City with 2000 yen and walks out with $72. The following
week, he walks in with 2000 yen, and is handed $66. He asks
the teller why he got less money that week than the previous
week.
  The teller says, "Fluctuations, sir."
  The Asian man storms out, and just before slamming the
door, turns around and shouts, "Fluc you Americans, too!"

A British pilot gets shot down behind enemy lines. He wakes up in a German hospital, his uniform gone, with a funny feeling in his left leg.

A German doctor comes to his bed and says:

"I am a doctor before I am a German, and I will treat you with the respect to which any patient is entitled," he says. "I must tell you, however, that it is quite possible we'll have to amputate your left leg.'

The pilot is shocked, but manages to say:

"Thank you for your kindness, doctor, and for agreeing to treat me although I am an enemy." He pauses, then says: "Do you think it would be possible to send my leg back to my family in England?"

The doctor is a bit surprise by this request, but he agrees. Unfortunately, a month later, the second leg has to go too, and again the pilot asks him to send it to England.

The doctor agrees. Another month goes by and he is forced to admit to himself that the pilot's right arm will soon have to come off. He breaks the news very gently to him and is not surprised to hear that the pilot would like his arm to be shipped home with the rest of his other bits. The doctor complies but, when comes the time for the right arm to come off, he is accompanied to the unfortunate pilot's bedside by two German security officers.

"So this is the pilot who gets his arms and legs sent to England," one of them says. "Tell me... you're not trying to escape, are you?"

Programming today is a race between software engineers striving to build bigger and better idiot-proof programs, and the Universe trying to produce bigger and better idiots. So far, the Universe is winning.

One day the Pope decides he's had enough of the 'No sex' rule, so he decides to treat himself to a bit of five-on-one in his bedroom. Half-way through, a window cleaner appears at his window and demands £5,000 to keep schtum, so the Pope pays him. A week later a cardinal comes round and notices how clean the windows are.

"How much did your window cleaner charge?" he asks.

"£5,000," the Pope replies.

"Christ, he must have seen you coming!"

While redecorating a church, three nuns become extremely hot and sweaty in their habits, so Mother Superior says, "Let's take our clothes off, and work naked."

The other two nuns disapprove, and ask, "What if someone sees us?"

But the Mother Superior says, "Don't worry; no one will see us. We'll just lock the door."

So the other nuns agree, strip down and return to work.

Suddenly, they hear a knock at the door, and grab their clothes in a panic.

Mother Superior runs to the door and calls through, "Who is it?"

"Blind man," a man's voice comes back.

So she opens the door, and lets in the blind man. He turns to the nuns and says, "Great tits, ladies. Now, where do you want these blinds?"

Two builders (Dave and Stuart) are seated either side of a table in a rough pub when a well-dressed man enters, orders a beer and sits on a stool at the bar. The two builders start to speculate about the occupation of the man in the suit...

"I reckon he's an accountant", Dave says.

Stuart: – No way – he's a stockbroker.

"He ain't no stockbroker ! A stockbroker wouldn't come in here!"

The argument repeats itself for some time until the volume of beer gets the better of Dave and he makes for the toilet. On entering the toilet he sees that the suit is standing at a urinal. Curiosity and the several beers get the better of the builder.

"Scuse me... no offence meant, but me and me mate were wondering what you do for a living?", he asked the well-dressed man.

"No offence taken! I'm a Logical Scientist by profession".

"Oh! What's that then?"

"I'll try to explain by example ...Do you have a goldfish at home?"

"Er ... mmm ... well yeah, I do as it happens!"

"Well, it's logical to follow that you keep it in a bowl or in a pond. Which is it?"

"It's in a pond!"

"Well then it's reasonable to suppose that you have a large garden then?"

"As it happens, yes I have got a big garden!"

"Well then it's logical to assume that in this town if you have large garden then you have a large house?"

"Actually yes, I've got a five bedroom house... built it myself!"

"Well, given that you've built a five bedroom house, it is logical to assume that you haven't built it just for yourself and that you are quite probably married?"

"Yes I am married, I live with my wife and three children".

"Well then it is logical to assume that you are sexually active with your wife on a regular basis?"

"Yep! Four nights a week!"

"Well then it is logical to suggest that you do not masturbate very often?"

"Me? Never!"

"Well there you are! That's logical science at work: from finding out that you had a goldfish, I've told you about your sex life!

"I see! That's pretty impressive... thanks mate!"

They both leave the toilet and Dave returns to his mate.

"I see the suit was in there. Did you ask him what he does?" Stuart asks Dave.

"Yep! He's a logical scientist!"

"What's that then?"

"I'll try and explain. Do you have a goldfish?"

"Nope".

"Well then, you're a wanker."

After a long time procrastinating, a man finally agrees to see a doctor about a lump on his belly, only if his grown-up son goes with him. On the appointed day, they receive the terrible news that he is suffering from cancer and that he doesn't have long to live. They are both shocked and the son decides to take his dad to his local for a pick-me-up. In the pub they find all his father's friends and his dad tell them in hushed tones that he is going to die of AIDS. The son is rather surprised and, when they find a table to sit at for a chat, he asks his dad: "Tell me; why did you tell your friends you're dying of AIDS? You don't have AIDS." "I know," the father replies, "but I don't want them screwing your mother after I'm gone!"

A Catholic priest and a nun are enjoying a rare round of golf on their day off. The priest steps up to the first tee and takes a mighty swing. He misses the ball entirely and says, "Sh*t, I missed."

The good Sister demands that he watches his language: but on his next swing, he does it again and shout,s "Sh*t, I missed."

"Father, I'm not going to play with you if you keep swearing," the nun complains.

The priest promises to hold his tongue, but on the fourth tee he misses again, and can't stop cursing.

The Sister is really mad now and says, "Father John, God is going to strike you dead if you keep swearing like that."

On the next tee, Father John continues his bad form. Again he instinctively cries out, "Shit, I missed."

Suddenly a terrible rumble is heard and a gigantic bolt of lightning strikes Sister Marie dead in her tracks. Then, from the sky, a booming voice can be heard... "Shit, I missed!" .

A man was sprawled out across three entire seats in his local cinema. When the usher came by and noticed this, he whispered to the man, "Sorry sir, but you're only allowed one seat."

The man groaned but didn't budge, and the usher became impatient.

"Sir," the usher repeated, "if you don't get up from there, I'm going to have to call the manager."

Again, the man just groaned, infuriating the usher, who then turned and marched briskly back up the aisle in search of his manager. In a few moments, both the usher and the manager returned and stood over the man. Together the two of them tried to move him, but with no success. Finally, they decided to call the police. Soon, a policeman arrived and surveyed the situation briefly.

"Alright, mate. What's your name?"

"Sam," the man moaned...

"Where you from, Sam?" the cop asked.
"The balcony."

Two old Englishmen and two old Irishmen enter a bar and see a sign that reads, "Old Timers' Bar: All Drinks 50p!"

When the old bartender spots them he calls out: "Come on in and let me pour you a drink! What'll it be?"

The four men each ask for a martini and the bartender duly serves them up and says: "That'll be 50p each, please."

They pay for their drinks, down them and order another round. Again, four excellent martinis are produced for just 50p each.

The old men pay up, but their curiosity is too much and one of the Irishmen asks "How can you afford to serve martinis as good as these for just 50p a piece?"

"Here's my story," the barman says. "I used to be a tailor in London, but I always wanted to own a bar. Last year I hit the lottery for £15 million and decided to open this place. I think our culture is far too disrespectful to its senior members, so every drink costs 50p: wine, whiskey, beer, anything. Guys like you are coming from all over – it's great."

"Wow! That's quite a story," says one of the Englishmen.

The four of them continue drinking and can't help but notice three other blokes at the end of the bar who don't have a drink between them. In fact, they haven't ordered anything the whole time they've been there.

The Englishman gestures at the men and asks the generous landlord, "What's with them?"

The bartender says, "They're from Scotland. They're waiting for Happy Hour."

The residents of a redneck town keep falling down a deep hole in the middle of its main street and always end up dying because the nearest hospital is located some 40 miles away. The mayor calls a town meeting to address the issue and asks for suggestions.

"We need our own hospital!" suggests one local.

"That's beyond our budget," answers the mayor. "Anyone else got any ideas?"

"I got a perfect idea," says another hick. "Just dig the hole next to the hospital."

Why doesn't Mexico have an Olympic team?

Because everybody who can run, jump or swim is already in the US.

Two boys get their grades from their female sex education teacher. One gets a D and the other an F.

"We should get her for this," says the first boy.

"Yeah," the second agrees. "I'm going to kick her right in the nuts."

Young Johnny was having nightmares, so his father Dave runs into his bedroom to wake him up. "Johnny, what's wrong?" Dave asks. "I dreamt that Auntie Sue had died," the boy replies. The father reassures him that his favourite aunt was perfectly fine, but the next day, coincidentally, aunt Sue died. That night, Johnny had another dream, this time that his grandfather was dead. As before, Dave enters his room to wake him up. Dave again reassures him that Grandpa is fine, but on the way home, the boy's grandad is tragically run over by a bus.

The next day, Johnny had another dream – just like before, the father asks what's wrong. This time, Johnny sobs, "I dreamt that my daddy had died."

So, the next day, Dave drives to work very slowly to avoid any accidents, eats nothing for fear of food poisoning and spends the whole day under his desk in case the roof caved in. When he gets home, his wife says to him, "I can't do you your cup of tea, dear. The milkman didn't come..."

A corporal announces:

"The platoon has been assigned to unload 'luminum..."

"Er, aluminium, not 'luminum, Sir" corrects a trooper.

"The platoon is going to unload 'luminum," repeats the corporal, "and the intellectual here is going to load shit."

A nun goes to confession. "Forgive me, father," she says. "I used horrible language this weekend."

"Go on," the priest says.

"Well," the nun continues, "I was playing golf and hit an incredible drive, but it hit a phone line and fell short after about only 100 yards."

"And you swore?" the priest asks.

"No," the nun says. "After that, a squirrel ran out and stole my ball."

"You swore then?" the priest asks.

"Well, no," the nun says. "Then, an eagle swooped down and grabbed the squirrel in his talons. As they flew away, the squirrel dropped my ball."

"Then you swore?" the father asks.

"No," she continues, "the ball fell on a big rock, rolled on to the green and stopped six inches from the hole."

The priest is silent for a moment and then finally says, "You missed the f**king putt, didn't you?"

A woman walks into the kitchen to find her husband stalking around with a fly swatter.

"What are you doing?" she asks.

"Hunting flies," he replies.

"Oh! Killing any?" she asks.

"Yep. Three males and two females," he replies.

Intrigued, she asks, "How can you tell?"

"Three were on a beer can and two were on the phone."

A man phones up his local building firm and says: "I want a skip outside my house."

"Go ahead; I'm not stopping you," the builder replies.

Stephen Spielberg is casting for a new film based around the great composers. Anyway to give the film a twist and some "oomph" he decides to cast the parts to the great action heroes of today. He calls Stallone, Arnie, Bruce Willis and Seagal into his office to hear who they would like to play.

"Well," started Stallone, "I've always admired Mozart. I would love to play him."

"Chopin has always been my favourite, and my image would improve if people saw me playing the piano" said Willis. "I'll play him."

"I've always been partial to Strauss and his waltzes," said Seagal. "I'd like to play him."

Spielberg was very pleased with these choices. "Sounds splendid."

Then, looking at Schwarzenegger, he asked, "Who do you want to be, Arnold?"

"I'll be Bach," Arnold replies.

Two blondes take a stroll in the forest. Suddenly, one blonde stops and looks down.

'Look at those deer tracks,' she says to her friend.

Her friend looks down and replies: 'These aren't deer tracks: they're wolf tracks.'

'No way. They're deer tracks.'

'You're completely wrong. These are WOLF tracks!'

They kept on arguing for half an hour, at which point they got killed by a train.

Why did Frosty the Snowman get excited?

He heard the snowblower coming.

After years of battling with himself, John finally went to a shrink.

"Doc," he said, "I've got trouble. Every time I get into bed, I think there's somebody under it. If I get under the bed, I think there's somebody on top of it. I KNOW there's no one in my bed or under my bed, but it doesn't matter, I have to check. You have to help me, it's been going on for years and I am going mad."

"It's all in your head. Just put yourself in my hands for two years," said the shrink. "Come to me three times a week, and I'll cure your fears."

"How much do you charge?" asked John, suspiciously.

"Fifty pounds per visit."

"Fifty pounds, three times a week, for two years?" chokes John. "No way!" and he storms off.

Six months later the doctor meets John on the street. "Why didn't you ever come to see me again?" asked the psychiatrist.

"Fifty quid a visit? A barman cured me for the price of a beer."

"Is that so?" says the doctor scornfully. "How?"

"He told me to cut the legs off the bed!"

A woman awakens during the night to find that her husband is not in bed. She puts on her robe and goes downstairs to look for him. She finds him sitting at the kitchen table with a cup of coffee in front of him. He appears to be in deep thought, just staring at the wall. She watches as he wipes a tear from his eye and takes a sip of his coffee.

"What's the matter, dear?" she asks tenderly. "Why are you down here at this time of night?" The husband looks up. "Do you remember when we were first dating, we were so young?" he asks. "Yes, I do," she replies.

The husband continues, his voice brimming with emotion. "Do you remember when your father caught us in the back seat of my car making love?" "Yes, I remember," says the wife.

The husband continues. "Do you remember when he shoved

the shotgun in my face and said, 'Either you marry my daughter, or I'll see that you go to jail for 30 years?'"

"I remember that," she replies softly, taking his hand. He wipes a tear from his cheek and says, "I would have got out today."

A native American Indian went to his father one day because his school was doing a project onto how people get their names and where names come from. He first asked, "Father, why was it that you named my first sister Buffalo Grazing?" The chief looked at his son and said, "On the morning after the birth of your first sister, I walked out of the hot, sweaty teepee and I looked around the plains. I saw great beauty around me, and I saw the fields where the graceful buffalo graze peacefully. I hoped that she would know peace like these fine animals, and decided to name her Buffalo Grazing." "That's great," said the son, "and why did you name my other sister Full Moon Shining?" "Well," said the chief, "on the evening of the birth of your other sister, I walked out of the hot, sweaty teepee and looked around me. It was still dark and the only light came from the moon above. I thought of the light of life that had just been breathed into the little one and decided to name her Full Moon Shining." "That's great dad,' said the boy. The father looked at his son once more, and said, "but why do you ask, Two Dogs Fucking?"

Usually the staff of the company play football. The middle level managers are more interested in tennis. The top management usually has a preference for golf. Findings:
As you go up the corporate ladder, the balls reduce in size.

Customer: I'd like a pair of stockings for my wife.
Storekeeper: Sheer?
Customer: No, she's at home.

Deep into an international flight, a guy finds himself desperate to go to the toilet. It is busy for ten, then twenty, then thirty minutes. He calls the stewardess and asks if he cannot just use the ladies' toilet, just this once. She says that that will be fine, but that he mustn't use any of the buttons that he'll see on the wall. The man says that's fine and he promises not to press any of the buttons. So he goes to the bathroom and does his business, but all the time he's looking at these four buttons on the wall next to the toilet. He gets really curious and says to himself that nothing could be that bad, and that he'll just try the first button. So, he presses the first button. There is a noise, and suddenly a warm, gentle, soothing jet of warm air sprays from the toilet, cleaning his arse. "This is fantastic," thinks the man. "I must try the second button." So he presses the second button. There is a noise and warm air come flowing up from the toilet, drying his arse. "This really is fantastic," he thinks to himself. "I've got to try the third button." So, he presses the third button. There is a noise and some gentle, soothing powder is deposited on his arse. "Unbelievable," he says to himself. "I really have to try the last button, which has the initials 'ATR' stamped upon it." So he presses the fourth button and the next thing he knows he is waking up in a hospital bed, surrounded by doctors and covered in bandages. There is blood all over the place and he is hooked up to a drip. "What the hell happened to me?" he asks the nearest doctor. "You pressed the ATR button, didn't you?" says the doctor. "Well, yes," says the man, "but I never knew what it meant!" The doctor replies, 'Automatic Tampon Removal!'

What is it that separates five nymphomaniacs from two drunks?
The cockpit door.

A couple go on vacation to a fishing resort in northern Minnesota. The husband likes to fish at the crack of dawn. The wife likes to read. One morning the husband returns after several hours of fishing and decides to take a nap. Although not familiar with the lake, the wife decides to take the boat out. She motors out a short distance, anchors and continues to read her book. Along comes a game warden in his boat. He pulls up alongside the woman and says, "Good morning Ma'am. What are you doing?"

"Reading a book," she replies.

"You're in a restricted fishing area," he informs her.

"As long as it is not a non-reading area, I am fine then, since I am not fishing?"

"The problem is that all the fishing equipment you need to fish with in this boat. I'll have to take you in and write you up."

"If you do that, I'll have to charge you with sexual assault," says the woman.

"But I haven't even touched you," says the game warden.

"Ah, but you could – you have all the equipment required."

A woman has been in a coma for several weeks, but one day nurses notice a slight response while washing her private parts. They rush to her husband and explain the surprise, suggesting a little oral sex might bring her round, to which he readily agrees. A few minutes later her monitor flatlines, showing no pulse or heart rate.

The nurses rush into the room crying, "What happened!?"

"I'm not sure," the husband replies sadly. "She may have choked."

Mr Cadbury and Ms Rowntree went off for the weekend.

It was After Eight.

She was from Quality Street

He was a Fishermans Friend

On the way they stopped at a Yorkie Bar.

He had a Rum and Butter.

She had a Wine Gum.

He asked her name. She said Polo, I'm the one with the hole.

(But I'm the one with the Nuts he thought)

Then he touched her Milky Way.

They checked in and went straight to the bedroom. Mr Cadbury turned out the light for a bit of Black Magic It wasn't long before he slipped his hand into her Snickers and felt the contrast of her Double Decker.

Then he showed her his Curly Wurly.

It was a Magic Moment as she let out of scream of Turkish Delight.

When he came out his Fun Sized Mars Bar felt a bit Crunchie.

She wanted more but he decided to take a Time Out. However, he noticed her Pink Wafers looked very appetising.

So he did a Twirl and had a Picnic in her Sherbert. At the same time he gave her a Gob Stopper!

Unfortunately Mr Cadbury had to go home to his wife Caramel.

Sadly, he was soon to discover he had caught V.D.

It turns out Ms Rowntree had a Box of Assorted Creams.

She really had been with All Sorts.

BB King's wife wants to surprise him for his birthday, so she goes to a tattoo parlour and has a big 'B' tattooed on each of her buttocks.

When BB gets home later that night, he opens the door to find his wife naked and bent over showing off her new tattoos. BB can't believe his eyes and screams, "Who the hell's Bob?"

Why did the chicken cross the playground?
To get to the other slide.

A Ukrainian woman bumps into the Chelsea football squad in a nightclub. She approaches John Terry and asks for his autograph on her breast. Terry agrees, and she obliges by lifting up her top so that he can sign her left one. She then asks Drogba for his autograph on her other breast. Drogba willingly agrees, and she obliges by lifting up her top so he can sign the right one. She then asks Mourinho for his autograph somewhere a bit more private. Jose agrees and the woman obliges by dropping her knickers. Suddenly, Mourinho turns white and says, 'On second thoughts, I think I'll pass. The last time I signed a Ukrainian twat it cost me £30 million.'

How do you tell a male hippo from a female hippo?
The male's the one with the remote.

A little old lady had two monkeys for years. One day, one of them died of natural causes. Overcome with grief, the second monkey passed away two days later. Not knowing what to do with the remains, she finally decided to take them to the taxidermist and have them stuffed. After telling the owner of her wishes, he asked her, "Do you want them mounted?"
"No. Holding hands will be fine," she said, blushing.

Little Johnny and his grandfather have gone fishing. After a while, Grandpa gets thirsty and opens up his cooler for some beer. Little Johnny asks, "Grandpa, can I have some beer, too?" "Can you stick your penis in your arsehole?" Grandpa asks back. "No." "Well, then you're not big enough." Grandpa then takes out a cigarette and lights up. Little Johnny sees this and asks for a cigarette. "Can you stick your penis in your arsehole?" Grandpa asks again. "No." "Well, then you're not big enough." Little Johnny gets upset and pulls out some cookies. His grandfather says, "Hey, those cookies look good. Can I have some?" Little Johnny asks, "Can you stick your penis in your arsehole?" Grandpa looks at Johnny and senses his trick so he says, "Well of course I can, I'm big enough." Little Johnny then says, "Well, go fuck yourself. These are my cookies."

A girl goes into the doctor's office for a check-up. As she takes off her blouse, the doctor notices a red 'H' on her chest. "How did you get that mark?" asks the doctor. "Oh, my boyfriend went to Harvard and he's so proud of it he never takes off his Harvard sweatshirt, even when we make love," she replies.

A couple of days later, another girl comes in. As she takes off her blouse, the doctor notices a blue 'Y' on her chest. "My boyfriend went to Yale," explains the girl, "and he's so proud of it he never takes off his Yale sweatshirt, even when we make love."

A couple of days later, another girl comes in. She takes off her blouse to reveal a green 'M' on her chest. "Do you have a boyfriend at Michigan?" asks the doctor.

"No, but I have a girlfriend at Wisconsin. Why do you ask?"

A wealthy couple decided to go out for the evening and the lady of the house gave their butler, Jervis, the night off. However, the wife didn't have a good time at the party, so she came home early alone, while her husband stayed on at the function.

When the woman walked into the house, she found Jervis by himself in the dining room. She called him to follow her, and led him into the master bedroom. She turned to him and said, "Jervis, I want you to take off my dress."

Jervis obeyed.

"Jervis," she continued. "Now I want you to take off my stockings and suspender belt."

Again, Jervis silently obeyed.

Both were breathing heavily as the tension between them steadily mounted.

She then looked sternly at him and said, "If I ever catch you wearing my clothes again, you're fired!"

This guy had been dating this girl for some time when she invited him over to her parents' house for dinner to meet them. When they got there, the guy realized he was so tense that he was starting to get really bad gas.

They sat down for dinner but he just couldn't hold it in any longer. A fart slipped out. The mother yelled "Spot!" The guy realized the family dog was under his chair, and was relieved that the dog had got the blame.

A few minutes later he let another one go and the mother again yelled "Spot!" Again, the boyfriend was relieved that the dog had been told off, so he decided he might as well get it all out, and let this huge fart go.

"Spot!" the mother yelled. "Get out from under there before he shits on you!"

The following advisory for American travellers heading for France was compiled from information provided by the U.S. State Department, the Central Intelligence Agency, the U.S. Chamber of Commerce, the Food and Drug Administration, the Centre for Disease Control and some very expensive spy satellites that the French don't know about. It is intended as a guide for American travellers only and no guarantee of accuracy is ensured or intended.

General overview

France is a medium-sized foreign country situated on the continent of Europe. It is bounded by Germany, Spain, Switzerland and some smaller nations of no particular consequence or shopping opportunities. France is a very old country with many treasures such as the Louvre and EuroDisney. Among its contributions to Western civilization are champagne, Camembert cheese, the guillotine, and body odour. Although France likes to think of itself as a modern nation, air conditioning is little used and it is next to impossible to get decent Mexican food. One continuing exasperation for American visitors is that the people wilfully persist in speaking French, although many will speak English if shouted at repeatedly.

The people

France has a population of 54 million people, most of whom drink and smoke a great deal, drive like lunatics, are dangerously over sexed and have no concept of standing patiently in line. Men sometimes have girls' names like Marie and they kiss each other when they hand out medals. American travellers are advised to travel in groups and to wear baseball caps and colourful pants for easier mutual recognition.

Safety

In general, France is a safe destination, although travellers are advised that France is occasionally invaded by Germany. By tradition, the French surrender more or less at once and, apart from a temporary shortage of Scotch whisky and increased difficulty in getting baseball scores and stock market prices, life for the visitors generally goes on much as before. A tunnel connecting France to Britain beneath the English Channel has been opened in recent years to make it easier for the French government to flee to London.

History

France was discovered by Charlemagne in the Dark Ages. Other important historical figures are Louis XIV, the Huguenots, Joan of Arc, Jacques Cousteau and Charles de Gaulle, who was President for many years and is now an airport.

Government

The French form of government is democratic but noisy. Elections are held more or less continuously and always result in a runoff. Parliament's principal preoccupations are setting off atomic bombs in the South Pacific and acting indignant when anyone complains. According to the most up-to-date State Department intelligence, the current President is someone named Jacques. Further information is not available at this time.

Economy

France's principal exports, in order of importance to the economy, are wine, nuclear weapons, perfume, guided missiles, champagne, high-calibre weaponry, grenade launchers, land mines, tanks, attack aircraft, miscellaneous armaments and cheese.

Conclusion

France enjoys a rich history, a picturesque and varied landscape and a temperate climate. In short, it would be a very nice country if French people didn't inhabit it, and it weren't still radioactive from all the nuclear tests they run. Remember no one ordered you to go abroad. Personally, we always take our vacation in Florida, and you are advised to do the same.

An elderly gentleman had serious hearing problems for a number of years. He went to the doctor, and was fitted with a set of hearing aids that allowed him to hear 100 per cent.

A month later, the gentleman went back for a check-up. The doctor said, "Your hearing's perfect. Your family must be really pleased for you."

The gentleman replied, "Oh, I haven't told my family yet. I just sit around and listen to the conversations. I've changed my will three times so far!"

To cut costs, a managing director is forced to sack an employee. After much thought, he narrows the choice down to two young members off the office: Jack and Jill. As the pair have near-identical performance records, he cannot decide who should go, so, after hours of deliberation, he comes up with an idea; the first person to go for a fag break on Monday morning gets axed.

Monday arrives and Jill walks in with a monstrous hangover. After a few minutes, she heads outside for a cigarette. The director walks over. "Jill, I'm so sorry," he says, "but due to circumstances beyond my control, I've got to lay you or Jack off..."

"OK," replies Jill. "Would you just jack off, then? I've got a bloody awful headache this morning."

A blonde has been in a taxi for some time when she realizes she doesn't have any money.

"I'm sorry", she says to the driver, "you'll have to go back, I forgot my purse and it is already £10."

The driver glances at her and says: "It's OK: I'll just stop in a dark alley and you can take off your bra."

"I can't do that: you'd be cheating yourself," the blonde replies.

"Cheating myself? How so?"

"This bra cost me only a fiver."

Why do bagpipers walk when they play?
To get away from the sound.

Three patients in a mental institution prepare for an examination given by the head psychiatrist. If the patients pass the exam, they will be free to leave the hospital and go back to a normal life. However, if they fail, the institution will detain them for five another years.

The doctor takes the three patients to the top of a diving board looking over an empty swimming pool, and asks the first patient to jump.

The first patient jumps head-first into the pool and breaks both arms.

The second patient, who has just witnessed what has happened, jumps enthusiastically into the empty pool and breaks both legs. The third patient looks over the side and backs off from the diving board. "Congratulations! You're a free man. Just tell me: why didn't you jump?" asked the doctor.

"Well, Doc, I can't swim!"

A psychiatrist and a proctologist became good friends and agreed to share offices to cut down on expenses. To economize even further, they had just one sign printed:
Dr. John Wayland, Psychiatrist
Dr. Stan Smith, Proctologist
SPECIALIZING IN ODDS AND ENDS

A man and woman have been married for what seems like for ever. They have eight grown-up children and countless grandchildren. On their sixtieth wedding anniversary they have a very candid conversation. The wife says to her husband, "Honey, since we are so old now and we've been together for so long, I'm going to be totally honest with you. Is there anything you'd like to know about me and our relationship over the past six decades that you'd like to ask me about? If there is, I promise that I will answer you with total honesty." The husband pauses for a while, and then says, 'Dear, this isn't easy for me to say, but there is actually something that has been eating away at me for quite a few years now. It's just that of all our kids, there's one who looks decidedly different from the others. You know the one I mean, I'm sure, and I'm sure it's nothing but, as I say, I've wondered about this for years and I would like to know if he had a different father from the rest of the kids.' The wife looks down at her feet and sighs loudly. 'Well, dear, I'm sorry to say it, but you're right. I cannot tell a lie: that child did indeed have a different father from all the others.' The husband looks miserable, but he's still curious. 'And who would that be?' he asks. 'Well, dear...' begins the wife slowly, '...you.'

Two men were out fishing, when they found a lamp floating in the water. One of the men picked it up and rubbed it, and straight away a genie appeared from the lamp. Unfortunately, it was a very low-level genie, and could only grant one wish. The men thought for a few minutes and then wished for the entire lake to be made of the best beer in the world. With a flash the wish was granted. All of a sudden, one of the men got really angry. "Dammit! Now we have to piss in the boat!"

A famous heart surgeon is having a friendly charity barbecue when he is approached by what appears to be a loudmouth.

'Hey, Doc,' the guy says, 'I'm the best mechanic in town. I can take an engine apart, take the valves out, clean them, tune them and after I put everything back together the baby will purr like a newborn kitten. We're basically doing the same job, so how come you get more money than me, hey?'

'Try to do that with the engine running,' the heart surgeon says softly.

John played golf every Saturday with his friend Harry. John was usually home by noon, so his wife was worried at 2pm when she hadn't heard from him.

Three o'clock came and went, then four. Finally, around 5pm, John walked in dragging his golf bag. "Where have you been? I was so worried!" his wife exclaimed.

"It was a really bad day at the golf course." John replied. "Harry had a heart attack and collapsed at the fourth hole."

"No! How awful," cried his wife.

"Yeah, it was pretty rough," said John. "Hit the ball... drag Harry... hit the ball... drag Harry..."

Two men in their nineties have been friends for decades, and after going through the war together, they now just meet a few times a week to play cards. One day they're playing together when one of them suddenly puts down his cards. "Listen, don't get mad at me, pal," he says. "I know we've been friends for years, but I realized the other day that I can't remember your name. I'm really embarrassed but my memory is fading fast. Please remind me."

For three minutes the other old fella just glares back at his mate, shaking his head. Finally, he stirs. "Look," he says, "how soon do you need to know?"

The Hunchback of Notre Dame returns home from a hard day's ringing the cathedral bells, and finds his beautiful wife standing in the kitchen holding a wok.

"Fantastic, Esmeralda," says the Hunchback, "I really fancy some Chinese food."

"Oh, no, not tonight, Quasi," she says, "I'm ironing your shirts."

1st Eskimo: Where did your mother come from?
2nd Eskimo: Alaska.
1st Eskimo: Don't bother; I'll ask her myself.

What did the redneck say to his girlfriend after breaking up with her?

"Can we still be cousins?"

A redneck, named Kenny, buys a donkey from a farmer for $100. The farmer agrees to deliver the donkey the next day.

The next day the farmer drives up and says, "Sorry, son, but I have some bad news; the donkey's dead."

Kenny replies, "Well, then, just give me my money back."

The Farmer says, "I can't do that. I went and spent it already."

Kenny says, "OK, then; just bring me the dead donkey."

The farmer asks, "What are you going to do with him?"

Kenny says, "I'm going to raffle him off."

A month later, the farmer meets up with Kenny and asks, "What happened with that dead donkey?"

Kenny says, "I raffled him off, like I said I was going to. I sold 500 tickets at two dollars a piece and made a profit of $998."

The farmer says, "Didn't anyone complain?"

Kenny says, "Just the guy who won: so I gave him his two dollars back."

A scientist is sharing a train carriage from Norfolk to London with a farmer. To pass the time, he decides to play a game with the farmer.

"I'll ask you a question and if you get it wrong, you have to pay me a pound," says the scientist arrogantly. "Then you ask me a question, and if I get it wrong, you get a tenner."

"You're on," says the farmer.

"OK; you go first," says the scientist.

The farmer thinks for a bit then says, "I know. What has three legs, takes ten hours to climb up a palm tree and ten seconds to get back down?"

The scientist is very confused and thinks long and hard about the question. Finally, the train is pulling into Waterloo. As it comes to a stop, the scientist takes out his tenner and gives it to the farmer.

"Well, you've got me stumped," says the scientist. "What does have three legs, takes ten hours to get up a palm tree and ten seconds to get back down?"

The farmer takes the tenner and puts it into his pocket. He then takes out a pound coin and hands it to the scientist.

"I don't know," he smiles.

A man moves to New York City from Suffolk, leaving two of his best friends behind. To keep their tradition of nightly drinks alive, every night he goes to a British-themed pub and orders three pints. After a month of this the barman is curious, and asks the man what he's doing. Touched by his story, the barman has the three pints ready for the man every time he comes in. One day, the man tells the barman to only give him two pints.

"My condolences," says the bartender, thinking that one of the man's friends has died.

"No, no," says the man, "they're both still alive. I've just quit drinking."

A man returns home a day early from a business trip and gets into a taxi at the airport after midnight. On the way back to his house, he asks the cabby if he would be a witness as he suspects his wife is having an affair and he intends to catch her in the act.

For £100, the cabby agrees. They arrive at the house and the husband and cabby tiptoe into the bedroom. The husband switches on the lights, yanks the blanket back and there is his wife in bed with another man.

The husband immediately puts a gun to the naked man's head.

The wife shouts, "Don't do it! This man has been very generous! I lied when I told you I inherited money. He paid for the Porsche I bought for you, your United season ticket, the house at the lake and your golf club membership and green fees."

Shaking his head from side to side the husband slowly lowers the gun and looks over at the cabbie and says, "What would you do?"

The cabby says, "I'd cover him up with that blanket before he catches a cold."

A man comes home from a poker game late one night and finds his wife waiting for him with a rolling pin.

"Where have you been?" she asks.

"Pack all your bags," he demands. "I lost you in a card game."

"How did you manage to do that?"

"It wasn't easy," he says. "I had to fold a royal flush."

Feeling uncertain about his love life, a frog calls up a psychic hotline.

"I can see that you're going to meet a beautiful young girl who will want to know everything about you," the psychic tells the frog.

"That's great," the frog says. "Will I meet this babe at a party?"

"No," the psychic says. "In her biology class next term."

Hear about the man who was banned from B&Q?

Some bloke in orange dungarees asked him if he wanted decking, so he got the first punch in.

One day, a man came home early from work and was greeted by his wife dressed in very sexy lingerie and high heels. "Tie me up," she purred, "and you can do anything you want." So he tied her up and went golfing.

Brother William is on his way back from teaching children at a local school. It is late at night and the Abbey's car that he is travelling in breaks down. He knows he hasn't run out of petrol because he just filled up so he opens up the bonnet and starts to have a look at the engine. A few minutes later a car pulls up next to him and the window is wound down.

A red-faced chap pops his head out and says, "Hello old chap, what's the matter with you then?"

"Piston broke I think," says the monk to which the man in the car replies, "Me too, but what's up with the motor?"

Two men are changing after a sweaty game of squash. One notices that the other has a cork up his arse. He says, 'Um, I couldn't help noticing, but how the hell did you get that cork up your arse?'

The other man says, 'Well, um, yes: it's a bit embarrassing, really. I was walking along a beach barefoot when I tripped over this old bottle. I pick it up, take the cork out and whoosh! Out pops a huge red man with a turban on his head, floating in space in front of me. He says "I am a genie. I grant you one wish. What will it be?" So I – rather foolishly, upon reflection – said, "No shit!"'

A drunken old bloke stumbles into the front door of a pub, walks up to the barman and says, "Give me a damn shot of vodka."

The barman tells him that he's had enough, so the old guy swears and walks out the front door.

A few minutes later, the same drunk comes in through the side door and stumbles up to the bar and demands a shot of vodka. The barman looks at him in disbelief and refuses to serve him again. The old man swears again and storms out.

Within minutes the same old bloke stumbles in through the back door and before he can say a word, the barman says, "Listen, I told you already twice that I'm not going to serve you, so get out of my bar, you drunken bastard."

The old guy looks at the bartender and says, "Damn; how many bars do you work at?"

Why wasn't Jesus born in Ireland? Because God couldn't find three wise men or a virgin.

What's the difference between Alex Ferguson and God?
God doesn't think he's Alex Ferguson

A man is standing at the Pearly Gates before St. Peter.

"All you need to have done is one good deed, and we will allow you passage into heaven."

The man says, "No problem. I was stopped at a crossroads once and saw a gang of blokes harassing a young woman. I got out of my car, walked up to the leader, who was over seven feet tall and must have weighed nearly 15 stone, and I told him that abusing a woman is a cowardly act and that I would not tolerate it. I then reached up, yanked out his nose ring and kicked him in the balls to make a point."

St. Peter is amazed and starts searching the man's life in his book in front of him and says, "I can't find that incident anywhere in your file. When did that happen?"

The man looks down at his watch and says, "Oh, about two minutes ago."

A famous Admiral and an equally famous General were fishing together in a boat when a sudden squall came up. They both fell in the water and spent some time spluttering, struggling helplessly and swallowing quite a quantity of the stuff, until the Admiral floundered his way back to the boat and pulled himself painfully in. Then he fished out the General.

Catching his breath, he puffed: 'Please don't say a word about this to anyone. If the Navy found out I can't swim, I'd be disgraced'.

'Don't worry,' the general said ruefully. 'Your secret is quite safe. I myself would hate to have my men find out I can't walk on water.'

A primary school teacher was trying to get her class to stop speaking in "baby talk" and insisting on "big people" words only.

She asked Chris what he had done over the weekend.

"I visited my Nana, Miss," said Chris.

"No, you went to visit your grandmother. We're using 'big people' words here, Chris!"

She then asked Rupert what he had done.

"I took a ride on a choo-choo, Miss," replied Rupert.

The teacher said, "No, Rupert, you took a ride on a train. You must remember to use 'big people' words."

She then asked little Johnny what he had done.

"I read a book, Miss," he replied.

"That's wonderful!" the teacher said. "What book did you read?"

Alex thought for a second, before saying, "Winnie the Shit, Miss."

An 85-year-old man visits his doctor to get a sperm count. The old fella's given a jar and told to bring back a sample. The next day he returns with an empty jar.

"What happened?" asks the doc.

"Well," the old man starts. "I asked my wife for help and she tried with her right hand and then with her left. Anyway, we got nothing. Then she tried with her mouth, first with her teeth in, then with her teeth out, still nothing. We even called Evelyn, the lady next door, but still nothing."

The doctor bursts out, "You asked your neighbour?!"

So the old man replies, "Yep, no matter what we tried, we couldn't get that damn jar open."

What do you call a snake that has taken Viagra?
A walking stick.

Jack and Bob are driving when they get caught in a blizzard. They pull into a nearby farmhouse and ask the attractive lady of the house if they can spend the night.

"I'm recently widowed," she explains, "and I'm afraid the neighbours will talk if I let you stay here."

"Not to worry," Jack says, "we'll be happy to sleep in the barn."

Nine months later, Jack gets a letter from the widow's attorney. After reading it, he quickly drives around to Bob's house.

"Bob, remember that good-looking widow at the farm we stayed at?"

"Yes, I remember her," says Bob.

"Did you happen to get up in the middle of the night, go up to the house and have sex with her?" asks Jack.

"Yes, I have to admit that I did," replies Bob.

"Did you happen to use my name instead of telling her your name?" asks Jack.

Embarrassed, Bob says, "Yeah, I'm afraid I did."

"Well, thanks," says Jack. "She just died and left me her farm!"

A large cup and two smaller ones go out for a meal at a posh restaurant. When the bill arrives, the small cups do a runner, leaving their pal to pay up.

A week later, the three are back and, once again, the large cup is left behind to settle the bill.

The waiter comes up to him, and says, "No offence, mate, but I think your two pals are taking you for a mug."

Rob is a commercial saturation diver for Global Divers in Louisiana. He performs underwater repairs on offshore drilling rigs. Below is an email he sent to his sister:

Hi Sue,

Just another note from your bottom-dwelling brother. Last week I had a bad day at the office. I know you've been feeling down lately at work, so I thought I would share my dilemma with you to make you realize it's not so bad after all.

Before I can tell you what happened to me, I first must bore you with a few technicalities of my job. As you know, my office lies at the bottom of the sea. I wear a suit to the office. It's a wetsuit. This time of year the water is quite cool. So what we do to keep warm is this: We have a diesel powered industrial water heater. This $20,000 piece of shit sucks the water out of the sea. It heats it to a delightful temperature. It then pumps it down to the diver through a garden hose, which is taped to the air hose. Now this sounds like a damn good plan, and I've used it several times with no complaints. What I do, when I get to the bottom and start working, is I take the hose and stuff it down the back of my wetsuit. This floods my whole suit with warm water. It's like working in a jacuzzi. Everything was going well until all of a sudden, my bum started to itch. So, of course, I scratched it. This only made things worse. Within a few seconds my arse started to burn.

I pulled the hose out from my back, but the damage was done. In agony I realized what had happened. The hot water machine had sucked up a jellyfish and pumped it into my suit. Now since I don't have any hair on my back, the jellyfish couldn't stick to it. However, the crack of my bum was not as fortunate. When I scratched what I thought was an itch, I was actually grinding the jellyfish into my ass. I informed the dive supervisor of my dilemma over the communicator. His instructions were unclear due to the fact that he along with five other divers were all laughing hysterically. Needless to say I aborted the dive. I was instructed to make three agonising in-water decompression stops totalling 35 minutes before I could reach the surface to begin my chamber dry decompression. When I arrived at the surface, I was wearing nothing but my brass helmet. As I climbed out of the water, the medic, with tears of laughter running down his face, handed me a tube of cream and told me to rub it on my bum as soon as I get in the chamber. The cream put the fire out, but I couldn't shit for two days because my arsehole was swollen shut.

Count Dracula is on the pull in Glasgow. He spends the night drinking Bloody Mary's in various clubs and biting on unsuspecting women's necks. He is heading for home, wandering along Argyle Street sometime before sunrise.

Suddenly he is hit on the back of the head. He looks round and sees nothing, but at his feet there is a small sausage roll. "Mmmm," he thinks. "What's going on here?"

A few yards further on and ... BANG. Smacked on the back of the head again! He whirls round as quickly as he can, nothing but a small triangular sandwich lying on the ground. How odd!

A few yards further along the street and... CRASH! Smacked on the back of the head again! He whirls round as quickly as he can, nothing. He's getting really angry now and only half surprised to notice a cocktail sausage lying on the ground.

He stands and peers into the darkness of the night. Nothing. He walks a few yards further on when he gets a tap on the shoulder. With a swirl of his cape and a cloud of mist he turns as fast as he can. He feels a sharp pain in his heart. He falls to the ground clutching his chest, which is punctured by a small cocktail stick laden with a chunk of cheese and a pickle.

On the ground dying, he looks up and sees a young female. With his dying breath he gasps, who the fuck are you?"

She replies: "My name is Buffet, the Vampire Slayer."

A young mother teaches her son to go to the bathroom by numbers. She teaches him the following lesson: 1. Unzip your flies. 2. Gently lift out your family jewels. 3. Pull back the foreskin. 4. Let nature take its course. 5. Slide the foreskin forward. 6. Replace the family jewels. 7. Zip back up.

The mother would often check that he was following instructions by listening outside the door of the bathroom. She would hear, 'One, two, three, four, five, six, seven. All done!' However, one day she was walking past the bathroom and was disturbed to hear, 'Three–five, three–five, three–five, three–five...'

A dyslexic man walks into a bra.

Plucking up his courage, a young man goes to a notorious massage parlour for the first time. As he's not sure when to ask for the dirty deed, he lies on the bed, getting more and more aroused.

After a few minutes, the masseuse notices his condition. "Perhaps sir would like some relief?" she says breathlessly.

The man gulps. "Yes please," he stutters.

With that the lady leaves the room.

She returns a full fifteen minutes later. "Well," she says, popping her head around the door. "Finished?"

Did you hear? Sir Clive Woodward is going into football, and is taking up a new position with Manchester United...

Apparently, it's so Wayne Rooney can continue playing with hookers.

Q: What do you call an intelligent, good looking, sensitive man?
A: A rumour

An old fella with a dodgy heart goes to see his doctor about some chest pains he's been experiencing.

When he gets home his wife asks him if he's been prescribed medication. "No, nothing like that," says the old man. "I'm going to make some lunch."

Wanting to give him some space, the wife lets her husband go. Ten minutes later she hears screams of pain coming from the kitchen and rushes in to find the old guy cooking a fry-up in a biscuit tin and burning his fingers whenever he touches it.

"What on earth are you doing?" she screams.

"Just following doctor's orders," says the old man. "He said the best thing I can do for my heart is to throw away the frying pan."

A man has huge feet. Wherever he goes, people take the mick. Sitting on the beach wall with his plates dangling in the water, a vicar strolls past and can see the man is upset, so he walks over and asks, "What's the matter?"

"I'm so depressed," replies the man. "Everywhere I go, people ridicule me for the size of my feet."

The vicar comes up with a plan and tells the man, "Dye your hair a brilliant green and that way, people will look at your hair and not your feet!"

The man thanks the vicar for the advice, goes to the nearest hair salon and has his hair dyed. He walks out feeling fantastic – better than he's felt in a long time. He bounds down the road and a passer-by shouts out, "Hey, you with the green hair!"

He turns around and shouts confidently back, "Yeah?"

"Ha, ha," laughs the passer-by, "You've got bloody massive feet, mate!"

What's the definition of a happy transvestite?

A guy who likes to eat, drink and be Mary.

A man was sick and tired of going to work every day while his wife stayed home. He wanted her to see what he went through so he prayed: "Dear Lord, I go to work every day and put in 8 hours while my wife merely stays at home. I want her to know what I go through, so please allow her body to switch with mine for a day. Amen."

God, in his infinite wisdom, granted the man's wish. The next morning, sure enough, the man awoke as a woman.

He arose, cooked breakfast for his mate, woke up the kids, set out their school clothes, fed them breakfast, packed their lunches, drove them to school, came home and picked up the dry cleaning, took it to the cleaners and stopped at the bank to make a deposit, went grocery shopping, then drove home to put away the groceries, paid the bills and balanced the check book. He cleaned the cat's litter box and bathed the dog. Then it was already one o'clock and he hurried to make the beds, do the laundry, vacuum, dust and sweep and mop the kitchen floor. He ran to the school to pick up the kids and got into an argument with them on the way home. He set out milk and cookies and got the kids organised to do their homework, then set up the ironing board and watched TV while he did the ironing. At 4:30 he began peeling potatoes and washing vegetables for salad, breaded the pork chops and snapped fresh beans for supper. After supper, he cleaned the kitchen, ran the dishwasher, folded laundry, bathed the kids and put them to bed. At 9 P.M. he was exhausted and, though his daily chores weren't finished, he went to bed where he was expected to make love, which he managed to get through without complaint.

The next morning, he awoke and immediately knelt by the bed and said, "Lord, I don't know what I was thinking. I was so wrong to envy my wife's being able to stay home all day. Please, oh please, let us trade back."

The Lord, in his infinite wisdom, replied, "My son, I feel you have learned your lesson and I will be happy to change things back to the way they were. You'll just have to wait nine months, though. You got pregnant last night."

A teacher says to her class, "I'm going to call on each of you and you're going to tell me what your father does for a living. Tommy, you're first."

Tommy says, "My father's a doctor."

The teacher says, "Jamie, what about you?"

Jamie says, "My father's a lawyer."

Finally, there's one boy left and the teacher says, "Billy, what does your father do?"

Billy replies, "My father's dead, miss."

Shocked, the teacher says, "I'm so sorry. What did he do before he died?"

Billy says, "He turned purple and collapsed on the dog, miss."

"Doc, I can't stop singing 'The green, green grass of home'."

"That sounds like Tom Jones syndrome."

"Is it common?"

"It's not unusual."

A man placed some flowers on the grave of his mother and was starting back toward his car when his attention was diverted to another man kneeling at a grave. The man kept repeating, "Why did you have to die?"

The first man approached him and said, "I don't wish to interfere with your private grief, but can I ask whom you're mourning for?"

The mourner took a moment to collect himself, then replied, "My wife's first husband."

Sure signs that your co-worker is a hacker:

You told him off once and your next phone bill was for £20,000.

He's won the Publisher's Clearing House sweepstakes three years running.

When asked for his phone number, he gives it in hex.

Seems strangely calm whenever the office LAN goes down.

Somehow manages to get Sky Sports on his PC at work.

Massive £40,000 contribution to the ritual Christmas booze trip to Calais made in one-cent increments.

His video dating profile lists 'public-key decryption' among turn-ons.

When his computer starts up, you hear, 'Good morning, Mr. President'.

You hear him murmur, 'Let's see you use that Visa card now, bitch!'

An architect, an artist and an IT guy were discussing whether it was better to have a wife or a mistress.

The architect said he enjoyed his time with his wife, building a solid foundation for an enduring relationship.

The artist said he enjoyed time with his mistress, because of the passion and mystery he found there. The IT guy said, "I like both."

The artist said "BOTH?"

The IT guy replied "Yeah. If you have a wife and a mistress, they will each assume you are spending time with the other woman and you can go to the office and get some work done."

To the optimist, the glass is half full.

To the pessimist, the glass is half empty.

To the IT guy, the glass is twice as big as it needs to be.

Some friends are playing a round of golf when they hear shouts in the distance. Looking across, they watch, amazed, as a buxom lady runs on to the fairway, pulls off some of her clothes and sprints up the course. Not two minutes later, two men in white coats appear and ask which way the woman has gone. They point up the course and the two men run off in that direction.

Bemused, the golfers carry on with their game, but are again disturbed by another man. This time he's staggering over the hill, panting with the effort of carrying two buckets of sand. Between wheezes, the newcomer too asks which way the woman has gone, and then totters away. Increasingly baffled, the golf party runs after the figure. "What the hell is going on?" they ask.

Gasping, the man explains. "That woman has escaped from our treatment clinic. She has acute nymphomania, and as soon as she gets all her clothes off, the nearest man is ravished."

"But why do you need two buckets of sand?" shout the golfers after him.

"Well, I caught her the last time she escaped," pants the man, "so it's my turn for the handicap."

A man walks into a bar. He has a frog attached to his forehead. He says to the barkeep, 'I'll have a gin and tonic, please.' The barman pours him the drink – all the while looking at the frog – and gives it to the man. 'I'm sorry to be so curious, sir, but I was wondering how on earth you ended up with that thing on you?' he asked. Quick as a flash the frog replies, 'I don't know; it started out as a wart on my bum five years ago!'

Bill gates has finally died and Satan greets him. "Welcome, Mr. Gates, we've been waiting for you," he purrs. "You've been a naughty boy, flooding the world with version after version of software that didn't work and not permitting any other software to exist. You are now in Hell and this will be your home for all eternity." Satan eyes Bill Gates and resumes his welcome speech: "But you're lucky, because I am in a good mood today and I will present to you three Hells for you to choose to be locked up in."

Satan takes Bill to a huge lake of fire in which millions of poor souls are tormented and tortured. He then takes him to a massive amphitheatre where thousands of people are chased about and devoured by starving nightmarish creatures. Finally, he takes Bill to a tiny room in which, to Bill's delight, there is a PC and, next to it, a cup of coffee. Without hesitation, Bill says: "I'll take this option."

"Fine," says Satan, locking up Bill in the room.

Outside, his second-in-command is waiting for him to process the next unfortunate soul.

"So he chose this room, master, as you predicted," the aide says. "But I don't understand. You gave him quite a nice room, and with a PC too..."

"Ah, but you see, this is no ordinary PC," Satan sniggers. "The Control, Alternate and Delete keys are missing and it's got Windows Vista!"

What do cookery books and science fiction have in common?
Men read them and think, "Well, that's not going to happen."

Why do gorillas have big nostrils?
Because they have big fingers.

A farmer has a prize cock which has sired hundreds of young. It used to take care of every single one of the farmer's 200 chickens. But one day the old cock dies and the farmer is forced to get himself a replacement. The farmer looks at all the ads in Farmers' Weekly and orders a mail-order rooster named Randy. A couple of days later the new cock arrives. It is a very impressive and fit-looking bird. Before the farmer lets the rooster loose to work on his chickens, he gives it a bit of a pep talk. "Now, look here, Randy," the farmer says, "I need you as a long-term investment. I don't need a new rooster for just the next couple of days: I need one for a very long time. So take it easy and pace yourself when you get in there, OK?" Randy nods and the farmer puts him into the coop. But no sooner have Randy's claws hit the ground than he is off at the first brace of hens. The farmer looks on amazed as he sees the rooster making his way through the entire flock, doing all of the hens first once and then twice! The rooster doesn't even pause for breath. When he's done, he looks around and sees a load of ducks out by the pond. He sprints over and does them too – twice each. The farmer, while obviously impressed, is worried that his superb new rooster won't even make it through the night if he's that horny already. The farmer's worst fears are confirmed the next morning when he leaves the house after breakfast: Randy is lying a hundred yards from the hen-coop with buzzards circling around him. The farmer, shaking his head, walks slowly up to the chicken and looks down at him. "What the hell did I tell you, Randy?" he begins, "I knew you wouldn't make it if you didn't pace yourself!" Randy opens one eye and looks up at the farmer, then up at the buzzards. "Sshhhh," he says. "They're getting closer!"

Little Johnny is excited because the circus has come to town and his Mum has got front row tickets for him. Finally the evening come and little Johnny and his Mum go off to the big top. Little Johnny sits there and enjoys the lions and the tigers and the jugglers and the trapeze artists, and finally, out comes little Johnny's favorites, the clowns. Johnny loves the clowns and their humorous japes until one of the clowns comes up to him and says: "Little boy, are you the front end of an ass?"

"No", replies little Johnny.

"Are you the rear end of an ass?"

'No", replies little Johnny again.

"In that case", chuckles the clown, "you must be no end of an ass."

Laughter fills the big top, little Johnny is distraught and he runs out of the circus and all the way home in tears.

When his Mum catches up with him, she says: "Little Johnny, don't worry, your Uncle Marvo, the master of lightning wit, backchat and repartee, is coming to stay tomorrow. We will take him to the circus and he will sort that nasty clown out."

At this news, little Johnny cheers and looks forward to the next night.

The next night comes and, sure enough, Uncle Marvo, the master of lightning wit, backchat and repartee arrives and the three of them set off for the circus. When they get there, little Johnny, his Mum and Uncle Marvo, the master of lightning wit, backchat and repartee sit down and enjoy the lions, the tigers, the jugglers and the trapeze artists and then out come the clowns. Again, little Johnny is enjoying their antics and again, one of the clowns comes up to him and say: "Little boy, are you the front end of an ass?"

"No", replies little Johnny again.

"Are you the rear end of an ass?"

'No."

"In that case", says the clown gleefully, "you must be no end of an ass."

Laughter fills the big top once more as little Johnny looks upset... Quick as a flash, Uncle Marvo, the master of lightning wit, backchat and repartee jumps up and shouts at the very top of his voice... "Fuck off you red nosed bastard!"

What is the worst thing that can happen to a bat while asleep?

The runs

A bright young Scottish lad named Gordie has the opportunity to go to university in London, so he packs his bags and says goodbye to his mother and leaves the highlands for the big city. After the first week his mother calls to see how her boy is holding up.

"I love it here Mother," Gordie tells her, "but these English students are the oddest people ever! Why, the boy who lives in the dormitory room next to me bangs his head against the wall until midnight every night. And the boy in the room above me stomps around until midnight every night. And the boy right below me blasts his stereo until midnight every night."

"Why don't you complain to the Dean of Students?" asks his mother.

"Well, it doesn't bother me much," answers Gordie. "I'm usually up until that time practicing my bagpipes anyway."

What do a farmer and a pimp have in common?

Both need a hoe to stay in business.

A man walks into a bar. He has a monkey with him. The man orders a drink, and while the man drinks it the monkey just runs wild around the whole bar, annoying everyone including the man. While the man is drinking, the monkey runs up to the pool table, climbs up a cue, grabs the cueball, sticks it in his mouth and swallows it. The barkeep walks up to the man and says, "Did you see what your bloody monkey just did?" "No, what did the little prick do this time?" replies the man. "He just swallowed the cueball from my pool table, that's what he just did", says the barkeep, angrily. "Well, hopefully it'll kill the little bastard because I'm fucking sick of him and his little tricks," says the man. He then finishes his drink and leaves. A couple of weeks later the same man enters the bar with the same monkey. He orders the same drink and the monkey runs wild around the whole bar, same as last time. While the man is drinking, the monkey finds some peanuts on a tray on the bar. He picks one up, sticks it up his arse, takes it out again and eats it. The bartender finds this disgusting, so he walks up to the man again. "Did you see what your bloody monkey just did?" "No, what did the little prick do this time?" sighs the man. "He just stuck a peanut up his arse, took it out and ate it," says the barkeep. "Well, what do you expect?" says the monkey's owner. "Ever since he ate that sodding cueball he has to measure everything first!"

A doctor says to his patient: "I have bad news and worse news."
   "Oh, dear; what's the bad news?" asks the patient.
   The doctor replies: "You only have 24 hours to live."
   "That's terrible," says the patient. "How can the news possibly be worse?"
The doctor replies: "I've been trying to contact you since yesterday."

Two whales, male and female, are swimming happily through the ocean.

On seeing a boat, the male says to his friend: "Hey, I've got a great idea! Let's swim up under that boat and blow out really hard through our blowholes!"

The female says, "Uh... I don't know..."

"Come on, it'll be fun: just this once!"

The female agrees and they swim up under the boat and blow out, capsizing the boat and sending the hapless sailors into the water.

As they are swimming away, the male says, "Wow! That was fun, wasn't it? Hey! I've got another idea! Let's swim back there and eat all the sailors!"

The female, exasperated, replies, "Look, I agreed to the blow job, but I'm not swallowing any seamen."

A mother and her young blonde daughter have just finished shopping for food and all the grocery is scattered all over the kitchen floor in plastic bags. While the mum busies herself putting things away, the daughter picks up a box of animal crackers and empties its content on the table, making quite a mess.

"What are you doing?" her mum yells.

"Well, it says on the box, 'Do not eat if seal is broken'. I'm looking for the seal."

The doctor entered the waiting room. "I have some good news for you, Mrs. Douglas."

"Pardon me," she interrupted coldly, "but it's Miss."

The doctor said, "I have some bad news for you, Miss Douglas.'

A man and a woman could not have children and spent a long time working out why this was. Eventually it turned out that it was the man's problem, so they decided to get the woman artificially inseminated. They booked an appointment at the clinic but at the last minute the husband was called away on urgent business, so the wife had to go alone. She walked into the clinic and was shown to her room for insemination. After a couple of minutes a doctor walked in and told her to remove her clothes from the bottom half of her body and to lie back on the bed with her feet in the stirrups. The woman complied. After she had done this, the doctor dropped his trousers and pants and began to walk towards her. "Er, doctor, what on earth are you doing?" she asked, a little worried. "What's the problem?" said the doctor. "Don't you want to get pregnant?" "Well, yes, doctor, I do..." began the wife. "Well, just lie back and think of England," said the doctor, "because we're out of the bottled variety and you'll have to take what's on tap!"

How do you know a blonde is having a bad day?
    Her tampon's behind her ear and she can't find her cigarette.

A boy catches his mum and dad having sex. The boy is curious and says, "What are you guys doing?"
    The dad replies back, "We are playing poker and your mum is the wild card."
    About an hour later the father cannot find his son. He hears a noise in the bathroom and goes to check it out.
    He finds his son jacking off and says, "What in the hell are you doing?"
    The boy replies, "I am playing poker."
    Then the dad says, "How are you playing poker without a wild card?"
    The boy replies, "With a hand like this, who needs a wild card?!"

The famous golf champion Tiger Woods was having a quiet holiday far away from the sport paparazzi, driving around North Wales in his Volvo. One evening, noticing that he is almost out of petrol, he stopped at a station to fill up. An old man came out from behind an antiquated counter and approached the car.

"Fill her up," Tiger Woods said, getting out of the car to stretch his legs. As he did so, a tee fell from his pocket and landed at the feet of the old timer. The petrol attendant picked it up, turned it around in his hands, obviously puzzled, for a full minute. Then, defeated, not able to figure out what it was, he turned to Tiger Woods and asked:

"Say, what is this, son?"

"Oh, this is called a tee," the champion answered. Seeing the lack of comprehension in the old timer's eyes, he elaborated: "It's to rest my balls on when I am taking long drives."

The man looked him up, then at his car and said admiringly:

'They really think of everything at Volvo.'

What kind of fun does a priest have? Nun.

A man and a woman started to have sex in the middle of a dark forest. After about 15 minutes of it, the man finally gets up and says, "Damn, I wish I had a torch!"

The woman says, "Me too; you've been eating grass for the past ten minutes!"

Why does a redneck's pulse race when he meets a woman wearing a leather skirt?

Because she smells like a new truck.

A young entrepreneur starts his own business. He is shrewd and diligent, so business keeps coming in. Pretty soon he realizes that he needs an in-house counsel, and so he begins interviewing young lawyers.

"As I'm sure you can understand," he starts off with one of the first applicants, "in a business like this, our personal integrity must be beyond question." He leans forward. "Mr. Peterson, are you an 'honest' lawyer?"

'Honest?' replies the job prospect. 'Let me tell you something about honesty. I'm so honest that my dad lent me £15,000 for my education and I paid back every penny the minute I completed my very first case.'

"Impressive. And what sort of case was that?"

"My father filed a small claims suit against me."

A man suffers from premature ejaculation, so he decides to see a doctor about it. The doctor says there is nothing physically wrong with the man, but that he has a mental block. The doctor suggests that to cure the problem the man should try to shock himself when he feels that he is about to ejaculate. The doctor suggests using a starting pistol: the man should fire it when he feels the need, and that this should help prevent the problem. The man thanks the doctor and runs off to the sports shop to get himself a starting pistol. He rushes home to his wife, whom he finds naked on the bed, all ready for him. Things go well, and they find themselves in the 69 position. Moments later, the man feels the urge to ejaculate, so pulls the trigger. The next day the man finds himself back at the doctor's surgery. The doctor asks, 'So, how did it go? Any improvements?' 'Not really,' begins the man. 'When I fired the pistol, my wife crapped on my face and bit three inches off my penis, and my neighbour jumped naked out of the cupboard with his hands in the air!'

A ventriloquist is visiting New Zealand when he stumbles across a small village and decides to have some fun. Approaching a man on his porch patting his dog, he says, "Can I talk to your dog?" The villager just laughs at him and says, "Are you stupid? The dog doesn't talk." "Are you sure?" asks the ventriloquist. Turning to the dog, he says: "Hello, mate, how's it going?" "I'm doin' all right," the dog replies. At this, the villager looks shocked. "Is this your owner?" "Yep," says the dog. "How does he treat you?" asks the ventriloquist. "Really well. He walks me twice a day, feeds me great food and takes me to the lake once a week to play." "Mind if I talk to your horse?" the ventriloquist asks the villager. The horse tells the ventriloquist that he is also treated pretty well. "I am ridden regularly, brushed down often and kept in a nice barn." "Mind if I talk to your sheep?" The ventriloquist then asks. In a panic, the villager turns around and shouts: "The sheep's a liar!"

A man was on a blind date. He had spent the whole evening with this woman he just couldn't stand: she was everything he didn't like in a woman, so he was really bored to death. Luckily he had prepared for just this eventuality and had asked one of his mates to call the restaurant he was eating at, just in case he needed a getaway plan. So when the call came, he rushed over to the phone and feigned surprise and shock. When he returned to the table, his date looked up and asked, "Is everything all right?" He replied, "Not really. I'm afraid I'm going to have to go: my grandfather just died." "Thank God for that," the woman said. "If yours hadn't, mine would have had to!"

Did you hear about the guy in hospital for sniffing curry powder?
  He's in a korma.

After listening to an elderly prostitute plead her case, Judge Poe calls a brief recess and retires to his chambers. En route, he bumps into a colleague, Judge Graham.

"Excuse me, Judge Graham," Poe asks. "What would you give a 63-year-old prostitute?"

"Let me think," Judge Graham replies. "Ten quid, tops."

A man in a hot-air balloon realized he was lost. He reduced altitude and spotted a woman below. He descended a bit more and shouted: "Excuse me, can you help me? I promised a friend I would meet him an hour ago, but I don't know where I am."

The woman below replied: "You are in a hot-air balloon hovering approximately 30 feet above the ground. You are between 40 and 41 degrees North latitude and between 59 and 60 degrees West longitude."

"You must be a civil engineer," said the balloonist.

"I am," replied the woman. "How did you know?"

"Well," answered the balloonist, "Everything you told me is technically correct, but I have no idea what to make of your information and the fact is I am still LOST. Frankly, you have not been much help so far."

The woman below responded: "You must be in management". "I am" replied the balloonist, "but how did you know?" "Well," said the woman, "You don't know where you are or where you are going. You have risen to where you are due to a large quantity of hot air. You made a promise which you have no idea how to keep. And you expect people beneath you to solve your problems. The fact is, you are in exactly the same position you were in before we met, but now, SOMEHOW IT'S MY FAULT!"

David Cameron is visiting an Edinburgh hospital. He enters a ward full of patients with no obvious sign of injury or illness and greets one.

The patient replies:

"Fair fa your honest sonsie face,
Great chieftain o' the puddin race,
Aboon them a' you take your place,
Painch, tripe or thairm,
As lang's my airm."

Cameron is confused, so he just grins and moves on to the next patient and says hello.

The patient responds:

"Some hae meat and canna eat,
And some wad eat that want it,
But we hae meat and we can eat,
So let the Lord be thankit."

Even more confused, the PM moves on to the next patient, who immediately begins to chant:

"We sleekit, cowerin, timrous beasty,
Thou needna start awa sae hastie,
Wi' bickering brattle."

Now seriously troubled, Cameron turns to the accompanying doctor and asks, "What kind of facility is this? A mental ward?"

"No," replies the doctor. "This is the serious Burns unit."

70-year-old George goes for his annual check-up. He tells the doctor that he feels fine, but often has to go to the bathroom during the night. Then he says: "But you know, Doc: I'm blessed. God knows my eyesight is going, so he puts on the light when I pee, and turns it off when I'm done!"

A little later in the day, Dr. Smith calls George's wife and says: "Your husband's test results were fine, but he said something strange that has been bugging me. He claims that God turns the light on and off for him when uses the bathroom at night."

Thelma exclaims: "That old fool! He's been peeing in the refrigerator again!"

Mr Rennie was an old man and he lived in a nursing home. One day he walked into the nurses' quarters and told the nurses his penis had died. None of them were shocked – this sort of thing happens all the time – and they just figured he was a bit bored and would get over it. A couple of days later, Mr Rennie bumped into one of the nurses walking down the corridor. His penis was hanging out of his trousers. The nurse said to him, "I thought your penis had died, Mr Rennie?" "It certainly did, young lady," he replied, "but today's the viewing!"

A priest is preparing a man for his passing over. Whispering firmly, the priest says, "Denounce the devil! Let him know how little you think of him!"

The dying man says nothing. The priest repeats his order. Still the man says nothing.

The priest asks, "Why do you refuse to denounce the devil and his evil?"

The dying man replies, "Until I know for sure where I'm headed, I don't think I ought to aggravate anybody."

A penguin is on holiday in Arizona. He's driving around the desert when he sees the oil light come on on his car. He quickly stops at the next garage, just up the road. He asks the mechanic if he can take a look at the car and the mechanic says he can but he'll have to do a couple of other things first, so could the penguin leave the car and come back soon? "Sure," says the penguin and he goes off to find an ice cream parlour thinking that, as a penguin in Arizona, a bowl of ice cream will cool him down nicely. Having no hands, it's not easy to eat ice cream if you're a penguin, so he ends up covered in ice cream and has to hurry back to the garage to see what's up with his car. He asks the mechanic what's up with it and the mechanic replies, "It looks like you've blown a seal." The penguin, shocked, says, "No, no: it's just ice cream, I promise!"

A woman had just given birth to her first baby. She was tired and haggard, but she noticed the baby was nowhere to be seen.

"Where's my baby?" she asks. "I want to see my baby."

The doctor, apologising, says: "Er, well, you see, mmm... I know it will come as a shock, but there's a problem with your baby: she has no arms..."

The mother is stunned. "Wh... What..? No arms?" Then she wails: "I don't care: she's my baby – I want to see my baby! I hurt all this time to get her: I want to see her!"

"Er..." says the doctor, eyes downcast, "you see, she has no legs either..."

The mother is speechless for a few seconds, then erupts in tears and wails: "I want to see my baby!"

The doctor relents and nods to the nurse outside, who brings in a cot. The blonde mother peers inside and her smile dies on her face. Inside the cot is a big ear.

"Is...is this my baby?" she whispers.

"Speak louder," says the doctor, "she's deaf."

What did the mother turkey say to her disobedient children?
"If your father could see you now, he'd turn in his gravy."

A guy sitting at a bar at Heathrow notices an attractive woman sitting next to him. He thinks to himself: "Wow, she's so gorgeous she must be a flight attendant. But which airline does she work for?"

Hoping to pick her up, he leans towards her and utters the Delta Airways slogan: "Love to fly and it shows?"

She gives him a blank, confused stare.

A moment later, the Singapore Airlines slogan pops into his head. He leans towards her again, "Something special in the air?"

She gives him the same confused look.

Next he tries the Thai Airways slogan: "Smooth as silk."

This time the woman turned to him and said, "What the fuck do you want, you freak?"

The man smiles, slumps back in his chair, and says "Ah. Air New Zealand!"

A man waiting to go in to heaven is told by St Peter, "Before I can let you in, I have one question. Have you ever cheated on your wife?" "No, never," replies the man. "OK," says St Peter, "have this top-of-the-range Porsche." The next man walks up and is asked the same question. "Yes, quite a lot," he replies. "OK," says St Peter, "have a Mini." The second man then drives around heaven in his Mini and he sees the other man sitting in his Porsche looking really sad. So he asks, "What's the matter? You've been given this top-of-the-range Porsche." The other man replies, "I just saw my wife on a push bike."

How did the redneck die drinking milk?

The cow sat on him.

An Aussie lass is trying to sell her old car but she is having a lot of problems because it has almost 230,000 miles on the clock.

One day, she reveals the problem to her mate.

"There is a possibility to make the car easier to sell, but it's not legal," says her mate.

"That doesn't matter," replies the Aussie lass, "if I can only sell the car."

"OK," says her mate. "Here's the address of a friend of mine. He owns a car repair shop. Tell him I sent you and he'll 'fix it'. Then you shouldn't have a problem any more trying to sell your car."

The following weekend the Aussie lass makes the trip to the mechanic.

About one month after that, her mate asks her, "Did you sell your car?"

"No," replies the Aussie lass. "Why should I? It only has 50,000 miles on the clock."

A local business is looking for office help. They put a sign in the window, stating: "HELP WANTED. Must be able to type, must be good with a computer and must be bilingual."

A short time afterwards, a dog trots up to the window and goes inside. He looks at the receptionist and wags his tail, then walks over to the sign, looks at it and whines. Getting the idea, the receptionist gets the office manager.

The manager says, "I can't hire you. The sign says you have to be able to type."

With that, the dog jumps down, goes to the typewriter and proceeds to type out a perfect letter.

The manager is stunned, but tells the dog, "The sign also says you have to be good with a computer."

The dog jumps down again and goes to the computer, where it enters and executes a spreadsheet perfectly.

By this time the manager is totally dumbfounded. He looks at the dog and says, "I realize that you are a very intelligent dog and have some interesting abilities. However, I still can't give you the job. You have to be bilingual."

The dog looks at the manager calmly and says, "Meow!"

A redneck trucker is driving down the highway when he hears a loud thump under his rig. He stops to check the damage, and then calls his boss.

"I hit a pig on the road, and he's stuck under my truck," he explains. "What should I do?"

"Shoot him in the head," answers the boss. "Then pull him out and throw him in the truck."

The driver does it, and then calls his boss back. "I did what you told me," he explains.

"So what's the problem?" snaps the boss.

The driver replies, "I don't know what to do with his motorcycle."

Brenda is at home making dinner, when her husband's work mate Bill arrives at her door.

"Brenda, can I come in?" he asks. "I've something to tell you."

"Of course you can come in. But where's my husband?" enquires Brenda.

"That's what I'm here to tell you, Brenda. There was an accident down at the Guinness brewery."

"Oh, God ,no!" cries Brenda. "Please don't tell me."

"I must, Brenda. Your husband is dead and gone. I'm sorry."

Finally, she looks up at Bill. "How did it happen?"

"It was terrible, Brenda. He fell into a vat of Guinness and drowned."

"Oh, my dear Jesus! Did he at least go quickly?" sobbed Brenda.

"Well, no, Brenda. Fact is, he got out three times to pee."

A man walks into a bar grinning his face off. "The beers are on me!" he says happily. "My wife has just run off with my best friend."

"That's a shame," says the barman. "Why aren't you sad?"

"Sad?" asks the man. "They've saved me a fortune. They were both pregnant."

Viruses are the bane of modern technology. Here is a list of dangerous new viruses you DON'T want to see spreading:

AIRLINE VIRUS
You're in London, but your data is in Inverness.

DAVID CAMERON VIRUS
It doubles the files on your hard drive while stating it is decreasing the number of files, increases the cost of your computer, taxes its CPU to maximum capacity and then uses Quicken to access your bank accounts and deplete your balances.

BILL GATES VIRUS
This dominant strain searches for desirable features in all other viruses via the Internet. It then either engulfs the competing viruses or removes their access to computers until they die out.

DIET VIRUS
Allows your hard drive to lose weight by eliminating the FAT table.

DISNEY VIRUS
Everything in the computer goes Goofy.

ELVIS VIRUS
Your computer gets fat, slow and lazy and then self-destructs, only to resurface at shopping malls and service stations across rural America.

FREUDIAN VIRUS
Your computer becomes obsessed with its own motherboard or it becomes very jealous of the size of your friend's hard disk.

LORENA BOBBITT VIRUS
It turns your hard disk into a 3.5-inch floppy.

POLITICALLY CORRECT VIRUS
Never calls itself a 'virus,' but instead refers to itself as an 'electronic micro-organism.'

SPICE GIRL VIRUS
Has no real function, but makes a pretty desktop.

STAR TREK VIRUS
Invades your system in places where no virus has gone before.

TEENAGER VIRUS
Your PC stops every few seconds to ask for money.

X-FILES VIRUS
All your icons start shape-shifting.

TOBACCO INDUSTRY VIRUS
It contends that there is no reliable scientific evidence that viruses can harm you computer or that it targets adolescent computer users.

Two turtles are camping. After four days hiking, they realize they've left behind a bottle opener for their beer.
The first turns to the second and says, "You've got to go back or else we've got no lager." "No way," says the second turtle. "By the time I get back you'll have eaten all the food."

The first turtle replies, "I promise I won't, OK? Just hurry." Nine full days pass and there's still no sign of the second turtle, so the first finally cracks and digs into a sandwich. Suddenly the second turtle pops out from behind a rock and yells, "I knew it! I'm definitely not going now!"

Miss Bea, the church organist, was in her eighties and had never been married. She was much admired for her sweetness and kindness to all. The pastor came to call on her one afternoon early in the spring and she welcomed him into her Victorian parlour. She invited him to have a seat while she prepared a little tea.

As he sat facing her old pump organ, the young minister noticed a cut glass bowl sitting on top of it, filled with water. In the water floated, of all things, a condom. Imagine his shock and surprise. Imagine his curiosity! Surely Miss Bea had flipped or something...!

When she returned with tea and cookies, they began to chat. The pastor tried to stifle his curiosity about the bowl of water and its strange floater, but soon it got the better of him and he could resist no longer.

"Miss Bea," he said, "I wonder if you would tell me about this?" pointing to the bowl.

"Oh, yes," she replied, "isn't it wonderful? I was walking downtown last fall and I found this little package on the ground. The directions said to put it on the organ, keep it wet and it would prevent disease. And you know... I haven't had a cold all winter."

A man walks into a pub with his dog on a lead.

The landlord says, 'That's a weird-looking dog. He's got stumpy legs, he's pink and he doesn't have a tail. I bet my rottweiler could beat him in a scrap.' They bet £50 and out in the backyard, the rottweiler is soon whimpering for mercy.

Another drinker says his pit bull will win and the bet is increased to £100. Another trip to the backyard, and when it's all over the pitbull is cowering behind his owner, who pays up and says, 'So what breed is he, anyway?'

The owner says, "Well, until I cut his tail off and painted him pink, he was the same breed as every other alligator."

A Welsh farmer was out on his hillside tending his flock one day when he saw a man drinking with a cupped hand from the stream which ran down from one of his fields. Realising the danger, he shouted over to the man, "Paid a yfed y dwr! Mae'n ych-y-fi!" (Don't drink the water! It's disgusting!)

The man at the stream lifted his head and put a cupped hand to his ear, shrugged his shoulders at the farmer, and carried on drinking. Realising the man at the stream couldn't hear him, the farmer moved closer. "Paid a yfed! Dwr ych-y-fi! Defaid yn cachu yn y dwr!" (Don't drink! Water's disgusting! Sheep crap in the water!) Still the walker couldn't hear the farmer.

Finally, the farmer ran right up to the man at the stream and once again said, "Dwr yn ych-y-fi! Paid a'i yfed!" (Water's disgusting! Don't drink it!)

"I'm dreadfully sorry," said the man at the stream in a curt English accent. "I couldn't understand a word you said, dear boy. Can't you speak English?"

"Oh, I see," said the farmer. "I was just saying, if you use both hands you could get more in."

Howard comes home one evening to find his wife crying.

"What's the matter, darling?" he asks.

"I don't know what to do," she says. "I'd prepared a meal for a special night in, but the dog ate it."

"Don't worry, dear," he says. "I'll get us another dog."

Little Johnny returned home from school, informing his father that he'd received an F in maths and a detention.

"What happened?" asked his dad.

"Well," little Johnny said, "the teacher asked, 'How much is two times three?' and I said 'Six'."

"But that's right!" said his father.

"Then," said Johnny, "she asked, 'How much is three times two?'"

"That's crap. What's the difference?" asked his father.

"That's what I said!"

Doctor Dave had slept with one of his patients and had felt guilty all day long. No matter how much he tried to forget about it, he couldn't. The guilt and sense of betrayal was overwhelming.

But every once in a while he'd hear that soothing voice within himself, trying to reassure him: "Dave, don't worry about it. You aren't the first doctor to sleep with one of their patients and you won't be the last. And you're single. Let it go..."

But invariably the other voice inside his head would bring him back to reality:

"Dave, you're a vet..."

Why did God create Adam before Eve?

To give him a chance to speak.

Why was the exhibitionist drinking window-cleaning fluid?

To stop himself from streaking.

Where do you get virgin wool from?

Ugly sheep.

A man walks into a pub with his wife. His wife sits down while he orders drinks and a friend of his at the bar asks him where he's been.

"On holiday," he replies.

"Where on holiday?" his friend asks.

"Spain."

"Whereabouts in Spain?"

"Some little village on the coast."

"What's it called?"

"I forget. What's the name of that plant that grows up the side of houses?" "Ivy."

"That's it," he says, "Ivy, what's the name of the village we stayed at in Spain?"

A guy with a black eye boards his plane and sits down in his seat. He notices immediately that the guy next to him has a black eye, too. He says to him, "Hey this is a coincidence, we both have black eyes; mind if I ask how you got yours?"

The other guy says, "Well, it just happened. It was a tongue twister accident. See, I was at the ticket counter and this gorgeous blonde with the most massive breasts in the world was there. So, instead of saying, 'I'd like two tickets to Pittsburgh,' I accidentally said, 'I'd like two pickets to Tittsburgh'... So she socked me a good one."

The first guy replied, "Wow! This is unbelievable. Mine was a tongue twister too. I was at the breakfast table this morning and I wanted to say to my wife: "Please pour me a bowl of Frosties, honey," but I accidentally said, "you ruined my life you evil fat slag."

Why did the leprechaun wear two condoms?

Ahh, to be sure, to be sure.

A doctor is having an affair with his young enthusiastic, if a bit dumb, nurse. The nurse gets pregnant and the doctor, of course, doesn't want his wife to know. So he says to his mistress:

"You go and lie low somewhere, say Italy, for a while, until the baby is due. When the baby is born, just send me a postcard with 'Spaghetti' written on it and I'll know. By this time, I'll have spoken to my wife."

"Why 'Spaghetti'?" she asks.

"Because you'll be in Italy, that's why," the doctor says, just on this side of panicking.

Not finding anything logical to reply to that, the girl agrees and flies off to Italy. After nine months, the doctor receives a call from his wife, who tells him she has just received the strangest postcard.

"Don't worry, honey," the doctor says. "I'm coming home and I'll explain everything."

Back home, he picks up the postcard, wondering what he is going to say to his wife, reads it, stares at it for a second or two and then topples over and dies of a massive heart attack.

Stunned, her wife re-reads the mysterious postcard through tears of grief. It says:

"Spaghetti, spaghetti, spaghetti, spaghetti, three with sausage and meatballs, one with mussels."

A man dies while having sex and his erection stays. At the funeral parlour they discuss the situation with his wife and she gives them permission to cut it off in order to get the lid on the coffin. The wife keeps the penis, and later that night steals back and shoves it up the dead man's rear end. The next day, at the funeral, she peers over the coffin and, noticing a tear in the old man's eye, says, "I told you it hurt, you heartless bastard!"

A man walked into a supermarket with his zip down. One of the lady cashiers walked up to him and said: "Your barracks door is open!"

This is not a phrase men usually use, so he went on his way looking a bit puzzled.

When he had just about done his shopping, a man came up to him and said: "Your fly is open!"

Our man zipped it up and finished his shopping. He then intentionally got into the line to check out where the lady was who told him about "his barrack's door". He was planning to have a little fun with her on his way out. When he reached her till, he said: "When you saw my barracks door open, did you see a soldier standing to attention in there?"

The lady thought for a moment then said: "No, no, I didn't. All I saw was a disabled veteran sitting on two duffel bags!"

A man bought a new fridge for his house. To get rid of his old fridge, he put it in the driveway and hung a sign on it saying: "Free to good home. You want it, you take it."

For three days the fridge sat there without even one person looking twice at it.

He eventually decided that people were too suspicious. It looked too good to be true. He changed the sign to read: 'Fridge for sale, £50.'

The next day someone stole it.

A young polar bear walks up to his dad one day and asks: "Dad, am I a pure polar bear? You know, not part black bear or grizzly bear or anything?" "Why no, son. You come from a long line of proud and strong polar bears. Why do you ask?" "Because I'm fucking cold."

Jake moves to Australia after working all his life in the City. He buys a farm in the remotest part of the outback he can find. His post arrives once a week, his groceries once a month and he can call the flying doctor on his radio if he has an emergency. One night, after six months of this, Jake is finishing his dinner when he hears a knock on the door. He walks up, opens it and sees a huge outbacker standing in front of him. "G'day, mate," says the outbacker. "I'm your nearest neighbour, Bruce Sheldon, from twenty miles east. I'm having a party Saturday night and I thought you might like to come along, mate."

"That'd be great," says Jake, "I haven't really spoken to anyone for six months. Thanks a lot."

Bruce is about to turn away, but instead says, "I think I'd better warn you, though: there'll be some serious drinking going on."

"Not a problem," says Jake, "I like a couple of pints myself."

Bruce is about to turn away again, but instead says, 'Better warn you though, there'll probably be some fighting, too.'

"Not a problem," says Jake, "I know how to keep out of trouble."

Bruce is about to turn away again, but instead says, "Better warn you though, there'll probably be some pretty wild sex, too."

"Not a problem," says Jake, "I've been alone for six months, remember. Now, what time should I show up?"

Bruce turns once more and says, "Whenever you like, mate: there's only going to be me and you there anyway!"

Woman: Can I get Viagra here?
Pharmacist: Yes.
Woman: Can I get it over the counter?
Pharmacist: If you give me two of them, you can.

What do accountants do when they're constipated?
Work it out with a pencil.

A man was leaving a cafe with his morning coffee when he noticed a most unusual funeral procession approaching the cemetery. A long black hearse was followed by a second hearse. Behind the second hearse was a solitary man walking a pit bull on a leash. Behind him was a queue of 200 men walking in single file. The man couldn't stand the curiosity, he respectfully approached the man walking the dog, "I am so sorry for your loss, and I know now is a bad time to disturb you, but I've never seen a funeral like this with so many people walking in single file. Whose funeral is it?

The man replied "Well that first hearse is for my wife."
"What happened to her?"
"My dog attacked and killed her."
He enquired further. "Well, who is in the second hearse then?"
"The mother-in-law. She tried to save my wife and lo-and-behold, the dog turned on her and killed her as well."
A poignant moment of silence passed between the men.
"Can I borrow the dog?"
"Yeah, join the queue!"

A retiring golf club president is making his final speech at his club's annual awards ceremony. "From 18-handicappers to pros, I've treated everyone equally," the emotional president begins. "We all live for this game. We're like a big family and after all these years together I only fell by the wayside once. While my darling wife sits beside me, I want to apologise to her and you, my beloved friends. In a mere moment of weakness, I betrayed her. It meant nothing – a one-night stand, that's all."

After this shocking revelation, the president sits down, ashamed. His wife rises, smiling as ever. "I, too, have a confession, darling," she says. "Before I met you, I was a man!" There are gasps around the room as the startled president staggers back to his feet. "You cheating bastard!" he exclaims. "All these years you played off the front tees."

An elderly gent was invited to his old friend's home for dinner one evening. He was impressed by the way his buddy preceded every request to his wife with endearing terms: Honey, My Love, Darling, Sweetheart, Pumpkin, etc. The couple had been married almost 70 years and clearly, they were still very much in love.

While his wife was in the kitchen, the man leaned over and said to his host, "I think it's wonderful that, after all these years, you still call your wife those loving pet names." The old man hung his head. "To be honest with you," he said, "I forgot her name about 10 years ago."

What do you say if someone tries to steal your gate?
Nothing; he might take a fence.

Young Justin has a swearing problem, and his father's getting tired of it.

He decides to ask a shrink what to do. The shrink says, "Negative reinforcement. Since Christmas is coming up, ask Justin what he wants from Santa. If he swears while he tells you his wish list, leave a pile of dog poop in place of each gift he requests."

Two days before Christmas, Justin's father asks him what he wants for Christmas. "I want a damn teddy bear lying beside me when I wake up. When I go downstairs, I want to see a damn train going around the damn tree. And when I go outside, I want to see a damn bike leaning up against the damn garage."

On Christmas morning, Justin wakes up and rolls into a pile of dog poop. Confused, he walks downstairs and sees another pile under the tree. He walks outside, looks at a huge pile of dog poo by the garage, and walks inside. His dad smiles and asks, "What did Santa bring you this year?"

Justin replies, "I think I got a goddamn dog, but I can't find the son of a bitch!"

A soldier is telling his friends that his sister just enlisted, disguising herself as a bloke.

"Wait a minute: she'll have to get changed and shower with the other blokes, won't she?" one of his friends points out.

"So what?"

"Well, won't they find out?"

"Probably," replies the soldier with a wink, "but who'll tell?"

In the 60s people took acid to make the world weird. Now the world is weird and people take Prozac to make it normal.

A man starts a new job, and his boss says, "If you marry my daughter, I'll make you a partner and give you a £1 million salary."

The man's puzzled, until he sees a picture of the girl – she makes Margaret Thatcher look hot. But after a moment he accepts, figuring the money's worth it, and they get married.

A year later the fella's up on a ladder hanging a picture and yells to his wife, "Bring me my hammer, please."

She mumbles, "Get the hammer, get the hammer," and grudgingly fetches the hammer.

The guy says, "Can you hand me the nails, please?"

She mumbles, "Get me some nails, get me some nails," and does so.

The guy starts hammering, hits his thumb, and yells, "Ow! Fuck me!"

She shuffles off, mumbling, "Get the bag, get the bag..."

Wife to husband: "Who was that lady I seen you with last night?"

Husband: "You mean 'I saw.'"

Wife: "OK, who was that eyesore I seen you with last night?"

Two aerials met on a roof, fell in love and got married.

The ceremony was rubbish but the reception was brilliant.

A rather embarrassed man goes to see his doctor and tells him: "Well, I have this problem, you see: I can't get it up for my wife any more, if you see what I mean."

"It's quite all right," the doctor says. "Get undressed and we'll see what the problem is." He does so, but can find nothing wrong with the patient.

"Come back tomorrow," he advises. "Bring your wife with you. I'd like to examine her too."

The anxious patient turns up the following day with his wife, as promised. The doctor has a quick look at the woman, then asks her to take her clothes off.

"Mmm... I see... Now turn around please. Mmmm...Can you crouch down for me? That's it. Gooooood, now get on all fours on the carpet. Yes, this way... Mmmm... It's OK, you can put your clothes back on."

While the wife is getting dressed, the doctor takes the husband aside and tells him:

"You're perfectly healthy. Don't worry. Your wife didn't give me an erection either."

After passing his driving test, Davey comes home and says, "Dad, can I use the car?"

His dad replies, "OK, son. But first, you have to mow the lawn every week for three months and get your hair cut."

Three months pass and Davey comes into the house and says, "Dad, the lawn's looked like Lord's for the last three months. How about letting me use the car now?"

The dad replies, "That's true. But, son, you didn't cut your hair."

So Davey says, "But dad: Jesus had long hair!"

"You're right," says Davey's dad. "And he walked everywhere."

There is a theory which states: if ever anybody discovers exactly what the Universe is for and why it is here, it will instantly disappear and be replaced by something even more bizarre and inexplicable. There is another theory which states: this has already happened.

A guy goes on holiday to the Holy Land with his wife and mother-in-law. While they are there, the mother-in-law dies. They go to an undertaker who explains that they can ship the body home for £5,000 or they can bury her in the Holy Land for only £150. The guy thinks for a while and then says, 'We'll ship her home.'

"Are you sure?" the undertaker asks. "That's an awfully big expense and we can do a very nice burial here."

The guy says, "Look, 2,000 years ago they buried a bloke here and three days later he rose from the dead. I just can't take that chance."

Tired of a listless sex life, a husband asks his wife during lovemaking "How come you never tell me when you have an orgasm?"

To which she replies, "You're never here!"

One night a guy takes his girlfriend home. As they are about to kiss each other goodnight at the front door, the guy starts feeling a little horny. With an air of confidence, he leans with his hand against the wall and, smiling, he says to her,

"Honey, would you give me a blow job?"

"Horrified, she replies, "Are you mad? My parents will see us!"

"Oh come on! Who's gonna see us at this hour?" he asks, grinning at her.

"No, please. Can you imagine if we get caught?"

"Oh come on! There's nobody around, they're all sleeping!"

"No way. It's just too risky!"

"Oh please, please, I love you so much?!?"

"No, no, and no. I love you too, but I just can't!"

"Oh yes you can. Please?"

Out of the blue, the light on the stairs goes on and the girl's sister shows up in her pyjamas, hair dishevelled and in a sleepy voice she says: "Dad says to go ahead and give him his blow job, or I can do it. Or if need be, mom says she can come down herself and do it. But for God's sake tell him to take his hand off the intercom!"

One day, a sweet little girl goes home to find that her dog has died. He is lying on the lawn on his back with his poor little legs sticking straight up in the air. She quickly runs to her father and asks him why her dog is lying down with his poor little legs in the air. "Well," her father explains, "that's because Jesus will be coming down to help poor doggy up to Heaven, and if his legs are up in the air like that it'll be a whole lot easier for him to go."

The very next day when the father comes home, the sweet little girl runs up to him in a dreadful state. "Daddy! Daddy! Mummy almost died today – I'm sure of it!"

"Oh, my!" says the father. "How do you know – is she OK?" "Yes, Daddy," the girl says, "She's OK now, but earlier on Mummy's legs were up in the air and she was shouting 'Oh Jesus, I'm coming, I'm coming' and if the postman hadn't been there to hold her down I think she'd be in Heaven now!"

A newlywed couple arrive back from their honeymoon to move into their tiny new flat.

"Care to go to bed?" the husband asks.

"Shh!" says his blushing bride. "These walls are paper-thin; the neighbours will know what you mean! Next time, ask me in code, like: 'Have you left the washing machine door open?' instead."

So, the following night, the husband asks: "I don't suppose you left the washing machine door open, darling?"

"No," she snaps back, "I definitely shut it." Then she rolls over and falls asleep.

The next morning, she wakes up feeling a little frisky herself, so she nudges her husband and says: "I think I did leave the washing machine door open after all..."

"Don't worry," says the man. "It was only a small load, so I did it by hand."

A man is rushed to his nearest hospital in New York, Our Holy Mother of BeJesus, after a heart attack. The surgeon performs heart surgery and the man survives no problem. Afterwards, the man is lying in his bed and one of the nuns is comforting him. "Don't worry sir, you'll be just fine, it's all over now," says the nun. "But we would like to know, sir, if you don't mind the asking, as to how you intend to pay your bill for the operation and the care. Would you be covered by an insurance policy?" "Well actually sister, I don't think I am," the man replies. "Oh dear," continues the nun, "maybe you've got a load of money lying around and you'd like to pay by cash?" "Er, no I don't think so sister," the man replies. "I'm not really a man of much material wealth". "Well," says the nun, "perhaps you've some close family who could help out?" "Well not really sister," the man replies, "I've just the one sister in County Kerry in the old country, but she's a spinster nun." The nun replies, "Nuns are not spinsters, sir, nuns are married to God." "In that case," says the man, "perhaps you could get my brother-in-law to foot the bill!"

You have reached the Mental Health Hotline:

- If you are obsessive compulsive, press 1 over and over and over again.
- If you are multiple personality, press 3, 4, 5, 6, 7 and 8.
- If you are hysterical, don't touch any buttons, something terrible might happen!
- If you are paranoid, there's no need to touch any buttons, we know who you are, we know where you live and we will be coming to get you very soon.
- If you are a psychopath, rip the cord out of the wall and run away with the phone.
- If you are an anal retentive psychopath, take the phone apart, place each piece in a plastic bag and then place all the plastic bags in one large paper bag. Then put the paper bag in the south east corner of your freezer.
- If you are depressed, don't press any buttons, it wouldn't do you any good anyway.
- If you are manic, press as many buttons as you can as fast as possible.
- If you are a kleptomaniac, go to your neighbour's house, steal their phone and call again.

A pissed-off wife is complaining about her husband spending all his free time in the local boozer, so one night he takes her along with him.

"What'll you have?" he asks.

"Oh, I don't know: the same as you, I suppose," she replies, so the husband orders a couple of whiskies and throws his down in one shot.

His wife watches him, then takes a sip from her glass and immediately spits it out. "Yuck; that's terrible!" she splutters. "I don't know how you can drink this stuff!"

"Well, there you go," cries the husband. "And you think I'm out enjoying myself every night!"

A woman is tidying up around the house one day when she hears a strange humming noise coming from her daughter's bedroom. The mother knocks on the door but just opens it immediately. She walks in and finds her daughter lying naked on the bed, pleasuring herself with a vibrator. The mother is a little shocked, but retains her composure and says, "What on earth are you doing that for, dear?" The daughter replies, "Well, mother, I am nearly 40 years old and I live at home with my parents. I never date guys, so I figure this is the nearest thing I'll get to a husband!"

That night her father can't sleep, so he wanders downstairs and hears a strange humming noise coming from the front room. He walks in and finds his daughter lying naked on the sofa, pleasuring herself with a vibrator. The father is a little shocked, but retains his composure and says, "What on earth are you doing that for, dear?" The daughter replies, "Well, father, I am nearly 40 years old and I live at home with my parents. I never date guys, so I figure this is the nearest thing I'll get to a husband!"

The next day the mother is once more tidying up around the house when she hears that same humming noise coming from the front room. She walks in, and to her surprise she sees her husband watching TV with the vibrator just placed on the sofa beside him. "What the hell are you doing?" she says to her husband, shocked. He replies, "Just watching the game with the son-in-law."

A man walks into a pub and immediately spots a gorgeous woman standing at the bar. The man strides up to her and, by way of a chat-up line, says, "Do you want to see some magic?"

"What sort of magic?" the intrigued lady asks.

"You come back home with me, have sex and then disappear."

In the distant future, a couple of humans land on a distant planet in their spaceship. They are greeted by a couple of natives of the planet, who look remarkably human and who speak the same language. They talk for hours, comparing everything on Earth and on the alien planet. Things are a lot closer than they would have all imagined and the aliens have computers and cars and television and guns and all the other things we have that make life great. Eventually the couples get on to social interaction and, in particuar, how they have sex on their respective planets. It turns out that the aliens have sex pretty much the same way that Earth people do, so the two men suggest that, in order to see the differences, the couples should swap partners and see how things are done on the other planets. The women both agree to this and they all retire for the night. The Earth woman is in the bedroom with the alien man and they both undress. She is a little worried because the alien's member is tiny: a couple of centimetres long and only about one thick, even when it's hard. "This isn't going to be easy," she says. "What's up?" says the alien, 'the size bother you? Not a problem." And he slaps himself on the forehead. As he does so, his member grows longer. He continues to slap and with each hit he gets bigger until he is very impressive-looking. "That's pretty good," says the Earth woman, "but it could do with being a bit thicker." "Not a problem," says the alien again and he begins pulling his ears. With each pull, his member increases in thickness until it is very impressive-looking. "Amazing!" exclaims the Earth woman, and they shag wildly all night.

The next day she meets her husband at breakfast. "How was it for you?" he asks her. "Well, I must admit, they've got some pretty exciting stuff over us," she replies, "but how was it for you?" "Well, I must admit I was a bit disappointed," he says, "I just got a headache. She kept slapping my forehead and pulling my ears!"

As I drove into the parking lot, I noticed that a pickup truck with a dog sitting behind the wheel was rolling toward a female pedestrian. She seemed oblivious to the fact, so I hit my horn to get her attention. She looked up just in time to jump out of the way of the truck's path and the vehicle bumped harmlessly into the curb and stopped. I rushed to the woman's side to see if she was all right. "I'm fine," she assured me, "but I hate to think what could have happened to me if that dog hadn't honked."

Two weeks ago was my 45th birthday. I wasn't feeling too good that morning, but as I walked into my office, my secretary Janet said, "Good morning, boss. Happy birthday." And I felt a little better that someone had remembered. I worked until noon, then Janet knocked on my door and said, "You know, it's such a beautiful day outside, and it's your birthday, let's go to lunch, just you and me." We went to lunch. On the way back to the office, she said, "You know, it's such a beautiful day. Let's go to my apartment." After arriving at her apartment she said, "Boss, if you don't mind, I think I'll go into the bedroom and slip into something more comfortable." "Sure!" I excitedly replied. She went into the bedroom and, in a few minutes, returned carrying a huge birthday cake – followed by my wife, children and dozens of our friends, all singing Happy Birthday. And I just sat there – on the couch – naked.

You might think life is rubbish, but imagine being an egg. You only get smashed once, you only get laid once and the only bird to sit on your face is your mother!

Why are there so many tree-lined boulevards in France?
  Germans like to march in the shade.

A woman gets on a bus, and immediately becomes involved in an argument with the driver when he calls her baby ugly. She pays her fare and storms off to get a seat, visibly upset. The man next to her asks "What's the matter, love?"

"It's that bloody driver, I've never been so insulted in all my life," she replies.

"OK," says the man. "You go down there and sort him out. I'll look after the monkey."

Alan and his friend Martin went out hunting. Martin had never hunted before, so he was following Alan's lead. Alan saw a herd of deer and told Martin to stay in the exact spot he was and to be quiet. A moment later, Alan heard a scream. He ran back and asked Martin what had happened. "A snake slithered across my feet," said Martin, "but that didn't make me scream. Then a bear came up to me and snarled, but I still didn't scream." "So why did you?" Alan asked, infuriated. "Well," Martin went on, "two squirrels crawled up my trousers and I heard one of them say, 'Should we take 'em home or eat 'em now?'"

A three-legged dog walks into a saloon in the Old West. He slides up to the bar and announces: 'I'm looking for the man who shot my paw.'

After surgery, a man wakes up drowsily in the hospital. He yells to the nurse, "I can't feel my legs!"

"Well, of course you can't," she replies. "You have just had your arms amputated."

What did Keith Richards say after being inducted into the hall of fame? 'It's a night I will remember for the rest of the night."

Two mates are out for an evening in a bar. They happen to go to the toilet at the same time. As they are standing there, Jim notices that Nick is pretty well-endowed and he can't help mentioning the fact. "Yeah," says Nick. "But it wasn't always like that, you know. I was sick of having only a small one, so I had a transplant from a doctor in Harley Street. It was pretty expensive – ten thousand pounds – but it was really worth it."

A few months later, the two mates find themselves next to each other in a toilet again. Jim says to Nick, "I thought about what you said last time, and I decided to get myself a transplant, too. You got well ripped off, mate – mine only cost a grand!" Nick leans across the urinals and has a quick look. "Not surprising," he says. "They've given you my old one!"

A woman and a man are involved in a really nasty car accident. Both their cars are totally demolished but neither of them is hurt. After they crawl out of their cars, the woman says, "So you're a man – that's interesting. I'm a woman. Wow, just look at our cars! There's nothing left, but we're unhurt. This must be a sign from God that we should meet and get acquainted."

The man feels great at having such good luck, so says, "Oh, yes; I agree with you completely! This must be a sign from the Lord!"

The woman continues, "And look at this – another miracle. My car is demolished, but this bottle of wine didn't break. Surely God wants us to drink this to celebrate our good fortune." She hands the bottle to the man, who nods his head in agreement, opens the bottle and drinks half the wine before handing it back to the woman.

The woman takes the bottle and immediately puts the cap back on. The man asks, "Aren't you having any?" The woman replies, "No. I think I'll just wait for the police!"

Fresh from her shower, a woman stands in front of the mirror, complaining to her husband that her breasts are too small. Instead of his standard response of reassuring her that that wasn't the case, her husband uncharacteristically comes up with a suggestion.

"If you want your breasts to grow, then every day take a piece of toilet paper and rub it between your breasts for a few seconds."

Willing to try anything, the wife fetches a piece of toilet paper and stands in front of the mirror, rubbing it between her breasts.

"How long will this take?" she asks.

"They'll grow larger over a period of years," he replies.

The wife stops. "Why do you think rubbing a piece of toilet paper between my breasts every day will make my breasts grow over the years?"

He shrugged and said, "Worked for your arse, didn't it?"

He lived and with extensive therapy, he may even walk again.

Three young female students all lived together in a flat and one night they all had dates at the same time. Around midnight they all got back and started comparing notes. The first girl says, 'You know what? You can tell a good date when you come back home and your hair's all messed up.' And the second girl says, 'You know what? You can tell a good date when you come back home and your makeup's all smeared.' The third girl says nothing, but just reaches under her skirt, removes her knickers and throws them against the wall. They stick there. 'You know what? That's a good date,' she says.

A couple were on their honeymoon, lying in bed, about ready to consummate their marriage, when the new bride says to the husband, "I have a confession to make, I'm not a virgin."

"Oh yeah? Who was the guy?"

"Tiger Woods."

"Tiger Woods, the golfer?"

"Yeah."

"Well he's rich, famous and handsome. I can see why you went to bed with him."

The husband and wife then made passionate love.

When they finished, the husband gets up and walks to the telephone.

"What are you doing?" asks the wife.

The husband says, "I'm going to call room service for some food."

"Tiger wouldn't do that."

"Oh yeah? What would Tiger do?"

"He'd come back to bed and do it a second time."

The husband puts down the phone and goes back to bed and makes love to his wife for a second time.

When they finish, he gets up and goes over to the phone.

"What are you doing?" She asks.

The husband says, "I'm still hungry so I was going to phone room service to order some food."

"Tiger wouldn't do that."

"Oh yeah? What would Tiger do?"

"He'd come back to bed and do it one more time."

The guy slams down the phone and goes back to bed and makes love to his wife one more time.

When they finish, he's gasping for air and glistening with sweat. He drags himself over to the phone and starts to dial.

The wife asks, "Are you calling room service?"

"No! I'm calling Tiger Woods to find out what the par is for this damn hole."

A doctor and his wife are sitting in front of the TV one evening and the good doctor is relaxing by throwing peanuts in the air and catching them in his mouth and eating them. It goes on for a while until the end of the program, when a comment his wife makes distracts him and the peanut lands in his ear. He tries to shake it out, to no avail. Trying to take it out with his little finger just manages to get the damn thing even deeper.

"Come on," says his worried wife. "Let's go to the hospital and get this out."

The doctor agrees, sighs heavily and puts his coat on, just as their daughter comes back from the cinema with her boyfriend. He explains what has happened while his wife is looking for the car keys. On hearing the story the boyfriend comes forward and says he can help.

He asks the good doctor to sit down again, unceremoniously sticks two fingers up his nose and tells him to blow as hard as he can. Sure enough, the peanut pops out of the doctor's ear and goes 'Ping!' against the mirror on the mantelpiece.

As the daughter and her boyfriend go through to the kitchen to get drinks, the doctor and his wife sit down to discuss their luck. "So," the wife says, "What do you think he'll become after he finishes school? A GP or a surgeon?"

"Well," replies the doctor, rubbing his nose, 'by the smell of his fingers, I think he's likely to be our son-in-law.'

A man was in a terrible accident in which his manhood was torn from his body. His doctor assured him that modern medicine could give him back his pecker, but that his insurance wouldn't cover the cost of the surgery.

The doctor said the price would be £3,500 for 'small', £6,500 for 'medium', £14,000 for 'large'.

The man called his wife on the phone and explained their options. When the doctor came back into the room, he found the man looking dejected. "Well, what have the two of you decided?" he asked.

"She'd rather have a new kitchen," the man answered.

It is the ophthalmologist's 40th birthday and, in the middle of the party, he is blindfolded and taken by the hand to a table in the centre of the dining room. His loving wife takes the blindfold off with a flourish and he finds himself in front of a huge cake with 40 eyes made of marzipan around it. The specialist stares at the cake and then erupts in laughter. He laughs so much a couple of his friends have to pick him up from the floor.

After a few minutes, wiping a tear of mirth from his eye, he says:

"I'm sorry: this is a great cake. It's just that I suddenly thought about my colleague Terry, who's a gynaecologist. It's his 50th birthday tomorrow."

A gentleman staying at the Ritz Hotel in London removes a card offering sexual services from a telephone box on Piccadilly. Back at the hotel, he rings the number. A lady with a silky-soft voice answers and asks if she can be of assistance. The gentleman says, "I'd like a blow job, some missionary work, a little doggy-style, some mild bondage, finishing off with a pearl necklace. What do you think?"

The lady says, "I think it sounds intriguing, sir, but you might like to press nine first to get an outside line."

A middle-aged man and woman meet, fall in love and decide to get married. On their wedding night they settle into the bridal suite at their hotel and the bride says to her new groom, "Please promise to be gentle; I'm still a virgin."

The startled groom says, "How can that be? You've been married three times before."

The bride responds, "Well, you see, my first husband was a psychiatrist and all he ever wanted to do was talk about it.

"My second husband was a gynaecologist, and all he ever wanted to do was look at it.

"And my third husband was a stamp collector and all he ever wanted to do was... God, I miss him!"

One afternoon, a wealthy lawyer is riding in the back of his limousine when he sees two men eating grass by the roadside. He orders his driver to stop and he gets out to investigate.

"Why are you eating grass?" he asks one man.

"We don't have any money for food," the poor man replies.

"Oh, come along with me then."

"But sir, I have a wife with two children!"

"Bring them along! And you, come with us too!" he says to the other man.

"But sir, I have a wife with six children!" the second man answers.

"Bring them as well!"

They all climb into the car, which was no easy task, even for a car as large as the limo. Once under way, one of the poor fellows says, "Sir, you are too kind. Thank you for taking all of us with you."

The lawyer replies, "No problem; the grass at my home is about two feet tall!

A wolf had been chasing a rabbit in the forest for an hour when they arrived near the Enchanted Oak, where the genie lived... They were making such a racket that they woke up the genie, who said (he was a bit of a hippy):

"OK, OK, I see that there is no sleeping in peace in here until you two have resolved your differences. Therefore, I am going to grant you three wishes and you'll go on your way much happier."

The wolf had the first go and he said: "I want all the wolves in this forest to be female."

The genie sighed and said that it now was so. He turned to the rabbit and said:

"What is your first wish, rabbit?"

"I'd like a helmet," the rabbit says, a faint smile on his face.

The genie finds it a bit odd, but a wish is a wish and the rabbit is fitted with a nice crash-helmet.

"I want all the wolves in this country to be female," says the wolf for his second wish. The genie sighs again but complies and all the wolves in the country become female.

"For my second wish, I want a motorcycle," the rabbit says.

The genie says "OK" and grants the rabbit a nice, powerful motorbike which goes very well with the helmet. The rabbit's smile is getting bigger now.

True to his character and showing remarkable consistency, the wolf says: "For my third wish, I want all the wolves in the whole WORLD to be female!"

Marvelling at the single-mindedness of the wolf's wishes, the genie complies and turns all the wolves in the world female. He then turns to the rabbit, who is grinning from ear to ear.

"So what is your last wish, rabbit?"

The rabbit straps the helmet on his head securely, climbs on the motorbike, revs up the engine and says: "I wish the wolf was gay!"

A man was knocking back the drinks in a bar. "I think you've had enough, mate," said the barman. "But I've just lost my wife," slurred the drunk indignantly. The barman said sympathetically: "Well, it must be hard losing a wife." The man replied, "Hard? It was almost impossible."

A blonde and a brunette are sitting in a pub having a drink when the brunette's boyfriend comes in with a bunch of roses. The brunette receives the flowers with apparent pleasure, but makes a face as soon as her boyfriend is off to get a drink from the bar.

"Crap: he's bought me flowers again", says the brunette.

"What's the matter with you? You don't like flowers?" asks her friend.

"Oh, I do," the brunette replies. "It's just that when he buys me flowers it means I'll have to spend the next two or three days with my legs wide open."

The blonde asks, "You don't have a vase?"

One afternoon, an elderly couple are relaxing in front of the TV. Suddenly, the woman is overcome with lust and says to her husband, "Let's go upstairs and make love." "Steady on," he replies. "I can't do both."

The Lone Ranger and Tonto are riding in the desert when hostile Apaches surround them.

The Lone Ranger turns to his trusted sidekick and says, "It looks like we're in trouble, old friend."

Tonto replies, "Who the hell are you, paleface?

Two men and a woman were sitting in a bar discussing their lives. The first man says, 'You know, I'm a YUPpie – that's Young, Urban Professional.' The second man says, 'Well, me and my missus, we're DINKs – that's Double Income, No Kids.' Then the first man asks the woman, 'So what are you?' She replies, 'I'm a WIFE – that's Wash, Iron, Fuck, Etcetera!'

The librarian noticed a young man sitting in front of the computer, staring at the screen, his arms across his chest. After 15 minutes, he realized that the young man hadn't changed his position and was still there, doing nothing, staring blankly at the screen. Puzzled, he went to him and asked:
    'May I help you?'
    'It's about time!' he answered, ' I pressed the Help button over twenty minutes ago!'

Two MPs are talking late at night in the House of Commons bar.
    "How do you choose the right person to back for Prime Minister?" says the younger politician.
    "Easy," says the old buffer. "Just adopt the same procedure as you would when choosing a taxi driver."
    "What's that?" says the young MP.
    "Just decide which one will cost you least and not get you killed."

Why did the blonde take a ladder into the bar?
    She heard the drinks were on the house.

David Beckham goes shopping, and sees something interesting in the kitchen department of a large department store.

"What's that?" he asks.

"A Thermos flask," replies the assistant.

"What does it do?" asks Becks.

The assistant tells him it keeps hot things hot and cold things cold. Really impressed, Beckham buys one and takes it along to his next training session.

"Here, boys, look at this," Beckham says proudly. "It's a Thermos flask." The lads are impressed.

"What does it do?" they ask.

"It keeps hot things hot and cold things cold," says David.

"And what have you got in it?"

"Two cups of coffee and a choc ice," replies David.

The Lord's prayer for blokes

Our beer

Which art in barrels

Hallowed be thy drink

Thy will be drunk

I will be drunk

At home as it is in the local

Forgive us this day our daily spillage

And lead us not into the practice

Of poncey wine tasting

And deliver us from alcopops

For mine is the bitter, the ale and the lager

Forever and ever, Barmen

A blonde is sitting at the counter in a bar with a glass of vodka with an olive in it. She tries to pick the olive up with the toothpick but it always eludes her, skidding to the other end of the glass. This futile exercise has been going on for half an hour when the man next to her, exasperated, snatches the toothpick from her hand and adroitly skewers the olive in one stroke.

"This is how you do it," he says to the blonde.

"Big deal," the blonde mutters darkly. "I already had him so tired out, he couldn't get away."

Dave and Jim worked as aeroplane mechanics in London. One day, the airport was fogbound and they were stuck in the hangar. Dave said, "I wish we had a drink."

"Me, too." replied Jim, "Y'know, I've heard you can drink jet fuel and get a buzz. You want to try it?" So they poured themselves a couple of glasses and got completely smashed.

The next morning, Dave woke up and was surprised at how good he felt. Then the phone rang and it was Jim. "Hey, how do you feel this morning?" he asked.

"I feel great," says Dave. "How about you?"

"I feel great, too." Jim responds. "Have you broken wind yet?"

"No," says Dave.

"Well, don't; I'm in Glasgow!"

During training exercises, a British Army lieutenant is driving down a muddy back road and encounters another jeep stuck in the mud with a red-faced colonel at the wheel.

"Your jeep stuck, sir?" asks the lieutenant as he pulled alongside.

"Nope," replies the colonel, coming over and handing him the keys,

"Yours is."

A robber escapes from prison and breaks into a house occupied by a young couple. He ties them up and leaves them alone in the bedroom for a while. As soon as they are alone, the husband turns to his young wife, skimpily dressed in her black nightie, and says, "Now listen, dear: this man probably hasn't had sex with a woman for years. If he wants to have sex, just go along with it and pretend that you're enjoying it. It will probably mean the difference between living and dying for us."

"I'm so glad you feel that way, my darling," said the wife, "because he just told me he loves your smooth skin and firm arse!"

A couple had children who were very inquisitive, so were finding it hard to communicate about 'adult' things like having sex. To avoid having to teach the children about the birds and the bees, they decide to use a code instead, using the word 'typewriter' as a substitute for sex.

A couple of days later the husband thinks it will be amusing to use the code for the first time, so he calls his five-year-old daughter over and says to her, 'Go and tell your mother that Daddy would like her to come up and type a letter, please." The girl goes off and comes back a couple of minutes later. She says, "Mummy says that she can't type a letter for Daddy today because she's got a red ribbon stuck in the typewriter."

A few days later the daughter comes up to the father and says, "Mummy told me to tell you that she can type that letter now.' The father says, 'Well, you go and tell Mummy not to worry because Daddy couldn't wait for the typewriter, so he decided to write the letter by hand!"

A female TV reporter arranges for an interview with a farmer, seeking the main cause of Mad Cow disease. "Good evening, sir. I am here to collect information on possible causes of Mad Cow Disease. Can you offer any reason for this disease?" she asks.

The farmer stares at the reporter, "Do you know that a bull mounts a cow only once a year?" he asks.

The embarrassed reporter replies: "Well, sir, that's a new piece of information, but what's the relation between this phenomenon and Mad Cow disease?"

"And, madam, do you know that we milk a cow twice a day?" he asks, ignoring her.

"Sir, this is really valuable information, but what about getting to the point?" she retorts.

"I am getting to the point, madam. Just imagine; if I was playing with your breasts twice a day and only having sex with you once a year, wouldn't you get mad?"

A guy comes home from work, walks into his bedroom, and finds a stranger making love to his wife. He says, "What the hell are you two doing?"

His wife turns to the stranger and says, "I told you he was stupid."

Five secrets to a great relationship
1. It is important to find a man who works around the house, occasionally cooks and cleans and who has a job.
2. It is important to find a man who makes you laugh.
3. It is important to find a man who is dependable and doesn't lie.
4. It is important to find a man who's good in bed and who loves to have sex with you.
5. It is important that these four men never meet.

Just after I got married, I was invited out for a night with the boys.

I told my wife that I would be home by midnight ... promise!

Well, the hours passed and the beer was going down way too easy. At around 3A.M. drunk as a skunk, I headed for home. Just as I got in the door, the cuckoo clock in the hall started up, and cuckooed three times.

Quickly I realized she'd probably wake up, so I cuckooed another nine times. I was really proud of myself, having a quick witty solution, even when smashed, to escape a possible conflict.

Next morning, the wife asked me what time I got in and I told her 12 o'clock. She didn't seem disturbed at all. Whew! Got away with that one! She then told me that we needed a new cuckoo clock. When I asked her why she said,

"Well, it cuckooed three times, said 'oh fuck,' cuckooed four more times, cleared its throat, cuckooed another three times, giggled, cuckooed twice more, and then farted."

It is Christmas, and a little boy is taken to the local Santa's Grotto to meet the big man himself. Santa picks the boy up, places him on his knee and begins to ask him about what he wants for Christmas. The boy says he doesn't really know what he'd like for Christmas so Santa makes some suggestions, spelling the words out as he does so, and prodding the boy's nose, so the boy can surely understand. Santa asks him if he'd like a B-I-K-E or a T-R-A-I-N and so on, but the little boy doesn't seem to want any of the 'normal' Christmas stuff. So Santa eventually says, 'Come on, kid: what do you want for Christmas?' The little boy replies, 'I want some P-U-S-S-Y and I know you've got some because I can smell it on your finger!'

While out on an expedition, a man is climbing over a fallen tree when his shotgun goes off, hitting him straight in the groin. Rushed to hospital, he awakes from his anaesthetic to find the surgeon has done a marvellous job repairing his damaged member. As he dresses to go home, the surgeon wanders over and hands him a business card.

"This is my brother's card. I'll make an appointment for you to see him."

The guy is shocked. "But it says here that he's a professional flute player. How can he help me?"

The doctor smiles. "Well," he says, "he's going to show you where to put your fingers so that you don't piss in your eye."

The only treatment to save this patient is a brain transplant. His family is gathered in the doctor's office, taking in the bad news.

'Er, Doctor, how much is this going to cost?'

'Well, it's about £600,000 for a male brain and £200,000 for a female brain,' the specialist answer.

The men in the room all sit up and start chuckling, a superior expression on their faces. The youngest daughter casts her eyes ceiling-ward and asks the doctor:

'And why is a female brain cheaper?'

'Oh, it's standard practise, Miss,' he replies. 'The brain has to be marked down because it's used.'

A London lawyer is representing a local train company in a lawsuit filed by a West Country farmer. The farmer's prize bull is missing from the section of field through which the railway passes. The farmer wants to be paid the market price for the bull and just before the case the lawyer immediately corners the farmer and tries to get him to settle out of court. The lawyer does his best selling job, and finally the farmer agrees to take half of what he was asking.

After the farmer signs the release and takes his pay-off, the young lawyer can't resist gloating a little over his success. Outside the High Court he shakes the farmer's hand and tells him, "You know, I hate to tell you this, old fella, but I put one over on you in there. I couldn't have won the case. The driver was asleep when the train went through your farm that morning. I didn't have one witness to put on the stand. I bluffed you!"

The rosy-cheeked farmer replies, "Well, I'll tell you, boy, I was a little worried about winning that case myself, because I'll be blowed if that bull didn't come home this morning."

A man gets on a plane and is surprised to be seated next to a parrot. He doesn't really say anything but thinks it a bit odd. When the stewardess comes around to see if anyone wants drinks she asks the man.

He says that he'd like a cup of coffee and as he says this the parrot squawks, "And get me a whisky on the rocks, bitch!" The stewardess is visibly shaken and walks off.

She comes back a few minutes later and hands the parrot his whiskey but she has forgotten the man's coffee. The man points this out and asks again. As he does so, the parrot squawks, "And bring me another whiskey on the rocks you slut!"

The stewardess goes off again and comes back – again with the parrot's drink but with no coffee for the man. The man is a bit sick of this so he decides to use the parrot's approach. So he barks, "That's twice I've asked you for coffee, you useless cow, what the hell do I have to do to get a friggin' drink around here?"

The next thing the man knows he's been picked up by two huge stewards and thrown out of the plane.

He has the parrot next to him and, as they both start their plunge to earth, the bird turns to him and says, "Phew-ee, for someone who can't fly, you sure are one gobby fucker!"

Riding the favourite at Cheltenham, a jockey is well ahead of the field. Suddenly, he is hit on the head by a turkey and a string of sausages.

He manages to stay on his mount and pull back into the lead, only to be struck by a box of Christmas crackers and a dozen mince pies over the last fence.

He again manages to regain the lead when he's hit by a bottle of sherry full in the face.

Eventually, he comes in second. Furious, he goes to the stewards' room to complain that he has been seriously hampered.

A man walks into a bar. It is totally empty apart from the barkeep, who walks over to serve him. The man buys his beer and sits down in a corner. He then decides he'd like a chaser, so he walks up to the bar again. The barkeep has just gone out back for a second but they guy hears a little squeaky voice say, 'Nice shirt, mate.' He looks around and he cannot see anyone anywhere. He turns around to go and sit down and hears a similar voice say, 'Great arse.' He spins around quickly but he cannot see anyone and the barkeeper is definitely still out back. The man is a bit put out so he decides to go and buy some smokes. As he approaches the cigarette machine he hears the most dreadful swearing, aimed at him. 'You miserable wanker piece of crap; you suck, you dumbarse twit!' The insults seem to be pouring from the machine, so he retreats and goes back to the bar. The bartender is back by this time, so the man asks him, 'Look, pal; what's going on with the funny voices in this place?' The bartender looks at him and says, 'Of course, well, you must mean the complimentary peanuts; and I'm sorry, but the cigarette machine is out of order!'

On a sunny, hot afternoon a man is sitting on his porch drinking iced lemonade in a deckchair as his wife grunts, groans and struggles with the lawnmower. The next-door neighbour can't believe her eyes and she storms over to the porch. 'You should be ashamed of yourself, you caveman, letting your wife mow the lawn on a day like this. You ought to be hung!' 'I am' says the man with a wry smile, 'and that's exactly why my wife is mowing the lawn.'

How do you make a dog drink?

Put it in the liquidizer.

A mortician was working late one night. It was his job to examine the dead bodies before they were sent off to be buried or cremated. As he examined the body of Mr Schwartz, he made an amazing discovery: Schwartz had the longest private part he had ever seen!

"I'm sorry, Mr Schwartz," said the mortician, "but I can't send you off to be cremated with a tremendously huge private part like this. It has to be saved for posterity." And with that the coroner used his scalpel to remove the dead man's privates.

The coroner stuffed his prize into a briefcase and took it home. The first person he showed was his wife. "I have something to show you that you won't believe," he said, opening his briefcase.

"Oh, my God!" she screamed, "Schwartz is dead!"

Brazilian forward Ronaldo walks into a Burger King in Milan and asks for two Whoppers.

"OK," says the cashier. "You're not fat, and you haven't lost it."

A lonely spinster, aged 81, decided that it was time to get married, so she put an ad in the local paper that read: "Husband wanted, must be in my age group (80s), must not beat me, must not run around on me and must still be good in bed! All applicants please apply in person."

On the second day she heard the doorbell. Much to her dismay, she opened the door to see a grey-haired gentleman sitting in a wheelchair. He had no arms or legs.

The woman said, "You're not really asking me to consider you, are you? Just look at you... you have no legs!" The old man smiled, "Therefore I cannot run around on you!" She snorted. "You don't have any arms either!" Again the old man smiled, "Nor can I beat you!"

She raised an eyebrow and gazed intently. "Are you still good in bed?" With that, the old gentleman leaned back, beamed a big broad smile and said, "I rang the doorbell didn't I?"

After the baby was born, the panicked Japanese father went to see the obstetrician.

"Doctor,' he said, 'I'm a little upset. You see, my baby daughter has red hair. She can't possibly be mine."

"Do not worry,' the doctor said genially. "Even though you and your wife both have black hair, one of your ancestors might have contributed red hair to the gene pool."

"This is impossible," the man insisted. "We're pure Oriental. There have never been redheads in any of our families."

"Well," said the doctor, "let me ask you this. How often do you have sex?"

The man seemed ashamed. "I've been working very hard for the past year. We only made love once or twice a month."

"There you have it!" the doctor said confidently. "It's just rust."

A man finds a magic lamp, rubs it and a genie pops out: "I grant you three wishes, but for every wish you make, your mother-in-law gets double whatever it is you request!"

The man agrees and the genie asks for his first wish.

"I want to have £100 million!" says the man. The genie duly grants his wish, but warns that his mother-in-law now has £200 million.

"For my second wish," says the man, "I want to be famous!"

No problem for the genie – the man is famous. But his mother-in-law is twice as famous.

Several quiet, thoughtful minutes pass before the man suggests his final wish: "Genie? Beat me half to death!"

A big Texan cowboy stopped at a local restaurant after a day of drinking and roaming around in Mexico. While sipping his tequila, he noticed a sizzling, scrumptious-looking platter being served at the next table. Not only did it look good, but the smell was wonderful.

He asked the waiter, "What is that you just served?"

The waiter replied: "Ah, señor, you have excellent taste! Those are bull's testicles from the bullfight this morning. A delicacy! But there is only one serving per day. If you come early tomorrow and place your order, we will be sure to save you this delicacy!"

The next morning, the cowboy returned, placed his order, and then that evening he was served the one and only portion of the special delicacy of the day.

After a few bites, and inspecting the contents of his platter, he called to the waiter and said, "These are delicious, but they are much, much smaller than the ones I saw you serve yesterday."

The waiter shrugged his shoulders and replied, "Si, señor. Sometimes the bull wins."

A Russian and an American wrestler make it to the final at the Olympics. Before the pair contest the gold medal, the American wrestler's trainer comes up to him and says, "Now, don't forget all the research we've done on this Russian. He's never lost a match because of this 'pretzel' hold he has. Whatever you do, don't let him get you in this hold! If he does, you're finished!"

The wrestler nods in agreement. As the match begins, the American and the Russian circle each other several times looking for an opening. All of a sudden the Russian lunges forward, grabs the American and wraps him up in the dreaded pretzel hold.

A sigh of disappointment goes up from the crowd, and the trainer buries his face in his hands.

Suddenly there is a horrible scream, and the crowd cheers. The trainer raises his head just in time to see the Russian flying up in the air. The Russian's back hits the mat with a thud, and the American weakly collapses on top of him, gets the pin and wins the match.

The trainer is astounded. When he finally gets the American wrestler alone, he asks, "How did you ever get out of that hold? No one has ever done it before!"

The wrestler answers, "Well, I was ready to give up when he got me in that hold, but at the last moment, I opened my eyes and saw this pair of balls right in front of my face. I thought I had nothing to lose, so with my last ounce of strength I stretched out my neck and bit those babies just as hard as I could. You'd be amazed how strong you get when you bite your own balls!"

What happens to someone fired from a job at a fairground? They sue for funfair dismissal.

A driver was stuck in a traffic jam. Suddenly, a man knocked at his window. The driver rolled down his window and asked, "What's up?" The man said excitedly, "President Bush has been kidnapped by terrorists. They will cover him in petrol and burn him if they don't get $10 million ransom." The driver asked, "And what do you want me to do?" "Well, we're going from car to car and collecting for the cause," answered the man. "Aha... And how much are people giving?", asked the driver. "Oh, somewhere around one or two gallons."

A little office prayer

Grant me the serenity to accept the things I cannot change, the courage to change the things I cannot accept and the wisdom to hide the bodies of those people I had to kill today because they annoyed me.

And also, help me to be careful of the toes I step on today as they may be connected to the arse that I might have to kiss tomorrow.

Help me to always give 100% at work...

12% on Monday

23% on Tuesday

40% on Wednesday

20% on Thursday

5% on Friday

And help me to remember...

When I'm having a really bad day, and it seems that people are trying to piss me off, that it takes 42 muscles to frown and only four to extend my fingers and tell them to eff off. Amen

Q. Why is divorce so expensive?
A. Because it's worth it.

During a training exercise, a commanding officer's jeep got stuck in the mud. The CO, seeing some men lounging around nearby, asked them to help him get unstuck.

"Sorry, sir," said one of the loafers, "but we've been classified dead and the umpire said we couldn't contribute in any way."

The CO turned to his driver and said, "Go and drag a couple of those dead bodies over here and throw them under the wheels to give us some traction."

A jaguar was walking pugnaciously through the jungle, intimidating the other animals. He spotted a monkey and ran up to it, pinning it against the trunk of a tree.

"Who is the fiercest animal in the jungle?" he roared.

"You: you are," the monkey squeaked.

Satisfied, the jaguar let him go and carried on, noticing with satisfaction that all the other animals were running away from him. He nonetheless managed to immobilize a peccary and growled in a terrifying manner:

"Who is the fiercest animal in the jungle?"

"You: you are," the peccary stammered, and the jaguar magnanimously lets him go.

The jaguar then spotted a lion having a siesta and, giddy with self-importance, made the mistake of running up to him.

"Who is the fiercest animal in the jungle?" he roared, eyes bulging.

Hearing this, the lion stood up, picked up the jaguar by the tail, swung him around faster and faster and finally released him to crash heavily into a banana tree.

"All right, all right," the jaguar said, standing up groggily and shaking his head to clear it. "Even if you don't know the answer, it's no reason to get pissed off."

There's this really vain surfer type. He jogs and he lifts weights and he stretches and he tones. He's admiring himself in the mirror one day and he notices that all of him looks great apart from his willy – it is the only part of him that doesn't have a tan. So he tries instant tan from all sorts of places and he tries tanning booths, but nothing works. Eventually he goes to see a doctor who tells him that because of the sensitive nature of the skin, he will only be able to tan his willy in natural sunlight.

So the man goes to the beach. Sadly, there are no nudist beaches near where he lives so he goes to a normal one and tries to get himself a tan without anyone noticing. He can't manage it, so he develops a plan: he digs a hole big enough to hide in and buries himself, apart from his willy, which he leaves sticking out, and his mouth. He puts on suntan lotion and falls asleep.

A few minutes later, a couple of little old ladies walk past and one of them notices the willy in the sand. She prods it a couple of times with her walking stick and gets it to wake up a little bit. Then she sight and says to her friend, "There's no justice, is there?" "What do you mean, dear?" her friend replies. The lady says, "Well, I've spent my life being curious about willies, enjoying them, asking for them, tasting them, praying for more of them, hoping they'll get bigger, and now here I am, 80 years old – they grow wild on the beach and I can't even squat down!"

Did you hear about the man who joined the nudist colony?
The first day was his hardest.

Why is getting a new girlfriend like joining the army?

You're forced to have a new haircut, a new set of clothes, and you only get information on a need-to-know basis.

A scientific study has found that the kind of male face a woman finds attractive can differ depending on where she is in her menstrual cycle. For instance, if she is ovulating, she is attracted to men with rugged and masculine features. If she is menstruating, she is likely to prefer a man doused in petrol and set on fire, with scissors shoved deep into his temple. Further studies are expected.

Upon hearing that her elderly grandfather had just passed away, Kate went to her grandparents' house to visit her 95-year-old grandmother.

When she asked how her grandfather died, her grandmother replied, "He had a heart attack while we were making love on Sunday morning."

Horrified, the woman told her grandmother that two people nearly 100 years old having sex would surely be asking for trouble.

"Oh no, my dear," replied granny. "Many years ago, we figured out that the best time to do it was when the church bells started to ring. It was just the right rhythm: nice and slow and even. Nothing too strenuous for us."

She paused to wipe away a tear, and continued, "He'd still be alive if the ice-cream van hadn't come along."

At 7am, a lone wife hears a key in the front door. She wanders down, bleary-eyed, to find her husband in the kitchen – drunk, with ruffled hair and lipstick on his collar. "I assume," she snarls, "that there's a very good reason for you to come waltzing in here at seven in the morning?"

"There is," he replies. "Breakfast."

An old man had a dog he just loved but this dog had the nasty habit of attacking anything that moved, including people. His friends told him if he had the dog fixed, he would lose his aggression and quit this behaviour. Thinking it might be a good idea, the old man had his dog fixed. A few days later he was in his front room when the postman came up the steps. The dog jumped up, went right through the door and attacked the postman. The old man ran out, pulled his dog away and began apologizing.

"I am so sorry," he said. "I don't know what to do or say. My friends told me he would quit attacking people if I had him fixed but it didn't work. I just don't know what to do."

The postman picked himself up and said, 'You should have had his teeth pulled: I knew when he came through the door he wasn't going to screw me.'

A man breaks down in a country lane. He's looking under the bonnet, when suddenly he hears, "It's your spark plugs, mate."

He looks around, but there's no one there – just two horses. So he goes back under the bonnet when suddenly he hears again, "It's your spark plugs, mate." He looks up and the brown horse is looking directly at him, saying, "It's your spark plugs, mate."

The man is so scared he runs for a mile and finds a pub, goes inside and immediately orders a double whisky.

"You look like you've seen a ghost," says the barman.

"Well, I almost have," the man says. "I broke down in the lane a mile back there, looked under my bonnet and suddenly this brown horse says 'it's your spark plugs mate'."

"Well, you can thank your lucky stars," says the barman, "the black horse knows bugger all about cars."

There was this man at a bar, just looking at his drink. He stays like that for half an hour. Then, this big trouble-making lorry driver steps next to him, takes the drink from the guy, and just drinks it all down. The poor man starts crying. The truck driver says, "Come on, man, I was just joking. Here, I'll buy you another drink. I just can't stand to see a man cry." "No, it's not that. This day is the worst of my life. First, I fall asleep, and I go late to my office. My boss, outraged, fires me. When I leave the building, to get my car, I found out it was stolen. The police said they could do nothing. I get a cab to return home, and when I leave it, I remember I left my wallet and credit cards inside. The cab driver just drives away. I go home, and when I get there, I find my wife in bed with the gardener. I leave home, come to this bar, and just when I was thinking about putting an end to my life, you show up and drink my poison."

What do you call a woman who knows where her husband is?
  A widow.

A NASA crew destined for a moon landing was training near a Navajo Indian reservation. A Navajo elder asked if he could send a message to the moon with the astronauts. The NASA crew agreed, then called in a translator. The message said, "Watch out for these guys. They have come to steal your land."

All of us could take a lesson from the weather. It pays no attention to criticism.

Tech Support: "Tell me, in the bottom left-hand side of the screen, can you see the 'OK' button displayed?"
  Caller: "Wow. How can you see my screen from there?"

A man is getting into the shower just as his wife is finishing up her shower when the doorbell rings. After a few seconds of arguing over which one should go and answer the doorbell, the wife gives up, quickly wraps herself up in a towel and runs downstairs.

When she opens the door, there stands Bob, the next door neighbour. Before she says a word, Bob says: "I'll give you $800 to drop that towel you have on." After thinking for a moment, the woman drops her towel and stands naked in front of Bob. After a few seconds, Bob hands her $800 and leaves.

Confused, but excited about her good fortune, the woman wraps back up in the towel and goes back upstairs. When she gets back to the bathroom, her husband asks from the shower "Who was that?"

"It was Bob the next door neighbour," she replies.

"Great," the husband says, "did he say anything about the $800 he owes me?"

Moral: If you share critical information pertaining to credit and risk in time with your stakeholders, you may be in a position to prevent avoidable exposure.

A young businessman is leaving the office late one night when he finds his boss standing over the shredder with a piece of paper in his hand.

"This is a very sensitive official document," says the boss. "My secretary's gone for the night. Can you make this thing work?"

"Sure," says the keen underling as he takes the paper, puts it in the shredder and hits the start button.

"Great," says his boss. "I just need the one copy, thanks."

Two nuns are driving down a road late at night when a vampire jumps on to the bonnet.

The nun who is driving says to the other, "Quick! Show him your cross."

So the other nun leans out of the window and shouts, "Get off our fucking car!"

Mike staggers home very late after another late night drinking session with his best mates and removes his shoes to avoid waking his missus. He tiptoes as quietly as he can towards the stairs but trips and knocks a vase on to the floor, which he then falls on to, cutting his buttocks. Managing not to shout, he stands up and pulls his pants down to examine the damage in the hall mirror. His backside is cut and bleeding, so he grabs a box of plasters and sticks them wherever he can see blood. He then hides the almost empty plaster box and stumbles into bed.

The next morning, Mike awakes with searing pain in both his head and arse, to see his wife staring at him.

"You were drunk again last night, weren't you?" she says.

"Why would you say such a mean thing?" he asks.

"Well," she says, "it could be the open front door. Or the broken glass at the bottom of the stairs. Or the drops of blood on the stairs. It could even be your bloodshot eyes: but mostly, it's all those bloody plasters stuck to the hall mirror!"

Bono's fronting the home leg of U2's latest world tour in Dublin when he asks the audience for some quiet. Then he starts to slowly clap his hands and, as he does so, says into the microphone, "Every time I clap my hands, a child in Africa dies." A voice from near the front pierces the silence, "Well, stop fucking clapping, then!"

A maths teacher leaves a letter for his wife one Friday night:

Dear Janet,
As you know, I am 56, and by the time you read this letter I will be settled in at the Luxor Hotel, tucking into my beautiful, sexy, 18-year-old teaching assistant.

When the teacher arrives at the hotel he finds that a letter has been left for him:

Dear John,
As you know, I too am 56, and by the time you read this letter I will be settled in at the Excelsior Hotel, tucking into my handsome, virile, 18-year-old toyboy. You, being a maths teacher, will appreciate that 18 goes into 56 a lot more times than 56 goes into 18!

An accordionist is driving home from a late- night gig. Feeling tired, he pulls into a service station for some coffee. While waiting to pay, he remembers that he locked his car doors but left the accordion in plain view on the back seat of his car! He rushes out only to realize that he is too late. The back window of his car has been smashed and somebody's already thrown in two more accordions.

A man is giving a colleague a lift to work and asks him if he talks to his wife after sex.
"Absolutely," he says. "If I can find a phone."

What do you get when you cross LSD with a birth control pill? A trip without the kids.

Two men were asked what they would like to be said about them at their funerals. The first one said, "I want someone to say I was the greatest footballer ever."

The other man said, "I want someone to say, 'He's moving; he's moving!'"

A city man, completely ignorant of country life, was visiting Wales. He stopped in an educational farm, had a look around and went to chat the farmer.

'Nice pigs you've got there,' he said. 'How big are they?'

The pig farmer put the pig's tail in his mouth and bobbed his head up and down.

'30 pounds,' he said to the city guy.

'What? I can't believe that's the way you weigh pigs! You're having me on!"

'No, I'm not', the farmer said. He then called his son over and asked him to weigh the pig. The son put the pig's tail in his mouth, bobbed his head a couple of times and said the pig weighed 30 pounds.

As the city guy still couldn't believe this was the way to weigh a pig, the farmer asked his son to go and get his mum so that she could weigh the pig too.

The boy left and came back alone a few minutes later, saying: 'Mum can't come: she's busy weighing the postman.'

A couple is lying in bed. The man says, "I am going to make you the happiest woman in the world."

The woman says, "I'll miss you."

Three sisters, aged 92, 94 and 96, live in a house together. One night the 96-year-old draws a bath. She puts her foot in and pauses. She hollers to the other sisters, "Was I gettin' in or out of the bath?"

The 94-year-old yells back, "I don't know. I'll come up and see." She starts up the stairs and pauses. "Was I going up the stairs or down?" she shouts.

The 92-year-old is sitting at the kitchen table having tea listening to her sisters. She shakes her head and says, "I sure hope I never get that forgetful."

She knocks on wood for good measure and then yells, "I'll come up and help both of you as soon as I see who's at the door."

One Sunday morning George burst into the living room and said, "Dad! Mum! I have some great news for you! I am getting married to the most beautiful girl in town, and her name is Susan." After dinner, George's dad took him aside. "Son, I have to talk with you. Your mother and I have been married 30 years and she's a wonderful wife... but she has never offered much excitement in the bedroom, so I used to fool around with other women a lot. Susan is actually your half-sister, and I'm afraid you can't marry her." George was broken-hearted. After eight months, he eventually started dating girls again. A year later he came home and very proudly announced, "Diane said yes! We're getting married in June." Again his father insisted on another private conversation, and broke the sad news: "Diane is your half-sister too, George. I'm awfully sorry about this." George was livid! He finally decided to tell his mother the truth about his father. "Dad has done so much harm. I guess I'm never going to get married," he complained. "Every time I fall in love, Dad tells me the girl is my half-sister."

"Don't worry about that," his mother chuckled, shaking her head. "He's not really your father."

A bloke goes into the Jobcentre in London and spots a job vacancy which reads, 'Wanted: single man, willing to travel, must have own scissors. £500 a week guaranteed, plus company car and all expenses.'

It sounds a bit too good to be true, so the bloke fronts up at the counter and quotes the job's reference number.

"Oh, that one," says the clerk. "It's a modelling agency here in London. They're looking for a pubic hair snipper. They supply girls who model underwear and before they go on the catwalk they report to you to snip off any wisps of pubic hair that are showing. It pays well, but there are drawbacks; it involves a lot of travel to exotic places and you have to get used to living in first-class hotels."

"Well, I'd still like to apply," says the bloke.

The clerk says, "OK, here's an application form and a rail ticket to Manchester".

"What do I wanna go to Manchester for?"

"Well," says the clerk, "that's where the end of the queue is at the moment."

An old boy sits down in his local and asks the barkeep, an old friend, for a drink. The old boy is wearing a big, old-fashioned stovepipe hat, a black jacket and waistcoat, and a false, square beard.

The barman serves him a drink and says, "You off to a party tonight, then?"

"Yup,' says the man, 'I've come as my love life."

"What are you going on about?" says the barman. "you look like Abraham Lincoln."

"Indeed I do," says the man. "My last four scores were seven years ago!"

A man drives his date up to Lovers' Lane and parks up.

"I have to be honest with you," the woman says as the man makes his move, "I'm a prostitute."

The man thinks about this for a bit and decides he's OK with it. He agrees to pay her £25 in advance and they get down to business.

After they finish, the man says, 'Now, I should be honest, too. I'm a taxi driver and it's going to cost you £25 to get back into town.'

A blonde walks into a bank in London and asks to see the manager. She says she's going to Hong Kong on business for two weeks and needs to borrow £5,000. The manager says the bank will need some kind of security for the loan, so the blonde hands over the keys to a new Ferrari. The car is parked on the street in front of the bank, she has the title and everything checks out. The manager and the tellers all enjoy a good laugh at the blonde and an employee of the bank then drives the Ferrari into the bank's underground garage and parks it there. Two weeks later, the blonde returns, repays the £5,000 and the interest, which comes to £15.41. The manager says, 'While you were away, madam, we checked your details and discovered you're a millionairess. What puzzles us is, why would you bother to borrow £5,000?' The blonde replies, 'Where else in London can I park my car for two weeks for only £15.41 and expect it to be there when I come back?'

One day in a jewellery shop a man is in the process of buying a really expensive necklace with a lovely silver locket on it. The jeweller asks him, "Would you like her name engraved on it?" The man has a think and then replies, "No: just put 'To my one and only love.' That way, if we split up and she throws it back in anger, I'll be able to recycle!"

Into a Belfast pub comes Paddy Murphy, looking like he'd just been run over by a train. His arm is in a sling, his nose is broken, his face is cut and bruised and he's walking with a limp.

"What happened to you?" asks Sean, the bartender.

"Jamie O'Connor and me had a fight," says Paddy.

"That little shit, O'Connor," says Sean, "He couldn't do that to you, he must have had something in his hand."

"That he did," says Paddy, "a shovel is what he had and a terrible lickin' he gave me with it."

"Well," says Sean, "you should have defended yourself, didn't you have something in your hand?"

"That I did," said Paddy. "Mrs. O'Connor's breast and a thing of beauty it was, but useless in a fight."

A little guy goes into an elevator, looks up and sees a huge bloke next to him. The man sees the little fella staring at him, looks down and says, "Seven feet tall, 350 pounds, 20-inch penis, three-pound left testicle, three-pound right testicle, Turner Brown."

The small guy immediately faints and falls to the floor. The tall man kneels down and brings him to, slapping his face and shaking him, "What's wrong with you?" he asks.

In a very weak voice, the little guy says, "Excuse me, but what exactly did you say to me?"

The tall man answers, "I saw the curious look on your face and figured I'd just give you the answers to the questions everyone always asks me. I'm seven feet tall, 350 pounds, 20-inch penis, three-pound left testicle, three-pound right testicle, and my name is Turner Brown."

"Thank God for that," the small guy says. "I thought you said, 'Turn around.'"

Q: How do you find a blind man in a nudist colony?
A: It's not hard.

What's the difference between bird flu and Man City? Bird flu has got to Europe.

A man gets taken on as a lorry driver at a new company but as he's about to sign his contract in the boss's office, he says, "I've got one demand. Since you employed me, you've got to hire my mate Dave too."

"Who's Dave?" says the boss, surprised at the demand.

"Dave's my driving partner. We're a team. He drives when I sleep, and I drive when he sleeps," the new employee says.

"OK," says the boss. "Answer this question satisfactorily and I'll hire your mate too. You're going down a hill, your brakes fail, and ahead of you is a bridge with an 18-wheeler jack-knifed across it. What would you do?"

"I'd wake Dave up," he replies.

"How the hell's that going to help?" says the boss.

"We've been working together 25 years," explains the new guy, "and he's never seen a wreck like the one we're about to have!"

In the middle of poker night John loses a £500 hand, clutches his chest, and drops dead on the floor. His mate Pete is designated as the guy who has to go and give his wife the bad news.

"Be gentle with her, Pete," one of the other players says. "They were childhood sweethearts."

So Pete walks over to the John's house, knocks on the door, and tries his best to be helpful. 'Your husband just lost £500 playing cards.'

"Tell that idiot to drop dead," shouts the wife.

"I'll tell him," Pete says.

How do you tell if a redneck's married?

There are tobacco-spit stains on both sides of the truck.

A little boy starts to notice the loud, heavy bouncing noises of his parents having sex at night. Curious, he asks his mother what the noises are. She doesn't really want to go into it, so just explains that she bounces on top of his father to help him to stay thin and to make his stomach smaller. 'I don't think it's going to work' says the boy. 'Whyever not?' asks the mother. 'Because every morning after you go to work, Elsie from next door comes over and blows Daddy back up again!'

A little girl walks in to the lounge one Sunday morning where her Dad is reading the paper.

"Where does poo come from?" she asks.

Father, feeling a little perturbed that his five-year-old daughter is already asking difficult questions, thinks for a moment and says:

"Well, you know we just ate breakfast?"

"Yes," replies the girl.

"Well, the food goes into our tummies and our bodies take out all the good stuff, and then whatever's left over comes out of our bottoms when we go to the toilet. That's poo."

The little girl looks perplexed, and stares at him in stunned silence for a few seconds and asks: "And Tigger?"

Pinocchio moaned to Gepetto that when he made love to his girlfriend she complained about splinters.

"Try some sandpaper, Pinocchio," advised Gepetto.

A month later Gepetto asked, "How's your love life, then? Is your girlfriend still complaining of splinters?"

"Who needs a girlfriend?" replied Pinocchio.

What did the fisherman say to the magician?

"Pick a cod: any cod."

A woman was in bed with her lover when she heard her husband opening the front door. "Hurry!" she said. "Stand in the corner!" She quickly rubbed baby oil all over him and then she dusted him with talcum powder. "Don't move until I tell you to," she whispered. "Just pretend you're a statue."

"What's this, honey?" the husband inquired as he entered the room.

"Oh, it's just a statue," she replied nonchalantly. "The Smiths bought one for their bedroom. I liked it so much, I got one for us, too." No more was said about the statue, not even later that night when they went to sleep.

Around 2 a.m., the husband got out of bed, went to the kitchen and returned a while later with a sandwich and a glass of milk.

"Here," he said to the statue, "eat something. I stood like an idiot at the Smiths' for three days, and nobody offered me as much as a glass of water."

Two little kids are in a hospital, lying on stretchers next to each other in the corridor outside the operating room.

The first kid leans over and asks, "What are you in here for?"

The second kid answers, "I'm in here to get my tonsils out, and I'm really scared."

The first kid says, "You've got nothing to worry about. I had mine out when I was four. They put you to sleep, and when you wake up they give you lots of jelly and ice cream. It's a breeze."

The second kid then asks, "So, what are you in here for?"

The first kid replies, "I'm going to be circumcised."

And the second kid says, "Whoa, good luck! I had that done when I was born. Couldn't walk for a year."

A lorry driver breaks down on the M6 with a cargo of live monkeys on board, bound for Chester Zoo. They need to be delivered by 9:00 am and the driver fears he will get the sack if they don't get there on time.

He decides to try and thumb a lift for his monkeys and eventually an Irish lorry driver pulls over.

"Where they going?" asks the Irish chap.

"Do us a favour mate and take these to Chester Zoo for me" says the driver, "and here's a hundred quid for your troubles."

"Happy days," says the Irish guy. He loads the monkeys onto his truck and gets on his way. The lorry driver goes about trying to fix his truck and is there for a good few hours when he notices the Irish guy coming back down the motorway, still with all the chimps on board.

Panicking, he flags him down again. "What are you playing at?" he fumes, "I told you to take them to Chester Zoo!"

"I did," the other says, "but there's still fifty quid left so now we're going to Alton Towers."

Jake was dying. His wife, Becky, was maintaining a candlelight vigil by his side. She held his fragile hand, tears running down her face. Her praying roused him from his slumber. He looked up and his pale lips began to move slightly, "My darling Becky," he whispered.

"Hush, my love," she said. "Rest. Shhh, don't talk."

He was insistent. "Becky," he said in his tired voice, "I have something I must confess to you."

"There's nothing to confess," replied the weeping Becky. "Everything's all right. Go to sleep."

"No, no, I must die in peace, Becky. I slept with your sister, your best friend, her best friend and your mother!"

"I know, darling," Becky whispered softly, "That's why I poisoned you."

Leaving London for Manchester, I decided to make a stop at one of those service stations on the motorway. I went to the WC. The first cubicle was taken so I went to the second one. I'd just sat down when I heard a voice from the next cubicle.

"Hi there, how's it going?"

Now I'm not the type to strike up conversations with strangers in WCs at service stations. I didn't know what to say, but finally I said, "...Not bad..."

Then the voice said, "So, what are you doing?"

I thought that was kind of weird, but I said, "Well, I'm just going to the bathroom, then I'm heading back north to Manchester..."

The voice interrupted, "Look, I'm going to have to call you back. Every time I ask you a question, this idiot in the next cubicle keeps answering me!"

In the middle of the night, a man phones the local vet to tell him his dog has swallowed a condom.

"You've got to help me," cries the man. "I don't know what to do."

"It's rather late," says the vet, "but, as it's an emergency, I'll be there as soon as I can."

"Hurry, please," says the owner.

"What should I do in the meantime?"

"Just keep the dog as still as you can," says the vet. "I'll get there as soon as possible."

After an hour, the vet is still driving when his mobile rings.

"I phoned earlier," says the caller. "My dog swallowed a condom."

"Yes, I know," replies the vet. "I'm going as fast as I can, but I'm stuck in traffic."

"You needn't bother," says the dog owner.

"Oh, no! Has the animal died?" cries the vet.

"No; we've found another condom in the drawer."

After marrying a younger woman, a middle-aged man finds that no matter what he does in the sack, she never achieves orgasm. So he visits his doctor for advice. "Maybe fantasy is the solution," says the doctor. "Why not hire a strapping young man and, while you two are making love, have him wave a towel over you?"

The doctor smiles. "Make sure he's totally naked; that way your wife can fantasise her way to a full-blown orgasm."

Optimistic, he returns home and hires a handsome young escort. But it's no use; even when the stud stands naked, waving the towel, the wife remains unsatisfied. Perplexed, the man returns to his doctor.

"Try reversing it for a while," says the quack. "Have the young man make love to your wife and you wave the towel over them."

And so he returns home to try again, this time waving the towel as the same escort pumps away enthusiastically. Soon, the wife has an enormous, screaming orgasm. Smiling, the husband drops the towel and taps the young man on the shoulder.

"You see?" he shouts triumphantly. "That's how you wave a bloody towel."

A big city promoter hears of a man who has 20 wives who he makes love to every day. Impressed, the promoter hires the man to exhibit his prowess on stage in London's West End. On opening night it all goes wrong, when the man makes love to only 10 of his wives before he collapses with exhaustion.

The curtain falls, and the promoter rushes up to his failed investment. "What happened?" he asks.

"I don't know," the man answers. "Everything went fine in rehearsal!"

A young man asked an old rich man how he made his money. The old guy stroked his worsted wool vest and said, 'Well, son, it was 1932 – the depth of the Great Depression. I was down to my last penny so I invested it in an apple. I spent the entire day polishing the apple and, at the end of the day, I sold it for two pence. The next morning, I invested those two pence in two apples. I spent the entire day polishing them and sold them at 5pm for 4p. I continued this system for a month, by the end of which I'd accumulated a fortune of £1.35. Then my wife's father died and left us two million pounds.'

Two village idiots are discussing safe sex:
   "So, matey, how do you protect yourself from AIDS?" says the first.
   "I wear a condom constantly," says the second.
   "Don't you ever take it off?" says the first.
   "Of course: when I go to the bathroom and when I have sex!" says the second.

Two elderly ladies had been friends for many decades. Over the years they had shared all kinds of activities and adventures. Lately, their activities had been limited to meeting a few times a week to play cards.

One day they were playing cards when one looked at the other and said, "Now don't get mad at me... I know we've been friends for a long time... but I just can't think of your name! I've thought and thought, but I can't remember it. Please tell me what your name is."
   Her friend glared at her. For at least three minutes she just stared and glared at her. Finally, she said, "How soon do you need to know?"

A worried man calls up his best mate in a panic. "I really need your advice, pal. I'm desperate and I don't know what to do."

His friend replies, "Sure; I'll try and help. What's wrong?"

The worried man explains: "For some time now, I've suspected that my wife may be cheating on me. You know the sort of thing; the phone rings, I answer, someone hangs up."

"That's terrible, mate," says his friend.

"That's not all," continues the worried man. "The other day, I picked up her mobile, just to see what time it was, and she went mental, screaming at me that I should never touch her phone again, and that I was checking up on her. So far I haven't confronted her about it. I sort of think, deep down, I don't really want to know the truth. But then, last night, she went out again and I decided to check up on her. I hid behind my car, which I knew would give me a good view of the whole street. That way, I could see which car she got out of on her return. Anyway, it was while I was crouched behind my car that I noticed some rust around the rear wheel arch. So: do you think I should take it into a body repair shop, or just buy some of that stuff from Halfords and try to sort it out myself?"

A man walks into a bar. 'Give me ten single shots of tequila, please, barman,' he says. 'Sure thing, sir,' says the barkeep, lines up ten shot glasses and fills them with tequila. The man chins them one after the other, in double-quick time. 'You must have had a great day,' says the barkeep. The man says, 'Yup, I just got myself my first blowjob today!' The barkeep says, 'Congratulations, sir; in that case, let me buy you the eleventh tequila – on the house!' The man says, 'No thanks, mate, but if ten of them can't get rid of the taste, I don't think eleven's going to do it!'

A gorilla and a rhino are best mates until one day, as the rhino bends over to drink at the watering hole the gorilla takes advantage of the situation and jumps him from behind. The rhino is furious and chases the gorilla all over the savannah. Half an hour later, still being chased by the rhino, the gorilla spots a tourist sitting in a chair, reading a newspaper. Quick as a flash, he knocks the tourist unconscious, strips him, hides him in the bush, puts on his clothes and sits down in his chair. Moments later, the rhino comes charging past and asks:

"Have you seen a gorilla around here anywhere?"

Holding the paper up to hide his face, the gorilla replies: "What, the one that rogered the rhino by the watering hole?"

"Oh, shit," says the rhino, "don't tell me it's in the papers already."

Little Jimmy is not doing well at maths, so his dad decides to enrol him in Catholic school, hoping for improvement. During Jimmy's first term, the little boy refuses to play with his friends in order to have more time to study and, for his first report, his dad is amazed to see an A+ for maths.

"What happened?" his dad asks.

"Do the nuns punish you if you do badly at maths?"

"No," little Jimmy replies, "but when I saw the little man on the wall nailed to the plus sign, I knew I had to do something."

Henry goes to confession and says, "Bless me Father, for I have sinned. Last night I was with seven different women." The priest quietly replies, "Take seven lemons, squeeze them into a glass and drink the juice without pausing." Henry, looking surprised, says, "Will that cleanse me of my sins, Father?"

"No," says the priest. "But it'll wipe that stupid grin off your face."

After striking gold in Alaska, a lonely miner walks down from the mountains and into a saloon in the nearest town.

"I'm lookin' for the meanest, toughest, roughest hooker you got," he says to the barman.

"We got her," he replies. "She's upstairs in the second room on the right."

The miner hands the pint-puller a gold nugget to pay for the lady of the night and two beers. He grabs the bottles, stomps up the stairs, kicks open the door and yells, "I'm looking for the meanest, roughest, toughest hooker in town."

The woman inside the room looks at the miner and says, "You found her!" Then she strips naked, bends over and grabs her ankles.

"How do you know I want to do you like that?" asks the miner.

"I don't," replies the hooker, "I want you to open me one of those goddamn beers first."

My friend drowned in a bowl of muesli. He was pulled in by the strong currants.

What did the elephant say to the naked man?
It's cute, but can you pick up peanuts with it?

Why do elephants drink?
To forget.

Who's the king of the hankies?
The handkerchief.

Two Microsoft programmers were walking across the Microsoft campus in Seattle when one of their colleagues appeared on a brand-new bicycle.

'Where did you get such a great bike?' asks the first programmer.

"Well, I was walking along yesterday minding my own business when a beautiful woman rode up on this bike. She threw the bike to the ground, took off all her clothes and said, "Take what you want.""

The second IT guy nodded approvingly. "Good choice; the clothes probably wouldn't have fitted."

A beautiful woman about to undergo a minor operation is lying on a trolley in a hospital corridor awaiting the doctors.

A man in a white coat approaches, lifts up the sheet and examines her naked body. He walks away and confers with another man in a white coat. He approaches and does the same thing.

When a third man approaches her, she asks impatiently, "These examinations are fine, but when are you going to start the operation?"

He shrugs and says, "Your guess is as good as mine, lady. We're just here to paint the corridor."

The Three Bears returned one sunny Sunday morning from a stroll in the woods to find the door of their little house open. Cautiously, they went inside.

After a while, big Daddy Bear's deep voice boomed out, "Someone's been eating my porridge!"

Mummy Bear gave a yelp. "Someone's been eating MY porridge!" she said.

Little Baby Bear rushed in, "Forget the damn porridge; some bastard's nicked the DVD player!"

The Lone Ranger is riding through the mountains when Indians attack. They drag him from his horse and bury him in the sand up to his neck, ready to kill him. Knowing he's about to kick the bucket, the Lone Ranger calls his horse over and whispers in his ear. The horse gallops off and returns a few minutes later with a gorgeous naked blonde girl on its back.

After surveying the scene she hops down out of the saddle and sits on his face, sighing and moaning as she writhes about. When she's finished the Indians dive in for the kill.

"Stop! I just want one more word with my horse," cries the Lone Ranger.

They agree and his steed trots over to hear his final words.

"I said 'Posse', you useless twat!"

An Irishman who had a little too much to drink is driving home from the city one night and, of course, his car is weaving violently all over the road.

A cop pulls him over. "So," says the cop to the driver, "where have ya been?"

"Why, I've been to the pub of course," slurs the drunk.

"Well," says the cop, "it looks like you've had quite a few to drink this evening."

"I did all right," the drunk says with a smile.

"Did you know," says the cop, standing straight and folding his arms across his chest, "that a few intersections back, your wife fell out of your car?"

"Oh, thank heavens," sighs the drunk. "For a minute there, I thought I'd gone deaf."

What do you call a judge with no thumbs?
Justice Fingers.

Things you would never know without the movies...

- All beds have special L-shaped cover sheets which reach up to the armpit level of a woman but only to waist level on the man lying beside her.
- The ventilation system of any building is the perfect hiding place. No-one will ever think of looking for you in there and you can travel to any other part of the building you want without any difficulty.
- Should you wish to pass yourself off as a German officer, it will not be necessary to speak the language, a German accent will do.
- A man will show no pain while taking the most ferocious beating but will wince when a woman tries to clean his wounds.
- Kitchens don't have light switches. When entering a kitchen at night, you should open the fridge door and use that light instead.
- If staying in a haunted house, women should investigate any strange noises in their most revealing underwear.
- Cars that crash will always burst into flames.
- Wearing a vest or stripping to the waist can make a man invulnerable to bullets.
- If you find yourself caught up in a misunderstanding that could be cleared up quickly with a simple explanation, for goodness sake, keep your mouth shut.
- Any person waking form a nightmare will sit bolt upright and pant.
- A cough is usually the sign of a terminal illness.
- All bombs are fitted with electronic timing devices with large red digits so you know exactly when they're going to go off.
- When in love, it is customary to burst into song.
- When confronted by an evil international terrorist, sarcasm and wisecracks are your best weapons.

- One man shooting at 20 men has better chances of killing them than 20 men firing at one man.
- Creepy music coming from a cemetery should always be investigated more closely.
- Most laptop computers are powerful enough to override the communication systems of any invading alien civilization.
- Freelance helicopter pilots are always eager to accept bookings from international terrorist organizations – even though the job will require them to shoot total strangers and will end in their own certain death as the helicopter explodes in a ball of flames.
- Most people keep a scrapbook of newspaper clippings – especially if one of their family or friends have died in a strange boating accident.
- All computer disks will work in all computers, regardless of software or operating systems.
- Police Departments give their officers personality tests to make sure they are deliberately assigned a partner who is their total opposite.
- When they are alone, all foreigners prefer to speak English to each other.
- Action heroes never face charges for manslaughter or criminal damage despite laying entire cities to waste by their actions.
- You can always find a chainsaw when you need one.
- Any lock can be picked by a credit card or a paper clip in seconds – unless it is the door to a burning building with a child trapped inside.
- You can tell if somebody is British because they will be wearing a bow tie.
- When driving a car, it is normal to look not at the road but at the person sitting beside you or in the back seat for the entire journey.

- An electric fence, powerful enough to kill a dinosaur will cause no lasting damage to an 8 year old child.
- Having a job of any kind will make fathers forget their son's eighth birthday.
- Honest and hardworking policemen are traditionally gunned down three days before their retirement.
- If you are blonde and pretty, it is possible to become a world expert in Nuclear Fission at age 22.
- The more a man and a woman hate each other, the more likely they will fall in love.
- If being chased through town, you can usually take cover in a passing St Patrick's Day parade – at any time of the year.
- All grocery shopping bag contain at least one stick of French bread.
- It's easy for anyone to land a plane, providing there is someone in the control tower to talk you down.
- Once applied, lipstick will never rub off – even when scuba diving.
- You're likely to survive any battle in any war unless you make the mistake of showing someone a picture of your sweetheart back home.
- The Eiffel Tower can be seen from any window of any building in Paris.
- People on TV never finish their drinks.
- The chief of police is always black.
- When paying for a taxi, never look at your wallet as you take out a note. Just grab one at random and hand it over. It will always be the exact fare.

Two cows are standing next to each other in a field. Daisy says to Dolly, "I was artificially inseminated this morning." "I don't believe you," says Dolly. "It's true, no bull!"

The kids filed back into class Monday morning. Their weekend assignment was to sell something, then give a talk on salesmanship.

Little Mary led off. 'I sold homemade biscuits and I made £30,' she said proudly.

"Very good," said the teacher.

Little Sally was next. 'I sold old magazines,' she said, 'I made £45.'

"Very good, Sally," said the teacher.

Eventually, it was Little Mikey's turn. He walked to the front of the classroom and dumped a box full of cash on the teacher's desk. '£2,467,' he said.

"How much!" cried the teacher, "What in the world were you selling?"

"Toothbrushes," said Little Mikey.

"Toothbrushes?" echoed the teacher, "How could you possibly sell enough toothbrushes to make that much money?"

"I found the busiest corner in town," said Little Mikey, "I set up a Dip & Chip stand. I gave everybody who walked by a free sample. They all said the same thing. 'Hey! This tastes just like dogshit!' Then I'd say, 'It is dogshit. Wanna buy a toothbrush?'"

An Essex girl is involved in a nasty car crash and is trapped and bleeding. The paramedics soon arrive on site.

"It's OK I'm a paramedic and I'm going to ask you some questions?"

"OK."

What's your name?"

"Sharon."

"OK Sharon, is this your car?"

"Yes."

"Where are you bleeding from?"

"Romford, mate."

After several unsuccessful years of searching for Mr Right, a woman decides to take out a personal ad. She ends up corresponding with a man who has lived his entire life in the Australian Outback; and, after a long-distance courtship, they decide to get married.

On their wedding night, she goes into the bathroom to prepare for the festivities. When she returns to the bedroom, she finds her new husband standing in the middle of the room, naked and all the furniture from the room piled in one corner.

"What's going on?" she asks.

"I've never been with a woman," he says. "But if it's anything like a kangaroo, I'm going to need all the room I can get!"

A blonde was playing Trivial Pursuit one night. When her turn came she rolled the dice and landed on 'Science & Nature'.

Her question was:

"If you are in a vacuum and someone calls your name, can you hear it?"

She thought for a long while and then asked, "Is it on or off?"

What do you call a man with no arms or legs playing the piano?

A clever dick.

What do you call a long line of actors?

A dole queue.

An ant and an elephant share a night of romance. Next morning the ant wakes up and the elephant is dead.

"Damn," says the ant. 'One night of passion and I spend the rest of my life digging a grave!'

A salesman checks into a futuristic hotel. Needing a haircut before his meeting, he calls reception to see if there's a barber on the premises.

"I'm afraid not, sir," the receptionist tells him, "but down the hall from your room is a vending machine that should serve your purposes."

Sceptical but intrigued, the salesman locates the machine, inserts £10 and sticks his head into the opening, at which point the machine starts to buzz and spin. Fifteen seconds later, he pulls out his head and looks in the mirror to see the best haircut of his life.

"That's amazing," he says before noticing another machine with a sign reading, "For 50p this machine will provide a service men need when away from their wives..." Very excited, he skips the rest of the description, and puts the coin in the slot.

"Oh, man. Do I ever need this!" he gasps, looking both ways and unzipping his fly. When the machine starts buzzing, he lets out a shriek of agony and almost passes out. Fifteen seconds later, it shuts off. With trembling hands, the man withdraws his member, which now has a button neatly sewn on the end.

A priest who has to spend the night in a hotel asks the girl in reception to come up to his room for dinner.

After a while he makes a pass at her, but she stops him and reminds him that he is a holy man.

"It's OK," he replies, "it's written in the Bible."

After a wild night of sex she asks to see where in the Bible it says it's OK.

The priest rolls over, takes the Gideon bible out of the desk by the bed and shows her the first page. On it, someone has scrawled: "The girl in reception will shag anyone."

A young woman on a flight from New York to London asks the priest sitting beside her, "Father, may I ask a favour?"

"Of course, my child. What may I do for you?"

"Well, I bought an expensive woman's electronic hair dryer for my mother's birthday," says the female passenger. "The dryer is unopened and well over the Customs limits, and I'm afraid they'll confiscate it. Is there any way you could carry it through Customs for me? Under your robes perhaps?"

"I would love to help you, my dear," says the man of the cloth, "but I must warn you: I will not lie."

"With your honest face, Father, no one will question you," replies the woman.

When they reach the Customs area, the women lets the priest go ahead of her. The Customs official asks, "Father, do you have anything to declare?"

"From the top of my head down to my waist, I have nothing to declare," answers the priest.

"And what do you have to declare from your waist to the floor?" says the official.

"I have a marvellous instrument designed to be used on a woman, but which is, to date, unused."

Roaring with laughter, the official says, "Go ahead, Father. Next."

A little old lady lives in a nursing home. She's losing her marbles and one day she walks up to one of the male patients and lifts up her skirt. She points down and says, 'Super pussy,' then drops her skirt and walks away.

She walks up to another male patient and lifts up her skirt. She points down and says, "Super pussy,' then drops her skirt and walks away.

Then she walks up to a third male patient and lifts up her skirt. She points down and says 'Super pussy' once more. The man looks up at her and says, 'I think I'll take the soup, thanks!'

A bloke was about to bring his new girlfriend home, so he warned his parrot not to make any offensive remarks; the parrot had a tendency to verbally abuse anyone who came into the house. The next night the guy walked in with his new girlfriend, and the parrot instantly began to insult her: 'Who's a fat cow, then? Who's been hit by a truck, then?'

The next day the infuriated man decided to shove the parrot in the freezer to teach it a lesson. About two minutes later the parrot called out, 'I'm sorry. I'm really sorry. I'm really, really sorry. I won't do it again!' The man let the parrot back out and said: 'I hope you behave, otherwise it's back in the cooler!'

For the next couple of months he didn't hear so much as a squeak out of the parrot. He couldn't believe how successful his freezer trick turned out to be. But finally one night the parrot got up enough courage to talk again.

'Excuse me, please,' the parrot said, very cautiously, 'but what exactly did the chicken do?'

What do you get after five days of non-stop sex?
A weak end.

A man walks into a bar one night. He goes up to the bartender and asks for a beer.

"Certainly, sir," replies the bartender. "That'll be one penny."

"One penny?!" exclaims the customer.

The barman replies, "Yes." So the guy glances over the menu and asks, "Could I have a nice juicy T-bone steak with chips, peas and a fried egg?"

"Certainly, sir," replies the bartender, "but all that comes to real money."

"How much money?"

"Four pence," the bartender replies.

"Four pence!?" exclaims the guy. "Where's the guy who owns this place?"

The bartender replies, "Upstairs with my wife."

"What's he doing with your wife?"

"Same as I'm doing to his business."

What makes men chase women they have no intention of marrying?

The same urge that makes dogs chase cars they have no intention of driving.

Tech Support: "What does the screen say now?"
Caller: "It says, 'Hit ENTER when ready'."
Tech Support: "Well?"
Caller: "How do I know when it's ready?"

Q: If the dove is the bird of peace, what is the bird of true love?
A: The swallow.

Hear about the flasher who was thinking of retiring?
He's sticking it out for a while longer

A woman rushes downstairs into the foyer of a large hotel and screams at the receptionist, "Check me out! I'm in a hurry!"

The receptionist eyes her up for a second and says, "Not bad, but your bum's a bit big."

After living in the remote wilderness of Norfolk all his life, an old man decides it's finally time to visit Norwich. In one of the shops he picks up a mirror and looks in it.

Not knowing what it is, he remarks, "How about that? Here's a picture of my dead daddy."

He buys the 'picture', but on the way home he remembers his wife, Lizzy, didn't like his father, so he hangs it in the barn, and every morning before leaving for the fields, he goes there to look at it. Lizzy begins to get suspicious of these many trips to the barn. One day after her husband leaves, she searches the barn and finds the mirror.

As she looks into the glass, she fumes, "So that's the ugly bitch he's runnin' around with..."

A blonde is taking a tour of a National Park and hears the guide say dinosaur fossils have been found in the area.

'Wow!' exclaims the blonde. 'I'd never have thought dinosaurs would come so close to the motorway.'

A blonde walks up to the counter of the local library and complains to the librarian:

'Here's your book back. It's the most boring book I have ever read. There's no plot whatsoever, and far too many characters.'

'Oh, thank you,' the librarian replies. 'You must be the person who borrowed our phone book.'

There were twin brothers by the name of Joey and John Jones. They had lived in the same fishing village all their lives. John was married and Joey had always been single. Joey owned a knackered old boat. One day, Joey's boat sank on exactly the same day that John's wife passed away.

A couple of days later a kindly old lady met Joey in the queue for the Post Office and she though he was John. She said to him, 'So sorry for your trouble: you must be feeling awful and I'm not surprised.' Joey, not at all worried about his crappy old boat, replied, 'Well, I couldn't care less. She was a pile of crap right from the very beginning. Her bottom was all lumpy and she always stank of old fish. The first time I got in her she leaked faster than anything I'd ever seen before in my life. She had a crack and a huge hole in front that kept getting bigger and bigger every time that I used her. I could handle her fine, but when someone else was using her she leaked like a bastard and that's what finished her off, I reckon: three or four blokes from out of town came over looking for a good time. I told them that she was fucked and much too creaky for all of them but they really thought she look all right. Anyway, all of them tried to get into her at the same time. It was just too much and she cracked right up the middle!' The little old lady fainted!

Three young boys are trying to figure out whose dad is best.

"My dad is so good he can shoot an arrow, run after it, get in front of it, and catch it in his bare hands," says the first lad.

"My dad is so good that he can shoot a gun, run after the bullet, get in front of it and catch it in his bare hands," says the second lad.

"I've got you both beat," says the third lad. "My dad works for the council, and he's so good he can get off work at five and be home by 4:30!"

What's six inches long, with a head on it, that women like to blow?
  Money.

NASA sends a space shuttle up with two pigs and a blonde on board. While the shuttle is taking off, the NASA command centre calls the first pig and asks, "Pig One, do you know your mission?"

The pig replies, "Oink oink. Get the shuttle into orbit and launch the trillion-dollar satellite. Oink oink."

Then Mission Control asks the second pig, "Pig Two, do you know your mission?"

The second pig replies, "Oink oink. Once Pig One has completed the trillion-dollar satellite launch, close hatch and land shuttle. Oink oink."

Then NASA asks the blonde, 'Blonde woman, do you know your mission?'

The blonde woman replies, "Um... Oh yeah: I remember now. Feed the pigs – and DON'T TOUCH A GODDAMNED THING!"

A guy comes to the military enlistment office.

"What would you like to be?" the officer asks him.

"A pilot," he answers.

"Good choice, son." The officer enrols the guy and sends him to study flying. Unfortunately, he doesn't have what it takes to be a pilot and fails his exams. He is sent back to the military enlistment office again.

"Sorry, but you can't be a pilot any more: I'm sure you can see that. Select something else."

The guy thinks for a few seconds and speaks:

"I want to be in the air defence."

"First a pilot, then air defence? Why AD?"

"If I can't fly, nobody will fly!" the guy answers pugnaciously.

Several men are in the changing room of a golf club when a mobile phone on a bench rings and a man answers. He switches to hands-free and everyone else in the room stops to listen.

"Hello," says the guy.

A female voice answers, "Honey, it's me. Are you at the club?"

"Yes," replies the man.

"I'm at the shops now and found this beautiful leather coat. It's only £1,000. Is it OK if I buy it?"

"Sure, go ahead if you like it that much," he says nonchalantly.

The woman goes on, "I also stopped by the Mercedes garage and saw the new models. I saw one I really liked."

"How much?" enquires the man.

"£60,000," says the spendthrift.

"OK, but for that price I want it with all the options," says the fella.

"Great!" says the woman. "Oh: and one more thing. The house we wanted last year is back on the market. They're asking £950,000."

"Well, then go ahead and give them an offer, but just offer £900,000," replies the man.

"OK. I'll see you later! I love you!" the woman signs off.

"Bye, I love you, too," says the man and hangs up.

The other men in the changing room look at him in astonishment.

Then the man asks: "Anyone know whose phone this is?"

My husband came home with a tube of KY jelly and said, "This will make you happy tonight." He was right. When he went out of the bedroom, I squirted it all over the doorknobs. He couldn't get back in.

An Indian chief had three wives, each of whom was pregnant. The first gave birth to a boy and the chief was so elated he built her a teepee made of deerhide.

A few days later the second gave birth, also to a boy. The chief was very happy and he built her a teepee made of antelope hide.

The third wife gave birth a few days later, but the chief kept the details a secret. He built this one a two-storey teepee, using hippopotamus hide. The chief then challenged the tribe to guess what had occurred.

Many tried and failed. Finally, one young brave declared that the third wife gave birth to twin boys.

"Correct," said the chief. "How did you figure it out?"

The brave replied, "It's elementary, really – the value of the squaw of the hippopotamus is equal to the sons of the squaws of the other two hides."

A cannibal comes back from holiday with one leg and half an arm missing.

His mate asks, "What the hell happened to you?"

"I didn't realize it was self-catering"

Two men are sitting in the doctor's office. The first man is holding his shoulder in pain, while the second man has ketchup in his hair, fried egg down the front of his shirt and two sausages sticking out of his pockets. After a while, the second man asks the other what happened. "My cat got stuck in a tree," the man says, gripping his arm. I went up after him and fell out. I think I've broken my shoulder. You?"

"Oh, it's nothing serious," the second man replies. "I'm just not eating properly."

Two cows were standing in a field. One cow says to the other, 'Moooooo.' The other says, 'I was just going to say that.'

A soldier at the Pentagon gets out of the shower, and realizes that his clothes are missing. He searches around for them, but accidentally locks himself out of his locker room, and finds himself completely naked in the halls of the world's most powerful military organization HQ. But, luckily, no one is around to see him.

So he runs as fast as he can to the elevator. When it arrives, it's empty. He breathes a sigh of relief and gets in. When the doors open on his floor, there is no one waiting outside. "This must be my lucky day," he says to himself. He is now only a few yards from his office.

Suddenly, he hears footsteps coming from around the corner. He hears the General's voice. There is no way he'll make it to his door in time, so he ducks into the closest office available, and finds himself in the laboratory for Research & Development. The Head Scientist looks up from one of her experiments with puzzled interest.

The soldier thinks quickly, stands up straight and salutes.

"I am here to report the partial success of the Personal Invisibility Device," he says.

"I see," the Head Scientist says. "The Shrink Ray seems to be working perfectly, too."

A young magician got a job working on a cruise ship with his pet parrot. The parrot would always steal his act by saying things like, "He has a card up his sleeve," or "He has a dove in his pocket." One day the ship sank and the magician and the parrot found themselves alone on a lifeboat. For a couple of days, they just sat there looking at each other. Finally, the parrot broke the silence and said, "OK, I give up. What did you do with the ship?"

What's brown and black and looks good on a lawyer?
    A doberman.

A masked man runs through the door of a sperm bank. He is brandishing a shotgun. He leaps over the counter and points the gun at the receptionist.

"Open the safe!" he barks at her.

"What?" she says. "There's no money here: we're a sperm bank, not a money bank."

"Just do it!" the guy continues. "Just open the damned safe and don't talk back. Don't make me hurt you, lady."

So the lady leads him out back and opens the safe. It is just a big refrigerator full of sperm samples.

"Now take a sample out," the guy snaps. The woman obliges. "Now, drink it," the guy says. "But it's sperm," the woman says. "Don't make me mad – just do it!" shouts the man.

Fearing the worst, the woman pops the cap off the bottle and drinks the sperm. She chokes a couple of times but drains the bottle.

"Another one," says the guy. She takes another bottle from the racks and drinks it. At that moment the man drops his gun and pulls of his mask. The woman cannot believe her eyes – the man who just had a gun at her head is her husband! "You see," he shouts at her, "it wasn't that bloody difficult, was it?"

Two women were playing golf. One teed off and watched in horror as her ball sailed towards a foursome of men playing the next hole. The ball hit one of the men, and he immediately clasped his groin, fell to the ground and rolled around in agony. The woman rushed down to the man and immediately began to apologise.

"Please allow me to help. I'm a physical therapist and I know I could relieve your pain if you'd allow me," she told him.

"Oh, no. I'll be all right. I'll be fine in a few minutes," the man replied, still in pain.

But she persisted, and he finally allowed her to help. She gently took his hands away and loosened his trousers, and put her hands inside. She began to massage him. She then asked, "How does that feel?"

He replied, "It feels great, but my thumb still hurts like hell."

"So, Cletus, how did your first day of upper school go?" asked Cletus' father.

"It was great, Daddy" said Cletus. "Teacher asked each one of us to count to one hundred. Some of the kids couldn't get past the number thirty, but I counted all the way to one hundred without making a single mistake. It was great."

"That's great, son. It's because you're from Arkansas."

The next day the father asked, "So how was school today, Cletus?"

Cletus said, 'It was fine. We had to say the alphabet in class today, Daddy. Some of the kids couldn't get past the letter Q but I got all the way from A to Z without any mistakes. It was great."

"That's great, son," said the father. "It's because you're from Arkansas."

After the third day, Cletus came back with a worried look on his face.

"What's the matter, son? No good news from school today" asked Daddy.

"Well, Daddy," said Cletus, "We had PE today, and after the lesson, in the shower, I noticed that I had the biggest weewee of anyone in the class. It must have been ten times longer and hairier than anyone else's. Is it because I'm from Arkansas?"

"Not quite, son,' said Daddy. 'It's because you're eighteen years old."

Two blokes are lying in bed when one turns to the other and says, "I don't think much of this wife-swapping."

God is talking to Adam and Eve one day during the Creation. "Well, you two, I only have a couple more goodies left to hand out before my job is done. Which one of you wants to be able to pee standing up?"

Adam raises his hand and yells "Me, me, pick me!" So God obliges.

God looks at Eve and says: "Well, sorry, Eve... but it looks like you're stuck with the multiple orgasms."

A pig farmer is worried because none of his pigs is getting pregnant. His pigs are his livelihood, so he calls the vet and asks him what on earth he can do to make his pigs procreate. The vet says that if the pigs really won't do the business he should really try artificial insemination. The farmer doesn't have a clue what artificial insemination is but he reckons it must mean he has to get the pigs pregnant by himself. So he loads them all into his truck, drives them to the woods and shags them all. The next day he calls the vet again and asks him how he will be able to tell if his pigs are pregnant. The vet tells him that the pigs will be lying down rolling in mud. The farmer looks out of the window and sees that all his pigs are really clean and all standing up in their field. So he herds them into his truck, drives them to the woods and shags them all again. The next morning the farmer gets up and looks at the pig field. All the pigs are still clean and all standing. So the farmer herds them yet again into his truck, drives them to the woods and shags them all. Early the next morning the farmer is exhausted so he asks his wife to have a look at the pigs to see if they are rolling in mud. His wife gets up, looks out at the pig field and says, "That's very odd: the pigs are all in your truck. Two of them are waving over here and one's tooting the horn!"

A drunk goes to the doctor complaining of tiredness and headaches. "I feel tired all the time," he slurs. "My head hurts and I'm not sleeping. What is it, Doc?"

Frowning, the doctor examines him before standing back. "I can't find anything wrong," he says. "It must be the drinking."

"Fair enough," replies the lush. "I'll come back when you sober up."

After fifty years of marriage to Lena, Ole becomes very ill and realizes that he will soon die. In bed one night, Ole turns to his wife.

"Lena," he asks. "When I am gone, do you think you will marry another man?"

Lena gives it some thought. "Well, yes," she says. "Marriage has been good to me and I think that I will surely marry again."

Ole is taken aback. "Why, Lena," he cries, "will you bring your new husband into our house?"

"This is a fine house," says Lena. "Yes, I think we will live here."

"But Lena," Ole gasps, "will you bring your new husband into our bed?"

Lena replies, "Well, yes; you made this bed, a good strong bed. Yes! Sure I will bring my new husband into this bed."

Ole gulps. "But Lena," he says in a quiet voice. "You won't let your new husband use my golf clubs, will you?"

Lena smiled at her husband. "Oh, Ole!" she grins, misty-eyed. "Of course he won't use your golf clubs! He's left-handed."

David Cameron calls Nick Clegg into his office and says, "Nick, I have a great idea! Let's go all-out to win back rural Britain."

"Great idea, Dave," says Nick. "How will we go about it?"

"Well," says Cameron, "we'll get ourselves tweed jackets, some wellies, a stick, a flat cap and a Labrador. Then we'll really look the part. We'll go to a nice old country pub, in one of those posh villages, and we'll prove we really enjoy the countryside."

"Right," says Clegg.

So a few days later, all kitted out and with the requisite Labrador at heel, they set off from London in a westerly direction. Eventually they find a lovely country pub and go up to the bar.

"Good evening landlord, may we have two pints of your best ale?" says Cameron.

"Good evening, Prime Minister," says the landlord, "two pints of best it is, coming up."

Cameron and Clegg stand by the bar drinking their beer and chatting, nodding now and again to those who come in for a drink.

The dog lies quietly at their feet when, all of a sudden, the door from the adjacent bar opens and in walks an old shepherd, complete with crook. He goes up to the Labrador, lifts its tail and looks underneath, shrugs his shoulders and walks back to the other bar. Moments later, another old shepherd comes in with his crook and repeats what the first shepherd did before scratching his head and going back to the other bar. Over the course of the next half hour or so several other locals come in, lift the dog's tail and go away looking puzzled. Eventually Cameron and Clegg can stand it no longer and call the landlord over.

"Tell me," says Cameron. "Why do all these old shepherds and locals come in and look under the dog's tail like that? Is it a local custom?"

"Good Lord, no," says the landlord. "It's just that word spread to the other bar that there was a Labrador in this bar with two arseholes."

A bank manager in America notices that one of his new cashiers lacks basic arithmetic skills. He calls the new man into his office. "Son, where did you say you studied finance again?" the manager asks.

"Yale, sir," the cashier replies.

"I see," says the bank manager, certain he must of pulled the wrong employee aside. "And what did you say your name was?"

"Yim Yohnson, sir," he replies.

Two Italian men are deep in conversation on a bus. The lady behind can't help but earwig on their conversation when she hears, "Emma come first. Den I come. Den two asses come together. I come once-a more. Two asses, they come together again. I come again and pee twice. Then I come one lasta time."

The woman, offended by what she has overheard, can't help but say something: "You foul-mouthed, sex-obsessed swine. In this country, we don't speak aloud in public places about our sex lives."

"Hey, coola down lady," says the Italian. "I'm a justa tellin' my frienda how to spella 'Mississippi'."

When the new patient is settled comfortably on the couch, the psychiatrist begins his therapy session.

"I'm not aware of the nature of your problem," the doctor says, "so perhaps you should start at the very beginning."

"Of course," replies the patient. "In the beginning, I created the Heavens and the Earth."

A mother and her young son are on a long-haul flight to America. The son, looking out of the plane's window, turns to his mum and says, "Mum, if big dogs have baby dogs and big cats have baby cats, why don't big planes have baby planes?"

Stumped for an answer, the mother suggests that her son ask the stewardess. The boy promptly gets out of his seat and wanders back to the service area.

"Excuse me," the boy says to the stewardess. "If big dogs have baby dogs and big cats have baby cats, why don't big planes have baby planes?"

"Did your mother tell you to ask me that?"

"Yes," he says.

The stewardess whispers in the boy's ear, "Tell your mother it's because British Airways always pulls out on time."

A little old lady answered a knock on the door one day, only to be confronted by a well-dressed young man carrying a vacuum cleaner.

"Good morning," said the young man. "If I could take a couple minutes of your time, I would like to demonstrate the very latest in high-powered vacuum cleaners."

"Get lost!" said the old lady. "I haven't got any money," and she proceeded to close the door. Quick as a flash, the young man wedged his foot in the door and pushed it wide open.

"Don't be too hasty!" he said. "Not until you have at least seen my demonstration." And with that, he emptied a bucket of horse poop all over her hallway carpet.

"If this vacuum cleaner does not remove all traces of this from your carpet, madam, I will personally eat the remainder."

"Well," she said, "I hope you've got a bloody good appetite, because the electricity was cut off this morning."

Four retired friends decide to go golfing. One of them pays the fees, while the other three go up to tee off. They are all bragging about their sons.

The first man says, "Well, my son's in construction, and he's so successful that he gave one of his friends a brand-new house for free."

The second man says, "Well, my son's a car salesman, and he's so successful that he gave one of his friends a Porsche for free."

The third man says, "Well, my son's a stockbroker, and he's so successful that he gave one of his friends a share portfolio for free."

At this point the fourth man arrives on the scene and they tell him, "We were just discussing how our sons were doing. Is yours successful?"

The man says, "Well, my son is an erotic dancer in a gay bar."

There is silence as the others look embarrassed for the man.

"I'm not really thrilled about the dancing, but still," the man continues, "he does pretty well anyway; his last three boyfriends gave him a share portfolio, a Porsche and a brand-new house for free!"

Two hydrogen atoms walk into a bar. One says, "I think I've lost an electron."

The other says, "Are you sure?"

"Yes, I'm positive..."

A General visits the infirmary to check on his men. He goes to the first soldier, lying in his bed and asks: "What's your problem, soldier?"

"Chronic syphilis, Sir."

"I see... And what treatment are you getting?"

"Five minutes with the wire brush and Dettol each day, Sir."

"As it should be! And what's your ambition?"

"To get back to the front, Sir."

"Good man," says the General, and goes to the next bed. "What about you? What's your problem, soldier?"

"Chronic piles, Sir"

"Nasty, that... what treatment are you getting?"

"Five minutes with the wire brush and Dettol each day, Sir."

"What an efficient infirmary this is! And what's your ambition, soldier?"

"To get back to the front, Sir."

"Good man," says the General, and goes to the next bed. "What's your problem, soldier?"

"Chronic gum disease, Sir."

"Unusual... And what treatment are you getting?"

"Five minutes with the wire brush and Dettol each day, Sir."

"This is really a top infirmary! And what is your ambition, soldier?"

"To be treated before the other two, Sir!"

A man weds his virgin bride and on the big night, strips off and jumps into bed for a grope. Taken aback, his new wife lays down the law. "I expect you to be as well-mannered in bed as you are at the dinner table, my love!"

"Oh right," says the man, backing off a bit. "Well, then; will you please pass the sex?"

A minister is winding up his sermon one Sunday in church.

"Next Sunday I am going to preach on the subject of liars: and in this connection, as a preparation for my discourse, I would like you all to read the seventeenth chapter of Mark," he says.

On the following Sunday, the vicar walks to the front of the church and says, "Now, then, all of you who have done as I requested and read the seventeenth chapter of Mark, please raise your hands."

Nearly every hand in the congregation shoots up.

The vicar looks stern and says, "You are the ones I want to talk to about lying. There is no seventeenth chapter of Mark."

There are two statues in a park, one of a nude man and one of a nude woman. They had been facing each other across a pathway for a hundred years when one day an angel comes down from the sky and, with a single gesture, brings the two to life. "As a reward for being so patient," says the angel, "you have been given life for 30 minutes to do what you've wished to do the most." Immediately, the two statues disappear off behind a shrubbery. The angel waits patiently as the bushes rustle and giggling ensues until, after fifteen minutes, the two return out of breath. The angel tells them, "Um, you have fifteen minutes left."

The male statue asks the woman statue, "Shall we do it again?"

"Oh, yes," she replies. "But let's change positions. This time, I'll hold the pigeon down, and you crap on its head."

Two men are walking home from work one hot, sweaty Friday in London. The first man says, 'First thing I'm going to do when I get home is rip my wife's knickers off!' 'Steady on, mate,' says the second. 'You've got the whole weekend: why are you in such a hurry?' The first man replies, 'They've been chafing my groin all day!'

There was a farmer with three daughters. One Saturday night they each had a date. One by one the dates arrived and the farmer answered the door each time.

The first fellow knocked on the door. The farmer answered and the fellow said, "Hello, Mr Farmer: my name is Joe, I'm here to take your daughter Flo out to eat some dough." "That's just fine," said the farmer, and off went Joe with the eldest daughter.

The second fellow knocked on the door. The farmer answered and the fellow said, "Hello, Mr Farmer, my name is Freddy, I'm here to take your daughter Betty out to eat spaghetti."

"That's just fine," said the farmer and off went Freddy with the middle daughter.

The third fellow knocked on the door. The farmer answered and the fellow said, "Hello, Mr Farmer, my name is Chuck –" "GET THE HELL OUT OF MY HOUSE!" yelled the farmer.

A minister was asked to dinner by one of his parishioners, whom he knew was a slovenly housekeeper. When he sat down at the table, he noticed that the dishes were the dirtiest that he had ever seen in his life.

"Were these dishes ever washed?" he asked his hostess, running his fingers over the grit and grime.

She replied, "They're as clean as soap and water could get them."

He felt a bit apprehensive, but blessed the food anyway and started eating. It was really delicious and he said so, despite the dirty dishes.

When dinner was over, the hostess took the dishes outside and yelled, to her dogs "Here, Soap! Here, Water!"

A man bought two birds from a pet shop, walked to the nearest cliff and jumped off. When he woke up in hospital, with most of his bones broken, he said to the nurse, "That's the first and last time I try budgie jumping."

Police arrested two kids the other day. One was drinking neat battery acid, and the other was eating fireworks. They charged one and let the other one off.

Three bulls, one large, one medium, and one small, are standing in the pasture. They've just heard a rumour that the farmer is bringing in a new, larger bull.

The largest bull of the three says, "Well, he ain't getting none of my cows."

The medium bull says, "He ain't getting none of my cows."

So the little bull says, "Well, if he ain't getting any of yours, then he sure as hell ain't getting one of mine."

Two days later, a truck pulls into the yard, and the farmer unloads the new bull. He's big and pissed off from having been cooped up for the long journey.

When the three bulls see him, the biggest bull says, "He can have my cows."

The medium bull says, "Yup, he can have mine, too."

The littlest bull, however, begins to paw the ground, snort and bellow.

"What the hell are you doing?" the other two ask.

"I'm just showing him I ain't a cow!"

Who was the last person to box Rocky Marciano?
His undertaker.

A surgeon was relaxing on his sofa one evening when the phone rang. The doctor calmly answered it and heard the familiar voice of a colleague on the other end of the line. "We need a fourth for poker," said the friend.

"I'll be right over," whispered the surgeon.

As he was putting on his coat, his wife asked, "Is it serious?"

"Oh, yes: quite serious," said the surgeon gravely. "Three doctors are there already!"

A family of England supporters head out one Saturday to get their new football kits. In the sports shop the son picks up a Scotland football shirt and says to his sister, "I've decided I'm going to be a Scotland supporter."

The sister is outraged at this, promptly whacks him round the head and says, "Go talk to your mother!"

The lad goes off and finds his mother. "Mum, I've decided I'm going to be a Scotland supporter and I want this shirt."

The mother is outraged and promptly whacks him round the head and says, "Go talk to your father."

Off goes the lad again and finds his father. "Dad, I've decided I'm going to be a Scotland supporter and I want this shirt."

The father is outraged, promptly whacks his son round the head and says, "No son of mine is ever going to be seen in that!"

About half an hour later, they're all back in the car heading home. The father turns to the son and says, "Son, I hope you have learned something today?"

The son turns to his dad and says, "Yes, I have."

"Good, son, what is it?" says the dad.

The son replies, "I've only been a Scotland supporter for an hour and I already hate you English bastards!"

Q. Do you know how New Zealanders practise safe sex?
A. They spray paint X's on the back of the sheep that kick.

A mounted policeman was on patrol one day when he comes across a little boy on a shiny new bicycle. The policeman leans down to the boy and says, "That's a nice shiny bike. Did Father Christmas bring it for you?"

"He sure did," says the boy, all pleased with himself. Then the cop sits back up and writes the boy a £25 fine.

"Next year, boy," he says, "ask Father Christmas to put a licence plate on it too."

The boy is really pissed off, so decides to get his own back. He looks up at the policeman and says,

"That's a fine horse. Did Father Christmas bring it for you?"

The policeman, thinking he will humour the boy, says, "He sure did," and is pretty pleased with himself. The boy then looks down underneath the horse and back up at the policeman before saying, "Next year, officer, perhaps you could ask Father Christmas to put the prick underneath the horse instead of on top!"

A new clinic, with several different specialists, opened in a trendy part of the city. Wanting to be different and creative with the design, the administration decided that each doctor's office door would, in some way, be representative of his practice.

So, when construction was complete... the eye doctor's door had a peep-hole, the orthopaedist's door had a broken hinge, the psychiatrist's door was painted all kinds of crazy colours. As for the gynaecologist's door, it was left open... just a crack.

A young woman was going to marry one of those elderly, wealthy eccentrics who want a virgin bride. Since she wasn't, she went to a doctor to reconstruct her hymen. The doctor told her that would cost around £500 to do it surgically, but that there was another way that would cost only £50 and could be done straight away in his office.

The woman agreed to try the cheap way, paid the money and lay down on the consultation bed, feet in the stirrups. The doctor worked on her for several minutes, then congratulated her on her forthcoming marriage and showed her the door.

After the honeymoon, the woman came back to the doctor and told him that it was perfect: the pain, the blood, everything was there.

"How did you do it?" she asked.

"Very simple," he replied. "I tied your pubic hair together."

A gorilla walks into a bar and orders a pint of lager. The barman charges him five quid and, after looking at him for a while, says, "Do you know, you're the first gorilla we've had in here for ages?"

"I'm not bloody surprised," replies the gorilla, "at a fiver a pint."

A cowboy walks into a bar and orders a whisky. When the bartender delivers the drink, the cowboy asks, "Where is everybody?" The bartender replies, "They've gone to the hanging." "Hanging? Who are they hanging?" "Brown Paper Pete," the bartender replied. "What kind of a name is that?" the cowboy asked. "Well," says the bartender. "He wears a brown paper hat, brown paper shirt, brown paper trousers and brown paper shoes." "How bizarre," said the cowboy. "What are they hanging him for?" "Rustling," said the bartender.

A mother and baby camel were talking one day when the baby camel asked, "Mum, why have I got these huge three-toed feet?"

"Well, son, when we trek across the desert your toes will help you to stay on top of the soft sand," the mother replied,

"OK," said the son.

A few minutes later, the son asked, "Mum, why have I got these great long eyelashes?"

"They are there to keep the sand out of your eyes on the trips through the desert."

"Thanks, Mum," replied the son, and went off to think on his own.

After a short while, the son returned and asked, "Mum, why have I got these great big humps on my back?"

The mother, now a little impatient with the boy, replied, "They're to help us store water for our long treks across the desert, so we can go without drinking for long periods."

"That's great, Mum: so we have huge feet to stop us sinking, and long eyelashes to keep the sand from our eyes and these humps to store water. But Mum..."

"Yes, son?"

"Why the heck are we in London Zoo?"

My mum said never marry a tennis player.

Love means nothing to them.

A man bursts into a busy pub, points to his left and shouts, "All the arseholes over that side!"

He then points to his right, and shouts, "All the dickheads get over that side!"

Suddenly, the hardest guy in the pub stands up and says, "Who are you calling a dickhead?"

The man points to his left and shouts, "Over there, arsehole!"

Brian returns home from the pub late one night, stinking drunk. He gets into bed with his sleeping wife, gives her a kiss and nods off. When he awakes a strange man is standing at the end of his bed in a long flowing white robe.

"Who the hell are you?" demands Brian. "What are you doing in my bedroom?"

"This isn't your bedroom," the man answers, "and I'm St Peter".

Brian is stunned. "You mean I'm dead? That can't be; I have so much to live for! I haven't said goodbye to my family. You've got to send me back straight away!"

"Well you can be reincarnated," the holy man says, "but there's a catch. We can only send you back as a hen."

Brian's devastated, but knowing there's a farm near his house, he asks to be sent back right away. A flash of light later, he's covered in feathers and pecking the ground. Within minutes he feels a strange feeling welling up inside him.

The farmyard rooster strolls over and says: "I can see you're struggling, mate. Don't worry; you're ovulating. Just relax and let it happen. You'll feel much better." And so he does.

A few uncomfortable seconds later, an egg pops out from under his tail and an immense feeling of relief sweeps through him. When he lays his second egg, the feeling of happiness is overwhelming and he realizes that being reincarnated as a hen is the best thing that has ever happened to him. The joy keeps coming but just as he's about to lay his third egg, he feels a massive smack on the back of his head and hears his wife shouting, "Brian, wake up you drunken bastard! You're shitting the bed."

Q: What do a Christmas tree and priest have in common?
A: Their balls are just for decoration.

Little Johnny walks past his parents' room one night and sees them making love. Puzzled, he asks his father about it the next morning. "Why were you doing that to mummy last night?"

His father replies, "Because mummy wants a baby."

The next night, Johnny spots mummy giving daddy a blowjob and the next morning he asks his father, "Why was mummy doing that to you last night?"

His father replies, "Because mummy wants a BMW."

A guy walks into the psychiatrist wearing only cling film for shorts.

The shrink says, "Well, I can clearly see you're nuts."

A man goes to a fancy dress party dressed only in his Y-fronts.

A woman asks, 'What are you supposed to be?"

"A premature ejaculation", the guy replies.

"What?"

"Yeah, look, I've just come in my pants."

What's black and white and red all over?

A cow that's just been murdered.

While making his rounds, a doctor points out an X-ray to a group of medical students.

"As you can see," he begins, "the patient has a limp because his left fibula and tibia are radically arched."

The doctor turns to one of the students and asks, "What would you do in a case like this?"

"Well," ponders the student, "I suppose I'd limp, too."

A duck walks into a bar and orders a beer.

The barman says: "Hey, you are a duck."

"Nothing wrong with your eyesight" observes the duck.

"Yeah but I mean, you can TALK!" says the barman.

"Guess your ears are fine too", answers the duck, "now can I have a beer please."

The barman serves the duck a pint and asks him: "So, what brings a duck like you to these parts?"

"Oh", says the duck, "I work on the building site across the road. We'll be here for a couple of weeks, and I'll most likely be in every lunch hour for a pint." The duck slurped down his beer, wiggling his tail happily.

Just as he said, the duck waddles over from his job at the building site and has his lunchtime lager. The next week, the circus comes to town on its annual round. The circus owner wanders in for a pint and the barman tells him about the talking duck.

"You should get this duck to join your circus", he says. "For a little consideration I could fix you up with this duck and you could make a lot of bucks. Everyone would love to see a talking duck, I think. Don't you?"

The circus man nods his agreement excitedly while sipping his beer and the barman agrees to talk to the duck about the circus.

The following day, the duck, once again, comes in for his regular lunchtime pint. The barman says to the duck: "You know, the circus is in town and yesterday I was chatting to the owner about you. He's very interested in you."

"Really?" says the duck.

"Yeah, you could make a lot of money there. I can fix it up for you easily."

"Hang on", said the duck, "you did say a CIRCUS, didn't you?"

"That's right."

"That's one of those big tent things, isn't it? With a big pole in the middle?"

"Yeah!"

"That's canvas isn't it?" said the duck.

"Of course", replied the barman, "I can get you a job there, starting tomorrow. The circus owner is dead keen on the idea."

The duck looked very puzzled. "But why would he want to hire a plasterer?"

Somebody complimented me on my driving the other day. They left me a note on my windscreen saying, "Parking Fine." So that was nice.

Two young nuns, freshly inducted into their order, were visiting the zoo when they stopped in front of the gorilla cage.

Something about them made the gorilla mad with desire and, after beating his chest for a while, he ran to the bars of the cage, pulled them open, jumped on one of the nuns and ravished her before going back into his cage, contented.

The nun picked herself up, brushed down her clothes and said to her friend: "Promise me never to talk about this – ever."

To which the other sister agreed.

Twenty-five years later, the two sisters found themselves together again and went to sit on a bench in a nearby park.

"I know I promised never to talk about this incident,' the nun said, 'but there's a question I've always wanted to ask you..."

"All right: ask your question, sister."

"Did it hurt?"

"Did it hurt?" the nun replied in a sad voice. "Oh, yes, it hurt. He never called ... he never wrote... he never sent flowers..."

A guy walks into a bar and orders a double whisky – straight. As he begins to drink he reaches into his wallet and pulls out a photograph. He takes a quick peek at it and then puts it back in his wallet quickly. He then finishes his whisky, calls the barkeep over and orders another. He begins to drink it and, as he does so, he reaches into his wallet and pulls out the photograph again, looks at it and then puts it away quickly. He continues doing this for about an hour.

Eventually the barkeep asks him, "Hey, mate, what's with the photo? I'm not worried by the amount you're drinking, I'd just really like to have a look at the pic – what on earth is it?"

The man replies, 'It's a photograph of my wife. When she starts to look good, I know it's time to go home!'

A man walks into a restaurant and orders a cheeseburger.

Later, the waitress brings his meal to him. He takes a bite out of it, and notices there's a small hair in the hamburger. He begins yelling frantically at the waitress, "Waitress, there's a hair in my hamburger! I demand to see what's going on!"

So the waitress takes him to the kitchen and, to his horror, he sees the cook take the meat patty and flatten it under his armpit. He says, "That's disgusting!"

The waitress replies, "You think that's disgusting? You should see him make doughnuts."

A man follows a woman with a parrot out of a cinema, stops her and says, "I'm sorry to bother you, but I couldn't help noticing that your bird seemed to understand the film. He cried at the right parts, and he laughed at the jokes. Don't you find that unusual?" "I do indeed," she replies. "He hated the book."

Q: What's the difference between purple and pink?
A: The grip.

Having just arrived at a Foreign Legion outpost, a raw recruit asks the corporal what the men do for recreation. The corporal smiles and says: "You'll see."

The young man is puzzled. "Well, you've got more than 100 men on this base and I don't see a single woman."

"You'll see," the corporal repeats.

That afternoon, 300 camels are herded into the corral. On a signal, the men go wild and sprint into the enclosure to grab a camel. The recruit sees the corporal hurrying past and grabs his arm.

"I don't understand," he says. "There must be over 300 camels and only 100 of us. Why is everybody rushing? Can't a man take his time?"

"What?" exclaims the corporal, wild-eyed. "And get stuck with an ugly one?"

Once upon a time, there lived an orphaned bunny and an orphaned snake who were both blind from birth. One day, the two met and decided to help one another out.

"Maybe I could slither all over you, and work out what you are," hissed the snake. "Oh, that would be wonderful," replied the bunny.

So the snake slithered all over the bunny, and said, "Well, you're covered with soft fur, your nose twitches, and you have a soft, cottony tail. I'd say that you must be a bunny rabbit."

The bunny then suggested to the snake, "Maybe I could feel you all over with my paw, and help you find out what you are." So the bunny felt the snake all over, and said, "Well, you're slippery, you have no backbone and no balls. I'd say you must be either a team leader, supervisor or management."

Did you hear about the new blonde paint?

It's not real bright, but it's cheap and it spreads easy.

Deep thoughts...

If you take an Oriental person and spin him around several times, does he become disoriented?

If people from Poland are called Poles, why aren't people from Holland called Holes?

Do infants enjoy infancy as much as adults enjoy adultery?

If a pig loses its voice, is it disgruntled?

If love is blind, why is lingerie so popular?

Why is the man who invests all your money called a broker?

When cheese gets its picture taken, what does it say?

Why is a person who plays the piano called a pianist but a person who drives a race car not called a racist?

Why do overlook and oversee mean opposite things?

Why isn't the number 11 pronounced onety-one?

"Go" is reportedly the shortest sentence in the English language. Could it be that "I do" is the longest sentence?

If lawyers are disbarred and clergymen defrocked, doesn't it follow that electricians can be delighted, musicians denoted and cowboys deranged?

If FedEx and UPS were to merge, would they call it Fed UP?

Western mothers feed their babies with tiny little spoons and forks. What do Chinese mothers use? Toothpicks?

Why do they put pictures of criminals up in the post office? What are we supposed to do, write to them? Why don't they just put their pictures on the postage stamps so the mailmen can look for them while they deliver the mail?

If it's true that we are here to help others, then what exactly are the others here for?

You never really learn to swear until you learn to drive.

No one ever says, "It's only a game" when their team is winning.

Ever wonder what the speed of lightning would be if it didn't zigzag?

If a cow laughed, would milk come out of her nose?

Whatever happened to Preparations A through G?

If four out of five people suffer from diarrhoea, does that mean that one enjoys it?

What's the difference between roast beef and pea soup?
Anyone can roast beef.

Two young boys go into a pharmacy, pick up a box of Tampax and walk to the counter.

"How old are you, son?" inquires the pharmacist.

"Eight."

"Do you know how these are used?"

"Not exactly," says the boy, "but they aren't for me. They're for my brother; he's four. We saw on TV that if you use these you'll be able to swim and ride a bike, and he can't do either."

One day, two old ladies are sitting outside their nursing home having a cigarette when it starts to rain. One of the old ladies whips out a condom, cuts the end off, puts it over her cigarette and continues smoking.

Maude: "What the hell is that?"

Mabel: "A condom; this way my cigarette doesn't get wet."

Maude: "Where did you get it?"

Mabel: "You can get them at any chemist."

The next day, Maude hobbles down to her local pharmacy and announces to the chemist that she wants a box of condoms. Obviously embarrassed, he looks at her, but very delicately asks what brand she would prefer.

Maude: "Doesn't matter, as long as it fits on a Camel."

The physical training instructor was drilling a platoon of soldiers.

'I want every man to lie on his back, put his legs in the air and move them as though he were riding a bicycle,' he explained. 'Now begin!'

After a few minutes, one of the men stopped.

'Why did you stop, Smith?' demanded the officer.

'I'm freewheeling for a while,' said Smith.

Passengers watch nervously as two men in pilots' uniforms and dark glasses use white canes to feel their way into the cockpit. The plane belts down the runway and the frightened passengers scream as the plane heads towards the end of the tarmac. Just in time, the plane soars into the sky and the relieved passengers all cheer and laugh at having been conned by the pilots' practical joke. In the cockpit one pilot says to the other, "You know, one day they're going to scream too late, and we're all going to die."

Q: What's the difference between purple and pink?
A: The grip.

A woman walks into an ice cream parlour and orders a scoop of chocolate ice cream.

The owner shakes his head apologetically and says, "I'm sorry, but we're all out of chocolate."

The lady looks confused and gazes down through the glass at all the ice cream tubs and then looks back up at the man and asks for a cornet of chocolate ice cream. The man replies a little annoyed, "Er, I'm sorry, but we're all out of chocolate."

The lady then seems to get the point and walks down to the end of the parlour. She then looks back up and says, "Excuse me? Can I get a litre of chocolate ice cream?"

At this point the owner explodes, "Miss, do me a favour please? Can you spell the 'straw' in strawberry?"

"Sure," says the woman. "S-T-R-A-W."

"Now can you spell the 'Van' in Vanilla?" says the owner.

"Yes. V-A-N," the lady says confidently.

"Now can you spell the fuck in chocolate?" the owner says smartly.

The lady looks up at the ceiling in thought then replies, "There is no fuck in chocolate."

"Exactly!" screams the owner.

A girl asks her boyfriend to come over Friday night and have dinner with her parents. Since this is such a big event, the girl announced to her boyfriend that after dinner, she would like to go out and make love for the first time.

Well, the boy is ecstatic, but he has never had sex before, so he takes a trip to the pharmacist to get some condoms. The pharmacist helps the boy for about an hour. He tells the boy everything there is to know about condoms and sex.

At the counter, the pharmacist asks the boy how many condoms he'd Like to buy: a 3-pack, 10-pack, or a family pack. "I'm really going to give it to this girl," the boy tells the pharmacist. "I intend to plug every orifice in her body at least twice." The pharmacist, with a laugh, suggests the family pack, saying the boy will be rather busy, it being his first time and all.

That night, the boy shows up at the girl's parents house and meets his girlfriend at the door. "Oh I'm so excited for you to meet my parents, come on in!"

The boy goes inside and is taken to the dinner table where the girl's parents are seated. The boy quickly offers to say grace and bows his head.

A minute passes, and the boy is still deep in prayer with his head down.

10 minutes passes and still no movement from the boy.

Finally, after 20 minutes with his head down, the girlfriend finally leans over and whispers to the boyfriend, "I had no idea you were this religious."

The boy turns and whispers back, "I had no idea your father was a pharmacist."

Q: What's worse than a male chauvinist pig?
A: A woman who won't do what she's told.

A priest and vicar from the local parishes are standing by the side of the road holding up a sign that reads, "The end is near! Turn yourself around now before it's too late!"

They plan to hold up the sign to each passing car.

"Leave us alone, you religious nuts!" yells the first driver as he speeds by.

Seconds later the men of God hear screeching tyres and a big splash from around the corner.

"Do you think," says one clergyman to the other, "we should just put up a sign that says 'Bridge Out' instead?"

On a recent transatlantic flight, a plane passes through a severe storm. The turbulence is awful and things go from bad to worse when one wing is struck by lightning. One woman in particular loses it. Screaming, she stands up in the front of the plane.

"I'm too young to die," she wails. "If I'm going to die, I want my last minutes on earth to be memorable! Is there ANYONE on this plane who can make me feel like a woman?"

For a moment there is silence. Everyone has forgotten their own peril. They all stared, riveted, at the desperate woman in the front of the plane.

Then an Italian man stands up in the rear of the plane. He is gorgeous: tall, well built, with dark brown hair and hazel eyes. He starts to walk slowly up the aisle, unbuttoning his shirt, one button at a time. He removes his shirt, muscles ripple across his chest... The woman gasps and he whispers: "Iron this and get me something to eat."

A local reporter goes to an old people's home to interview an ageing but legendary explorer. After hearing many incredible tales, he asks the old man to tell him about the most frightening experience he ever had on his travels.

"Once, I was hunting tigers in the jungles of India. I was on a narrow path and my native guide was behind me carrying my rifle. Just then, the largest tiger I've ever seen leapt out in front of us. I turned around for my weapon only to find that the native had fled. The tiger pounced at me with a mighty 'Roarrrr!' I'm sorry to say I soiled myself."

The reporter says, "Sir, don't be embarrassed. Under those circumstances anyone would have done the same."

"No, not then," the old man replies. "Just now, when I went 'Roarrrr!'"

Two women walking home drunk need to pee, so they duck into a graveyard. They have no bog roll, so one woman uses her pants and throws them away. The other uses a ribbon from a wreath. The next day their husbands are talking. "We'd better keep an eye on our wives," says one man. "Mine came home without her knickers." "You think that's bad," says the other man. "Mine had a card up her bum saying, 'From all the lads at the fire station, we'll never forget you.'"

A man with a 25 inch long penis goes to his doctor to complain that he is having a problem with this cumbersome instrument and has had more than one complaint.

"Doctor," he asks, in total frustration, "is there anything you can do for me?"

The doctor replies, "Medically son, there is nothing I can do. But, I do know this witch who may be able to help you." The doctor gives him directions to the witch.

The man calls upon the witch and tells his story.

"Witch, my penis is 25 inches long and I need help. Can

anything be done to help me? You are my only hope."

The witch stares in amazement, scratches her head, and then replies: "I think I may be able to help you with your problem. Do this. Go deep into the forest. There you will find a pond. In this pond, you will find a frog sitting on a log. This frog has magic powers. Say to the frog, "Will you marry me?" When the frog says no, you will find five inches less to your problem."

The man's face lights up and he dashes off into the forest. He calls out to the frog, "Will you marry me?" The frog looks at him dejectedly and replies, "NO."

The man looks down and suddenly his penis is 5 inches shorter. "WOW," he screams out loud, "This is great!" His penis is still too long at 20 inches though, so he asks the frog to marry him again. The frog rolls its eyes back in its head and screams back, "NO!"

The man feels another twitch in his penis, looks down and it was another 5 inches shorter. "This is fantastic!" He looks down at his penis again still 15 inches long and thinks for a moment. "Fifteen inches is still a monster, just a little less would be ideal."

Grinning, he looks across the pond and yells out, "Frog will you marry me?" The frog looks back across the pond shaking its head. "How many times do I have to tell you? NO, NO, NO!!!"

What do you call the sweat that's produced when a Norfolk couple have sex?
  Relative humidity.

Thirty-four ways to annoy people in the office:

1. Leave the photocopier set to reduce 200%, extra dark, 17-inch paper, 99 copies.
2. Develop an unnatural fear of staplers.
3. Every time someone asks you to do something, ask if they want fries with that.
4. If you have a glass eye, tap on it with your pen while talking to others.
5. Insist that your email address is: emperor-of-the-zorg@companyname.com.
6. Encourage your colleagues to join you in a little synchronised chair dancing.
7. Reply to everything someone says with, "That's what YOU think."
8. Practice making fax noises.
9. Highlight irrelevant material in scientific websites and "cc" them to your boss.
10. Make beeping noises when a large person backs up.
11. Finish all your sentences with the words "in accordance with prophecy".
12. Signal that a conversation is over by clamping your hands over your ears.
13. Disassemble your pen and "accidentally" flip the cartridge across the room.
14. Holler random numbers while someone is counting.
15. Adjust the tint on your monitor so that all people are green and insist to others that you like it that way.
16. Staple papers in the middle of the page.
17. Publicly investigate just how slowly you can make a croaking noise.

18. Wave to strangers from your office window.

19. Put decaf in the coffee maker for three weeks. Once everyone has gotten over their caffeine addictions, switch to espresso.

20. TYPE ONLY IN UPPERCASE.

21. type only in lowercase.

22. Don't use any punctuation anytime anywhere ever and I mean never do you understand.

23. Buy a large quantity of orange traffic cones and re-route the office.

24. Repeat the following conversation a dozen times: "Do you hear that?", "What?", "Never mind, it's gone now."

25. As much as possible, skip rather than walk.

26. Try playing the William Tell overture (the Lone Ranger theme) by tapping on the bottom of your chin. When nearly done, announce: "No, wait I messed it up" and repeat.

27. Ask people what sex they are. Laugh hysterically after they answer.

28. While making presentations, occasionally bob your head like a parakeet.

29. In the memo field of all your cheques, write "for sensual massage".

30. Stomp on little plastic ketchup packets.

31. Send email to the rest of the company to tell them what you're doing. For example, "If anyone needs me, I'll be in the bathroom, in Stall #3."

32. Ask your co-workers mysterious questions and then scribble the answers in a notebook. Mutter something about "psychological profiles".

34. Tell your boss, "It's not the voices in my head that bother me, it's the voices in your head that do."

Two nuns walk into an off-license and pick up the biggest bottle of whiskey that they can find. When they get to the cash-till the salesman says, 'I'm not sure that I can sell booze to you ladies now can I? I didn't think you were supposed to drink that stuff.' 'Don't be worrying yourself about that now will you,' replies one of the sisters, 'it's not for lowly nuns like us, 'tis for the Holy Mother Superior – she has constipation!' 'Oh well sister,' says the salesman, 'I'm so sorry, in that case, have the bottle on the house and wish her my best.' The nuns thank him and leave quietly.

A couple of hours later the salesman shuts up the shop and leaves. As he is walking to the bus stop he hears laughing and sees the two nuns sitting on a park bench laughing their heads off, rolling around and drinking all the whiskey he gave them. He is disgusted and runs over to them. 'You lied to me sisters!,' he begins, 'you told me that whiskey was for the Holy Mother Superior's constipation.' 'And so it is,' replies one of the nuns, 'and so it is – when the Holy Mother Superior sees us she's sure to shit herself!'

A man was pulled over by the police one day because his car didn't have any hubcaps on his tyres.

"What's the charge, officer?" asked the man.

The cop replied, "Indecent exposure."

"Indecent exposure!" exclaimed the fella.

The cop responded, "Yes! You can't just ride around with your nuts showing!"

Two Aussie girls walk up to the perfume counter in a superstore and pick up a sample bottle.

Shazza sprays it on her wrist and smells it: "That's quite nice, don't you think, Cheryl?"

"Yeah; what's it called?" says Cheryl to the assistant.

"Viens à moi," comes the reply.

"Viens à moi; what does that mean?" asks Shazza.

"Viens à moi, ladies, is French for 'come to me'," says the assistant haughtily.

Shazza takes another sniff and offers her arm to Cheryl saying, "That doesn't smell like come to me. Does that smell like come to you, Cheryl?"

A man walks into a Silicon Valley pet store looking to buy a monkey.

The owner points towards three identical-looking monkeys in politically-correct, animal-friendly, natural mini-habitats.

"The one on the left costs £500," says the owner.

"Why so much?" asks the customer.

"Because it can program in C," answers the owner.

The customer inquires about the next monkey and is told, "That one costs £1,500, because it knows Visual C and Object-Relational technology."

The startled man then asks about the third monkey. "That one costs £3,000," answers the store owner.

"£3,000!" exclaims the man. "What can that one do?"

The owner replies, "To be honest, I've never seen it do a single thing, but it calls itself a consultant."

How do historians know the Indians were the first people in America?

They've seen their reservations.

A dustman is going along the street picking up the wheelie bins. He gets to one house where the bin hasn't been left out so he has a quick look for it, and then knocks on the door. Eventually a Japanese man answers.

"Harro", he says.

"Alright mate, where's your bin?" asks the dustman.

"I bin on toiret" replies the Japanese man, looking perplexed.

"No mate, where's ya dust bin?"

"I dust bin on toiret I told you," says the Japanese man.

"Mate", says the dustman, "you're misunderstanding me... Where's your wheelie bin?"

"Okay, okay", says the Japanese man. "I wheelie bin having a rank."

An artist is summoned to paint a picture of General Custer's last thoughts on the anniversary of his death. Two weeks later, the artist comes back with a picture of a cow with a hole in it. Through the hole, there are two Indians having sex.

The historical council is not pleased with the picture, so the members ask the artist to explain the meaning of the picture.

The artist says, "It's simple. The meaning is this. 'Holy cow! Look at the fucking Indians!'"

The Mayor of London is worried because pigeon crap is ruining the streets and it's costing a fortune to keep them clean.

One day a man arrives at the London Assembly building and offers the Mayor a proposition: 'I can rid your beautiful city of its plague of pigeons without cost to the city, but you must promise not to ask me any questions: or, you can pay me £5 million and ask one question.' The Mayor considers the offer and accepts.

Next day the man climbs to the top of the London Assembly building, opens his coat and releases a blue pigeon that flies up into the sky. All the pigeons in London see it and they follow it out of the city. The next day the blue pigeon returns completely alone to the man and the Mayor is suitably impressed.

Even though the pigeon fancier-charges nothing, the Mayor presents him with a cheque for five million quid.

"You have done the city and the people of London a wonderful service," he declares, "but I have paid you five million pounds so that I can ask you one question."

"Fire away," says the man.

"By any chance, do you know where we can find a blue Australian?" the Mayor asks.

A team of elephants had agreed to play a game of football against a team of ants. Things were going well for the ants – more agile and nimble than the elephants – when the referee whistled loudly.

Everybody from both teams gathered around the remains of an unfortunate ant, now completely squashed to bits on the pitch.

"There you are," an ant complained bitterly. "You just can't trust the big people to play fair!"

"I didn't want this to happen,' the elephant said guiltily. "I just wanted to trip him over."

Two men meet while walking their dogs through a graveyard. One says to the other, "Morning."

The second man replies, "No: just walking the dog."

The SAS, the Parachute Regiment and the police go on a survival weekend to see who's the best. After basic exercises, the trainer sets them their next task – to catch a rabbit for supper.

First up, the SAS. Infrared goggles on, they drop to the ground and crawl into the woods. They emerge with a rabbit shot clean between the eyes. "Excellent," says the trainer. Next up, the Paras. They finish their cans of lager, smear on camouflage cream and go. They eventually emerge with the charred remains of a rabbit. "A bit messy, but well done," says the trainer.

Lastly, in go the police, walking slowly, hands behind backs. After an eternity they emerge with a squirrel in handcuffs. "Are you taking the mickey?" asks the trainer. The police team leader nudges the squirrel, who squeaks: "Alright! Alright! I'm a friggin' rabbit!"

A driver was pulled over by a policeman for speeding.

As the officer was writing the ticket, he noticed several machetes in the car. "What are those for?" he asked suspiciously. "I'm a juggler," the man replied. "I use those in my act." "Well, show me," the officer demanded.

The driver got out the machetes and started juggling them, eventually doing seven at one time. Seeing this, the driver of another car passing by said to his passenger, "Remind me never to drink and drive. Look at the test they're giving now."

An old couple were sitting on the porch one afternoon, rocking in their rocking chairs. All of a sudden, the old man reaches over and slaps his wife. "What was that for?" she asks. "That's for 40 years of rotten sex!" he replies. His wife doesn't say anything, and they start rocking again. All of a sudden, the old lady reaches over and slaps her husband hard across the face. "Well, what was that for?" he asks. "That's for knowing the difference!"

An elderly Italian man asked a local priest to hear his confession:

"Father, during the Second World War a beautiful woman knocked on my door and asked me to hide her from the Nazis. I hid her in my attic"

The priest replied, "That was a wonderful thing you did."

"It's worse father, I told her she must repay me with sexual favours."

"You were both in great danger and would have suffered terribly if you were caught, God will balance the good and the evil and judge you kindly. You are forgiven."

"Thank you father. That's a great load off my mind. I have one more question."

"Yes?" prompted the priest.

"Should I tell her the war is over?"

A group of second-, third- and fourth-year primary school kids are accompanied by two women teachers on a field trip to the local racetrack to learn about horses. Soon after arriving it's time to take the children to the toilet, so it's decided that the girls will go with one teacher and the boys with the other.

The teacher assigned to the boys is waiting outside the men's room, when one of the boys comes out and tells her that none of them can reach the urinal. Having no choice, she goes inside, helps the boys with their pants and begins hoisting the little boys up one by one to help them pee.

As she lifts one, she can't help but notice that he's unusually well endowed.

Trying not to show that she was staring, the teacher says, "You must be in the fourth."

"No, miss," he replies in a thick Irish brogue. "I'm in the seventh, riding Silver Arrow, but thanks for the fumble."

A farmer is having trouble with his prize stud bull, which has a herd of 300 cows to sort out. It won't do what's required of it, so the farmer takes it to the vet. Without even examining the animal, the vet hands the farmer a small bottle of pills and says, "Grind one of these into its feed, stand back and watch it go!"

Two weeks later, the farmer returns to the vet and says, "Veterinary, that was truly incredible. I did what you said and as soon as he'd eaten the feed he leaped over the fences and screwed all 300 cows in less than an hour!"

The vet says, "So what's the problem then – why are you back?"

The farmer says, "Well, I was wondering: it's a bit personal, but I've got a hot date with a 21-year-old tonight and I could really do with one of those tablets. I'm not really the man I used to be, after all"

"Well, I can't really let you have a whole one", says the vet, "but I guess a quarter of a pill wouldn't do much harm!"

So he gives a quarter-pill to the farmer, who goes off to prepare for his date. A few days later, the farmer is back at the vet's again.

"What is it this time?" asks the vet.

"Well, the pill worked fine – 40 times that one night," says the farmer.

"So what's up, then?" asks the vet. "

Well, now I need something for my wrist," says the farmer. "She never showed up!"

"It's just too hot to wear clothes today," said Jack as he stepped out of the shower. "Honey, what do you think the neighbours would think if I mowed the lawn like this?"

"Probably that I married you for your money," she replied.

A blonde began a job as a primary school counsellor and she was eager to help. One day during break she noticed a girl standing by herself on one side of the playing field while the rest of the kids enjoyed a game of footy at the other. The blonde approached and asked if the girl was alright. The girl said she was. A little while later, however, the blonde noticed the girl was in the same spot, still by herself. Approaching again, the counsellor offered, "Would you like me to be your friend?" The girl hesitated, then said, "OK," looking at the woman suspiciously. Feeling she was making progress, the blonde then asked, "Why are you standing here all alone?" "Because," the little girl said with great exasperation, "I'm the goalie!"

Why did the horse win the Nobel Prize?
    Because he was out standing in his field

What's black and white and tells the Pope to get lost?
    A nun who's just won the lottery.

At one American university, students in the psychology class are attending their first lecture on emotional extremes.
    "Just to establish some parameters," says the professor to a student from Arkansas, "what is the opposite of joy?"
    "Sadness," replies the diligent student.
    "And the opposite of depression?" he asks of a young lady from Oklahoma.
    "Elation," she says.
    "And you, sir," he says to a young man from Texas, "what about the opposite of woe?"
    The Texan replies, "Sir, I believe that would be 'giddy up'."

Little Billy was famous for his rectal prowess but it was starting to disrupt classes, so the teacher called him back after school to discuss the problem with him.

She began by asking him why he kept breaking wind all the time when he knew it offended many people.

"Well, miss, it's because I'm the best and I'm really proud of myself. I want to share my gift with the world."

"So, in that case," said his teacher, "if I can do it better than you, will you stop doing it in the classroom?"

Little Billy said he surely would, mainly because he didn't think she would be able to do it better than him.

So the teacher set up the test: she placed two pieces of paper covered in chalk dust on the floor, the idea being to blow as much dust as possible from the paper.

Little Billy steps forward first, drops his trousers and pants and crouches down over the paper. He rips out his best effort and it clears most of the chalk dust from the page.

At the teacher's turn, she hitches up her skirt, drops her knickers and squats over her piece of paper. She lets fly a huge blast that completely clears the chalk dust and also blows the paper across the room.

Little Billy is impressed and asks the teacher if she can repeat what she's just done. She is flattered, so agrees to do it just one more time. As she crouches down, Little Billy takes a quick peek up her skirt. "Hey, that's not fair,' he begins. 'No wonder you won, miss: yours is double-barrelled!"

Justin Beiber, Lady Gaga, Madonna and Radiohead are on a sinking ship. Who gets saved?

The world of music.

Things to do to have the military psychiatric nurses worry over your case:

Jam tiny marshmallows up your nose and try to sneeze them out while on parade.

When one of your roommates says, "Have a nice day!" tell them you have other plans and remind them you are in the Army to die.

During your next roll-call, sneeze and then loudly suck the phlegm back down your throat.

Find out what a frog in a gun barrel really looks like.

Make a list of things you have done in your life and a list of the people you have ever met, then pin them on the wall and shoot them repeatedly.

Dance naked in front of the flagpole on the Winter Solstice.

Put your uniform on backwards, then go to breakfast as if nothing was wrong.

Thumb through 'Gun Monthly', making little cooing noises.

Drive your tank in reverse.

On parade, drop a rabbit on the ground and stop to admire its fluffy coat for fifteen minutes, dragging the other conscripts around you.

At the Clintons' one morning, Hillary is reading the papers when she sees a story that Monica Lewinsky turns 31 years old that day. Not being able to resist a dig at her husband, she looks across at Bill over her cornflakes and says, "You know, it says here that Monica Lewinsky is 31 today."

"Oh, really?" replies an awkward Bill.

Not wanting to let her straying husband off the hook just yet, she gives him another dig. "She's certainly grown up fast, hasn't she, Bill?"

"Yes," says Bill, shooting her an irritated glance. "It seems like only yesterday she was crawling around the White House on her hands and knees."

Three old men were drinking around a pub table. At the table next to them sat a young girl.

The first man said, "I think it's spelt w-o-o-m-b." And the second replied, "No, it must be w-o-o-o-m-b-h." The third said, "No, no, you both have it wrong – it's w-o-o-m."

At this, the young lady could stand it no longer. She got up and said, "It's spelt w-o-m-b, you fools."

"Listen, love," said one of the old men. "Have you even heard an elephant fart underwater?"

Three blokes with dogs walk into a pub. The first orders a bottle of beer, and when it comes, his dog pours it for him. The second orders a beer, and his dog opens some crisps. The third orders a beer, but when it comes, his dog just sits there.

"Your dog doesn't do any tricks?" asks the first guy.

"He's a blacksmith," says the third.

"What do you mean?"

"If you pour beer over him, he'll make a bolt for the door."

A tramp asks a man for two quid.

The man asks, "If I give you the money, will you just use it to buy booze?" The tramp replies, "No."

The man says, "Good, but will you just gamble it away then?" The tramp replies, "No."

Then the man offers, "OK, tell you what then, I'll give you two quid if you come home with me so my wife can see what happens to a man who doesn't drink or gamble."

In the canteen:

"Pass me the chocolate pudding, would you?"

"No way, Jose!"

"And why not?"

"It's against regulations to help another soldier to dessert!"

Two friends were playing golf when one pulled out a cigar. He didn't have a lighter, so he asked his friend if he had one.

"Yep," he replied and pulled out a 12-inch Bic lighter from his golf bag.

"Wow!" said his friend, "Where did you get that monster?"

"I got it from the genie in my golf bag."

"You have a genie? Could I see him?"

The other bloke opens his golf bag and out pops a genie. The friend asks the genie, "Since I'm a friend of your master, will you grant me one wish?"

"Yes, I will," the genie replies. The friend asks the genie for a million bucks and the genie hops back into the golf bag and leaves him standing there, waiting for his million bucks. Suddenly, the sky darkens and the sound of a million ducks flying overhead is heard.

The friend tells his golfing partner, "I asked for a million bucks, not a million ducks!"

He answers, "I forgot to say; he's a bit deaf. Do you really think I asked him for a 12-inch Bic?"

With a screech of brakes, an ambulance pulls up at the local casualty ward and a hippie is wheeled out on a hospital trolley. The doctor questions the man's hippie friends about his situation.

"So what was he doing then?" asks the physician. "Acid? Cannabis?"

"Sort of," replies one of the hippies, nervously thumbing his kaftan, "but we ran out of gear, so I skinned up a home-made spliff."

"And what was in that?" asks the doctor.

"Um... I kind of raided my girlfriend's spice rack," says the hippie. "There was a bit of cumin, some turmeric and a little paprika."

"Well, that explains it," the doctor replies, looking at them gravely. "He's in a korma."

Derrick wanted to purchase a gift for his new sweetheart. As they had not been dating for very long he decided that a pair of gloves would strike the right note, not too romantic and not too personal. Accompanied by his sweetheart's sister he went to Harrods and bought a dainty pair of white gloves. The sister purchased a pair of panties for herself at the same time. During the wrapping the shop assistant mixed up the two items and the sister got the gloves and the sweetheart got the panties. Without checking the contents the young man sealed the package and sent it to his sweetheart with the following note:

Dear Maria,

I chose these because I noticed that you are not in the habit of wearing any when we go out in the evening. If it had not been for your sister I would have chosen the long ones with the buttons, but she wears short ones that are easier to remove. These are a delicate shade, but the lady I bought them from showed me the pair that she had been wearing for the past three weeks and they were hardly soiled at all. I had her try yours on for me and she looked really smart in them even though they were a little tight on her. She also told me that her pair rubs her ring which helps keep it clean and shiny, in fact she had not needed to wash it since she had begun wearing them. I wish I were there to put them on for you for the first time, as no doubt many other hands will touch them before I have a chance to see you again.

When you take them off remember to blow into them before putting them away as they will naturally be a little damp from wearing. Just think how many times my lips will kiss them during the coming year. I hope that you will wear them for me on Friday night.

All my love Derrick

P.S. The latest style is to wear them folded down with a little fur showing.

One fine day in the forest, Mr Rabbit is on his daily run when he sees a giraffe rolling a joint.

"Oh, Mr Giraffe!" he calls. "Why do you do drugs? Come run with me instead!" So the giraffe stops and runs with the rabbit.

Then they come across an elephant doing lines of cocaine.

"Oh, Mr Elephant, why do you do drugs? Come run with us instead." So the elephant stops snorting, and goes running with the other two animals.

Then they spy a lion preparing a syringe. "Oh, Mr Lion," cries the rabbit, "why do you do drugs? Come run with us instead."

But no – with a mighty roar, the lion smashes the rabbit to smithereens. "No!" cry the giraffe and elephant. "Why did you do that? All he was trying to do was help you out!"

The lion growls. "That rabbit always makes me run around the forest when he's whizzing his tits off."

When the husband finally died, his wife put the usual death notice in the paper, but added that he died of gonorrhoea. No sooner were the papers delivered when a good friend of the family phoned and complained bitterly, "You know very well that he died of diarrhoea, not gonorrhoea."

The widow replied, "I nursed him night and day so of course I know he died of diarrhoea, but I thought it would be better for posterity to remember him as a great lover rather than the big shit he always was."

A soldier serving in Hong Kong got quite upset when his girlfriend wrote to him, breaking off their engagement and asking for her photograph back. Out of spite, the soldier went out and collected from his friends all the unwanted photographs of women that he could find, bundled them all together and sent them back with a note saying, "Regret cannot remember which one is you. Please keep your photo and return the others."

A competition is running on a local radio station.

'Right,' says the DJ. 'If you can give a word in normal, everyday use that's not in the dictionary then you win £100.'

Only one light comes on the phone banks and the DJ punches it quickly.

"Hi, caller. What's your word?" says the DJ.

"GOAN," says the caller.

"How do you spell that?" says the DJ.

"G-O-A-N," the caller replies.

"Well, that's certainly not in the dictionary, but before you get the money can you tell me how you would use it in a sentence?"

"Goan fuck yoursel..." The DJ cuts him off and apologises to his audience for the bad language. Thankfully, another call comes in and the DJ is relieved to be able to move on.

"What's your word, caller?" he enquires.

"SMEE," says the caller.

"And how do you spell that?" says the DJ.

"S-M-E-E," says the caller.

"Well, you're correct SMEE isn't in the dictionary," says the DJ, "but before we give you the money can you tell me how you would use that in a sentence?"

"Smee again," says the caller. "Now goan fuck yourself."

A boy goes to the Jobcentre and says, "I'd like to work in a bowling alley."

"Ten pin?" says the man behind the desk.

"No, permanent," says the boy.

A young man, freshly promoted to the rank of second lieutenant, takes possession of his new office. He lovingly arranges a set of plaques and medals in prominent view on his desk and puts up a full-length mirror in which he spends some time wondering whether his shoulder buttons need another polish. Then a young soldier comes in.

Wishing to pass for a hotshot, the second lieutenant picks up the phone, waves the soldier to stand at attention and wait. He then starts throwing in the names of a few Generals, hints at a golfing date, whispers the name of and describes the amorous behaviour of a fictitious young lady and various bullshit. This comedy lasts for ten minutes, when he hangs up and turns his attention to the soldier.

"Can I help you, soldier?"

"Yes, sir; I'm here to activate your phone line."

A bunch of first-year medical students were receiving their first anatomy class with a real dead human body. They all gathered around the surgery table with the body covered with a white sheet. The professor started the class by telling them: "It is absolutely necessary to have two important qualities as a Doctor of Medicine: the first is that you're not disgusted by anything involving the human body."

As an example, the professor pulled back the sheet, rolled the body over and stuck his finger in the butt of the corpse, withdrew it and stuck it in his mouth. "Go ahead and do the same thing," he told his students.

The students freaked out, hesitated for several minutes, but eventually took turns sticking a finger in the butt of the dead body and sucking on it. When everyone finished, the professor looked at them and said: "The second most important quality is observation. I stuck in my MIDDLE finger and sucked on my INDEX finger. Now learn to pay attention."

Raul, Ronaldo and Beckham were all in Real Madrid's canteen, eating their packed lunches. Raul looked at his and said, "Tapas again! If I get tapas one more time, I'm jumping off the top of the Bernabeu."

Ronaldo opened his lunchbox and exclaimed, "Burritos! If I get burritos again, I'll do the same."

Beckham opened his lunch box and said, "Ham and cheese again. If I get a ham and cheese sandwich one more time, I'm jumping too."

The next day, Raul opened his lunchbox, saw some tapas and jumped to his death. Then Ronaldo opened his lunchbox, saw a burrito and jumped too.

Finally, Beckham opened his lunchbox, saw some ham and cheese sandwiches and followed the others in a fatal plunge.

At the funeral, Raul's wife was weeping. She said, "If I'd known how tired he was of tapas, I never would have given it to him again."

Ronaldo's wife also wept and said, "I could have given him tacos or enchiladas! I didn't realize he hated burritos so much."

Everyone turned to Victoria Beckham, dressed in black Versace.

"Hey, don't look at me," said Victoria. "David made his own lunch."

Dave says to Phil, "You know, I reckon I'm about ready for a holiday, only this year I'm gonna do it a little different. The last few years, I took your advice as to where to go. Two years ago you said to go to Tenerife; I went to Tenerife, and Marie got pregnant. Then last year, you told me to go to the Bahamas; I went to the Bahamas, and Marie got pregnant again."

Phil says, "So what you gonna do different this year?"

Dave says, "This year, I'm takin' Marie with me..."

A man buys a new car, but returns the next day, complaining that he can't figure out how the radio works. The salesman explains that the radio is voice-activated.

"Watch this!" he says... "Beatles!"

Sure enough, Eleanor Rigby starts blaring from the speakers.

The man drives away happy, and for the next few days, every time he says a band's name he gets their greatest hits.

One day, a dangerous driver runs a red light and nearly creams his high-tech car, but he swerves in time to avoid them.

"Assholes!" he yells. All of a sudden the German national anthem, sung by Coldplay, comes on the radio...

Two elderly women were eating at a restaurant one morning. Ethel noticed something funny about Mabel's ear and she said, "Mabel, did you know you've got a suppository in your left ear?"

Mabel answered, "I have? A suppository?" She pulled it out and stared at it. Then she said, "Ethel, I'm glad you saw this thing. Now I think I know where my hearing aid is."

Little Johnny's dad picks him up after school because Johnny has been trying out for a part in the school play. Johnny's all excited and his dad says, 'So, son, it looks like you got a part – that's great!' and Johnny says, 'Yes, dad, I did: I get to play the part of a man who's been married for a quarter of a century.' 'That's great, son,' says his father, 'and if you keep trying harder and harder, one day you'll get a speaking part!'

The police chief was putting the new recruits through their paces and explaining to them how their new job might throw up some difficult issues. "For instance," he says, "what would you do if you had to arrest your wife's mother?"

One of the recruits raises his hand and says, "Call for back-up, sir."

A woman stopped by unannounced at her recently married son's house. She rang the doorbell and walked in.

She was shocked to see her daughter-in-law lying on the couch, totally naked. Soft music was playing and the aroma of perfume filled the room.

'What are you doing?" she asked.

"I'm waiting for my husband to come home from work," the daughter-in-law answered. "This is my love dress," the daughter-in-law explained.

"Love dress? But you're naked!"

"My husband loves me to wear this dress," she explained. "It excites him to no end. Every time he sees me in this dress, he instantly becomes romantic and ravages me for hours on end. He can't get enough of me."

The mother-in-law left. When she got home, she undressed, showered, put on her best perfume, dimmed the lights, put on a romantic CD and laid on the couch waiting for her husband to arrive.

Finally, her husband came home. He walked in and saw her laying there so provocatively. "What are you doing?" he asked.

"This is my love dress," she whispered, sensually.

"Needs ironing," he said. "What's for dinner?"

A guy returns home one day and says to his girlfriend, "Look, I've bought the new Oasis CD."

"Why did you do that?" the girlfriend laughs. "We don't even have a CD player!"

"So what?" says the chap. "Have I ever asked why you keep buying bras?"

A man is dining in a fancy restaurant and there is a gorgeous redhead sitting at the next table. He has been checking her out since he sat down, but lacks the nerve to talk with her.

Suddenly she sneezes and her glass eye comes flying out of

its socket towards the man.

He reflexively reaches out, grabs it out of the air and hands it back.

"Oh my, I am sooo sorry," the woman says as she pops her eye back in place.

"Let me buy your dinner to make it up to you," she says.

They enjoy a wonderful dinner together and afterwards the theatre followed by drinks.

They talk, they laugh, she shares her deepest dreams and he shares his.

After paying for everything, she asks him if he would like to come to her place for an intimate night-cap...and stay for breakfast the next morning.

The next morning, she cooks a gourmet meal with all the trimmings. The guy is amazed! Everything had been incredible!

"You know," he said, "you are the perfect woman. Are you this nice to every guy you meet?"

"No", she replies, "you just happened to catch my eye."

Politics are supposed to be the second oldest profession. I have come to realize that it bears a very close resemblance to the first.

Sky have just won the rights to screen the first World Origami Championships from Tokyo. Unfortunately, it's only available on paper view...

Two old women are sitting in their retirement home.

The first woman says, "When my first child was born, my husband bought me a mansion in Jersey."

The second woman says, "Fantastic."

The other woman brags, "When my second child was born my husband bought me a Rolls-Royce."

"Fantastic," the other woman replies.

"And when my third child was born, my husband bought me the most expensive diamond bracelet they had at Tiffany's."

"Fantastic," says the second old lady.

"So what did your husband buy you when your first child was born?" says the bragging old dear.

"He sent me to charm school," the quiet one replies.

"What the hell for?"

"So instead of saying, 'Who gives a shit?' I could learn to say, 'Fantastic'."

A resident in a posh hotel breakfast room calls over the head waiter one morning.

"Good morning, sir," says the waiter. "What would you like for breakfast today?"

"I'd like two boiled eggs, one of them so undercooked it's runny and the other so overcooked it's tough and hard to eat. Also, grilled bacon that has been left out so it gets a bit on the cold side; burnt toast that crumbles away as soon as you touch it with a knife; butter straight from the deep freeze so that it's impossible to spread and a pot of very weak coffee, lukewarm."

"That's a complicated order, sir," said the bewildered waiter. "It might be quite difficult."

The guest replied, "Oh? I don't understand why. That's exactly what I got yesterday."

A dyslexic goth sold his soul to Santa.

Before an England vs Scotland friendly, Wayne Rooney goes into the England changing room, only to find all his team-mates looking a bit glum.

"What's the matter, lads?" he asks.

"We're having trouble getting motivated for this game, Wayne," replies Becks. "We know we're playing for national pride but it's only Scotland. We can't really get all that excited."

Rooney looks at them and says, "Well, I reckon I can beat them single-handed. You lads have the afternoon off and watch from the pub."

So Rooney goes out to play Scotland all by himself and the rest of the squad nip off to the pub for a few pints. After a few jars they wonder how the game is going, so they get the landlord to put it on the TV. A big cheer goes up as the screen reads, "England 1 – Scotland 0 (Rooney, 10 minutes)". A few more pints of lager later, and Ashley Cole shouts out, "It must be full-time now, let's see how he got on."

They look up at the TV and see "England 1 (Rooney, 10 minutes) – Scotland 1 (Ferguson, 89 minutes)." The England team can't believe it – Rooney has managed a draw against the entire Scotland team. They all rush back to the stadium to congratulate him but find him in the dressing-room, sobbing, with his head in his hands. He refuses to look at them.

"I've let you down, lads," says Rooney.

"Don't be daft!" says Becks. "You got a draw against Scotland all by yourself, and they only scored in the 89th minute!"

"No, no; I have let you down," insists Rooney. "I got sent off in the 12th minute."

According to a recent survey, men say the first thing they notice about a woman is their eyes and women say the first thing they notice about men is they're a bunch of liars.

Paris Hilton, filming on location in London, rushes into a local post office. She advances to the counter, flutters her eyelashes and tells the clerk, "I just have to get an urgent message to my mom who's in America."

The clerk informs the heiress that it costs £100 if she wants it sent immediately. She replies, 'But I don't have that much cash on me, and I must get a message to her straight away; it's soooo urgent! I'll do anything to get a message to her.'

"Anything?" the young clerk asks.

"Yes, anything!" replies the blonde.

He leads her back to the office and closes the door. He tells her to kneel in front of him and unzip his trousers. She does. "Take it out," he says. She does this as well.

She looks up at him, his manhood in her hands, and he says, "Well... what are you waiting for? Go ahead and do it."

Paris brings her lips close to it and shouts, "Hello? Mom?"

A blonde goes to the electrical appliance sale and finds a bargain.

She stops a salesman and says: "I'd like to buy this TV, please."

"Sorry, we don't sell to blondes," the salesman replies.

She storms out of the shop and hurries home, where she dyes her hair. She comes back to the same shop and again tells the salesman: "I'd like to buy this TV, please."

"Sorry, we don't sell to blondes," he replies again.

"How did he recognize me?" she wonders. Mortified, she rushes back home again and goes for the complete disguise this time – haircut, new colour, new outfit, big sunglasses – then waits a full day before returning to the shop.

"I'd like to buy this TV, please," she says to the same man.

"Sorry, we don't sell to blondes," he replies.

Frustrated, she exclaims, "But how do you know I'm a blonde?"

"Because that's not a TV, it's a microwave," he replies.

A man goes to the doctor and says, "Doctor, I'm having some trouble with my hearing." "What are the symptoms?" asks the doctor. The man replies, "A yellow TV cartoon family."

A blonde went to the hospital emergency room with the tip of her left index finger blown off.

"How did this happen?" the doctor asked.

"Well you see, I was trying to commit suicide," the blonde replied.

'By shooting your finger?' the doctor asked, baffled.

'No, silly! First I put the gun to my chest and I thought, 'I just paid £6,000 for these boobs: no way I am blowing them off.' Then I put the gun in my mouth but I thought, 'I just paid £2,000 to get my teeth fixed: the teeth are staying!' So I put the gun in my ear and I thought, 'This is going to make a loud noise,' so I put my finger in my other ear before I pulled the trigger.'

A sandwich walks into a bar.

The barman says, "Sorry we don't serve food in here."

A cowboy walks into a saloon and says, "Who painted my horse's balls yellow?"

Suddenly, a huge, mean-looking cowboy stands up and says, "I did."

So the first guy looks up at him and says, "Great; the first coat's dry."

Three guys are on a trip to Saudi Arabia. One day, they stumble into a harem tent with over 100 beautiful women inside. They start getting friendly with all the women, when suddenly the Sheik storms in.

"I am the master of all these women. No one else can touch them except me. You three men must pay for what you have done today. You will be punished in a way corresponding to your profession."

The Sheik turns to the first man and asks him what he does for a living.

"I'm a policeman," says the first man.

"Then we will shoot your penis off!" says the Sheik.

He then turns to the second man and asks him what he did for a living.

"I'm a fireman," says the second man.

"Then we will burn your penis off!" says the Sheik.

Finally, he asks the last man, "And you: what do you do for a living?"

And the third man answers, "I'm a lollipop salesman!"

God is sitting in Heaven when a scientist says to him, "Lord, we don't need you any more. Science has finally figured out a way to create life out of nothing. We can now do what you did in the beginning."

"Oh, is that so? Tell me," replies God.

"Well," says the scientist, "we can take dirt and breathe life into it, thus creating man."

"Well, that's interesting. Show me," booms God.

So the scientist bends down to the earth and starts to breathe on the soil.

"Oi!" says God. "Get your own dirt."

What's the punishment for bigamy?
    Two mothers-in-law.

A man walks into a bank and says to the clerk, "I want to open a bloody account, you total, utter moron!"

"I'm sorry, sir?" says the clerk, taken aback

"I said I want to open a bloody account, you dim-witted fool."

Offended by the attitude of the man, the clerk warns the customer that he doesn't have to put up with this sort of abuse and promptly leaves.

Returning with the manager, he explains the situation.

"Well, sir, it seems we have a problem," says the manager.

"You're right," says the man, "I've won £50 million quid and want to open an account with you."

"I see," says the manager looking at his clerk, "so it's this idiot here that's the problem then."

A jump-lead walks into a bar.

The barman says, "I'll serve you, but don't start anything."

Halfway through the first half of a school football game, the coach calls one of his nine-year-old players aside and asks, "Do you understand what co-operation is? What a team is?"

The little boy nods in the affirmative.

"Do you understand that what matters is whether we win or lose together as a team?" demands the coach.

The little boy nods.

"So," the coach continues, "I'm sure you know, when you're called offside, you shouldn't argue, swear, attack the ref or call him an idiot. Do you understand all that?"

Again the little boy nods.

The coach continues, "And when I take you off so another boy gets a chance to play, it's not good sportsmanship to call your coach a twat, is it?"

Again the little boy agrees.

"Good," says the coach. "Now go over there and explain all that to your dad."

It was the last day of nursery school and all the children had bought presents for their teacher whom they'd never see again. Because it was the last day, the teacher decided to make a game of guessing what the presents were. First of all the sweetshop owner's daughter comes up with a box. It is quite heavy so the teacher shakes it and says, "Is this full of sweets?"

"Yes, miss, it is" replies the little girl.

Then the flower shop owner's son comes up with a box. It is very light, so the teacher shakes it and says, "Is this some flowers?"

"Yes, miss, it is," replies the little boy.

Then the wine merchant's son comes up with a box. It is very heavy, so the teacher shakes it a little and notices that it is leaking a bit. She touches a drop of the liquid with her finger and tastes it. "Is this full of wine?" she says.

"No, miss," comes the reply. So the teacher tries another drop and then says, 'Is this full of champagne?'

"No, miss," comes the reply.

"In that case I give up," says the teacher, "what's in the box?" "A puppy," the boy says.

Two friends are sitting at a bar shooting the breeze over a couple of jars.

"I got my wife a diamond ring for her birthday," says one guy.

"Didn't you tell me she wanted an SUV?" asks his pal.

"Yeah, but I couldn't find a fake Range Rover."

A little girl is in line to see Santa. When it's her turn, she climbs up on Santa's lap. Santa asks, "What would you like Santa to bring you for Christmas?" The little girl replies, "I want a Barbie and Action Man." Santa looks at the little girl for a moment and says, "I think Barbie comes with Ken." "No," says the little girl. "She comes with Action Man, she fakes it with Ken."

What goes "Oooooooooooo"?

A cow with no lips.

An inflatable pupil goes to his inflatable school and is having a really bad day. Bored in his history lesson he gets up and walks out. Walking down the corridor he sees the inflatable headmaster.

Walking towards him and he pulls a knife out and stabs him. He runs out of the school. As he gets outside he thinks again "I hate school" and pulls his knife out and stabs the inflatable school.

He runs off to his inflatable home. Two hours later his inflatable Mum is knocking at his inflatable bedroom door with the inflatable police. Panicking, inflatable boy pulls out the knife and stabs himself.

Later on in the evening he wakes up in inflatable hospital and sees the headmaster is in the inflatable bed next to him. Shaking his deflated head more in sorrow than in anger, the headmaster gravely intones:

"You've let me down; you've let the school down but, worst of all, you've let yourself down"

Another Essex girl was involved in a serious crash; there's blood everywhere. The paramedics arrive and drag the girl out of the car till she's lying flat out on the floor.

"Right, I'm going to check if you're concussed."

"Ok."

"How many fingers am I putting up Sharon?"

"Oh my God I'm paralysed from the waist down!"

A boy comes home from school looking sheepish. "Dad," he moans, "we had a class spelling contest today, and I failed on the very first word."

"Ah, that's OK, son," says his father, looking over his glasses at him. "What was the word?"

The son looks miserable. "Posse," he replies.

His father bursts out laughing. "Well, no wonder you couldn't spell it," he roars. "You can't even pronounce it."

Two physicians boarded a flight out of Seattle. One sat in the window seat, the other sat in the middle seat. Just before takeoff, an attorney got on and took the aisle seat next to the two physicians.

The attorney kicked off his shoes, wiggled his toes and was settling in when the physician in the window seat said, "I think I'll get up and get a coke."

"No problem," said the attorney, "I'll get it for you."

While he was gone, one of the physicians picked up the attorney's shoe and spat in it.

When he returned with the coke, the other physician said, "That looks good, I think I'll have one, too."

Again, the attorney obligingly went to fetch it and while he was gone, the other physician picked up the other shoe and spat in it. The attorney returned and they all sat back and enjoyed the flight. As the plane was landing, the attorney slipped his feet into his shoes and knew immediately what had happened.

"How long must this go on?" he asked. "This fighting between our professions? This hatred? This animosity? This spitting in shoes and pissing in cokes?"

A woman walks into a Lexus dealership. She browses around, then spots the perfect car and walks over to inspect it. As she bends to feel the fine leather upholstery, a loud fart escapes her.

Very embarrassed, she looks around nervously to see if anyone has noticed her little accident and hopes a sales person doesn't pop up right now.

But, as she turns back, standing next to her is a salesman. "Good day, madam. How may we help you today?"

Very uncomfortably, she asks, "Sir, what is the price of this lovely vehicle?"

He answers, "Madam, I'm very sorry to say that if you farted just touching it... you're going to shit yourself when you hear the price."

A man and woman were having a secret affair. One afternoon they're in her bedroom, about to start making illicit love, when they are interrupted by the sound of a door slamming downstairs.

"Oh, no – it's my husband," says the woman. "He must have forgotten something." She quickly pulls on a dressing gown and goes down to greet her husband, while her lover jumps out of the bedroom window.

He isn't injured, but since he is totally starkers, he dives behind a bush to hide.

About an hour later, a nudist group runs by, doing a marathon. The man quickly jumps out of his hiding place and joins them.

After a while, he gets talking to the nudist running next to him.

"So, how long have you been a nudist?" the out-of-breath runner asks the fugitive lover.

"Not long," he replies.

"What about that?" the nudist said, pointing to the condom the man is still wearing.

"Oh, it was raining when I came out," the man replies.

A nurse walks into a ward to see patients early in the morning.

"Well, nurse, it seems to me you got up from the wrong side of the bed this morning," says one patient.

"Why do you say that?"

"You're wearing the surgeon's slippers."

A blonde walks down the street and sees a banana peel a hundred yards ahead. "Here we go again," she sighs.

A man goes into a bar and sees a friend at a table, drinking by himself.

"You look terrible," says the man. "What's the problem?"

'My mother died in August,' says the friend, 'and left me £25,000.'

"Gee, that's tough," replies the man.

'Then in September,' the friend continues, staring deep into his glass, 'my father died, leaving me £90,000.'

"Wow! Two parents gone in two months. No wonder you're depressed."

'And last month my aunt died, and left me £15,000.'

"Three close family members lost in three months. How sad," says the man in a comforting tone.

"Then this month," his friend goes on, "absolutely nothing!"

What's the Aussie for foreplay?

Brace yourself, Sheila!

Where do they have parties on a ship?

Where the funnel be.

A lady goes into a bar and sees a cowboy with his feet propped up on a table. He has the biggest feet she's ever seen. The woman asks the cowboy if what they say about men with big feet is true.

The cowboy replies, "Sure is; why don't you come back to my place and let me prove it?"

The woman spends the night with him. The next day, she hands the cowboy a hundred dollars.

Blushing, he says, "I'm flattered; nobody has ever paid me for my prowess before."

The woman replies, "Well, don't be. Take this money and go buy yourself some boots that fit!"

Redneck Bubba's pregnant sister is in a serious car accident and she falls into a deep coma. After nearly six months she wakes up and sees that she is no longer pregnant. Frantically she asks the doctor about her baby. The doctor replies, "Ma'am, you had twins – a boy and a girl – and your babies are fine. Your brother came in and named them."

The woman thinks to herself, "Oh no! Not Bubba; he's an idiot!"

Expecting the worst, she asks the doctor, "Well, what's the girl's name?"

"Denise," the doctor answers with a smile. The new mother thinks, "Wow! That's a beautiful name! I guess I was wrong about my brother. I really like the name Denise."

She then asks the doctor, "What's the boy's name?"

The doctor replies, "Denephew."

What's yellow and smells like bananas?
Monkey vomit.

After hearing a couple's complaints that their sex life isn't what it used to be, the sex counsellor suggests they vary their position.

"For example," he says, "you might try the wheelbarrow. Lift her legs from behind and off you go."

The eager husband is all for trying this new idea as soon as they get home.

"Well, OK," the hesitant wife agrees, "but on two conditions. First, if it hurts you have to stop right away, and second you have to promise we won't go past my parents' house."

What is a man's view of safe sex?
A padded headboard.

One Saturday, an older man and a sexy brunette walk into an expensive fur store.

"Show the lady your finest mink coat!" the man tells the owner.

The owner retrieves the store's best mink. The young woman tries it on and loves it.

'Sir,' the owner whispers to the man, 'that fur costs £25,000.'

"No problem," the man replies, "I'll write you a cheque."

"You can pick up the coat on Monday, after the cheque clears," the owner says.

On Monday, the man returns to the store on his own.

"How dare you show your face in here?" the owner screams. "There wasn't a penny in your account!"

"Yeah; sorry about that," the man says with a smile, "but I wanted to thank you for the best weekend of my life!"

In the beginning God created Eve. And she had three breasts. After three weeks in the garden, God came to visit Eve.

"How're things, Eve?" He asked.

"It is all so beautiful, God," she replied. "The sunrises and sunsets are breathtaking, the smells, the sights, everything is wonderful but I just have this one problem. It's these three breasts you've given me. The middle one pushes the other two out and I am constantly knocking them with my arms, catching them on branches, snagging them on bushes, they're a real pain," reported Eve.

"That's a fair point," replied God, "but it was my first shot at that you know. I gave the animals, what, six? So I just figured you'd need half, but I see that you are right. I'll fix that up right away!"

So, God reaches down and removes the middle breast, tossing it into the bushes. Three weeks passed and God once again visited Eve in the garden. "Well, Eve, how's my favourite creation?" He asked.

"Just fantastic," she replied, "but for one small oversight on your part. You see, all the animals are paired off. The ewe has her ram, the cow has her bull, all the animals have a mate, except me. I feel so alone."

God thought for a moment. "You know, Eve, you're right. How could I have overlooked this! You do need a mate and I will immediately create Man from a part of you!"

"Now, let's see... where did I put that useless tit?"

A boy's mother is pregnant, so she has to go off to hospital. The night before she goes, the boy chances upon her in the bathroom and sees hair between her legs. He asks, "What's that, Mummy?" and she tells him, "It's my washcloth, dear."

A couple of weeks later the mother is back from hospital but she had to have her pubic hair shaved during the birth. The boy chances in on her again and notices that her hair has gone. He asks, "What happened to your washcloth, Mummy?" and his mother replies, "I lost it dear."

A couple of days later the boy is running through the house shouting, "Mummy, I found your washcloth," so his mother stops him and says, "What do you mean, dear?"

"I found your washcloth, Mummy," the boy says again. The mother finds this pretty odd but decides to go along with it so she asks him, "And where did you find it, dear?"

So the boy says, "The maid has it now, and she's washing Daddy's face with it!"

A woman went to her psychiatrist because she was having problems with her sex life. The psychiatrist asked her many questions. Finally, he asked, "Do you ever watch your husband's face while you're having sex?"

"Well, yes, I actually did once," replied the woman.

"And tell me, how did your husband look?" asked the psychiatrist.

"Angry: fuming, actually," replied the woman.

At this point, the psychiatrist felt that he was getting somewhere and said, "Well, that's interesting. Why do you suppose that might have been?"

"He was looking at me through the window!"

A blonde walks into a clothing store. She looks around for a while and finally picks out a scarf and brings it to the counter to pay for it. As she seems very please with her purchase, the cashier is surprised to see her again a hour or so later, holding the scarf out for a refund.

"But this colour goes so well with your hair," the shop assistant remarks. "Why do you want to return it?"

"Because it's too tight!" the blonde says.

A drunken priest is pulled over for speeding. Smelling alcohol on the Father's breath and noticing a wine bottle on the passenger seat, the copper asks, "Sir, have you been drinking?"

The minister replies, "Just water."

"Then tell me," the policeman enquires, "How is it that I can smell wine?"

The minister looks down at the bottle and exclaims, "Good Lord, He's done it again!"

A deaf mute strolls into a chemist's shop to buy a packet of condoms. Unfortunately the mute cannot see any of his required brands on the shelves, and the chemist, unable to decipher sign language, fails to understand what the man wants. Frustrated, the deaf mute decides to take drastic action. He unzips his trousers and drops his penis on the counter, before placing a £5 note next to it. Nodding, the chemist unzips his own trousers, slaps his mammoth shlong down on the counter next to the mute's pecker, then picks up both notes and stuffs them in his pocket.

The now-furious deaf mute begins to grunt angrily at the chemist, waving his arms wildly.

"Sorry," says the chemist, shrugging his shoulders, "but if you can't afford to lose, you shouldn't gamble."

After a DIY store sponsored Ellen Macarthur's solo sea voyage, a man went into the store to congratulate them. "Well done for getting a yacht to leave the UK on November 28, 2004, sail 27,354 miles around the world and arrive back 72 days later," said the man. "Absolutely amazing."

"Well, thank you," replied the startled employee.

"Now, is there any chance you could let me know when the kitchen I ordered 96 days ago will be delivered from your warehouse 13 miles away?"

Three men, John, Jack and Jim, are shipwrecked and washed up on the shores of Africa. They turn inland looking for food and safety but are captured by cannibals. The cannibal king tells them that normally they eat everything they find in the forest, but that he will give them a chance to live if they pass a small test. The test is in two parts: for the first part, all they have to do is gather ten pieces of the same type of fruit in the forest. 'Easy enough', the men think, and they all run off quickly. First of all John comes back with his arms full and walks up to the king of the cannibals. 'I have brought apples, O cannibal king', he says. The cannibal king then explains the second part of the trial... 'You will have each piece of fruit forcibly inserted into your arsehole without any pain, pleasure or sentiment to be shown on your face. Any sentiment or sound whatever will cause you to be skinned alive and eaten.' So John is bent over and the second part of the trial begins. The first apple goes in easily but the second one is bigger and John winces as it is forced. As he cries out, he is carried away, prepared for the pot and eaten. Shortly Jack comes back with his hands full and walks up to the king of the cannibals. 'I have brought blackberries, O cannibal king', he says. The cannibal king explains the second part of the trial and Jack grins to himself as he bends over. The insertion begins. First one berry, then two, then three, then four, then five, then six, then seven, then eight. Jack keeps his cool throughout but suddenly, on the ninth berry, he bursts out laughing and is taken away, prepared for the pot and eaten.

The two men meet up in Heaven. John says to Jack, 'What happened to you then? I saw that you picked berries and I'd have thought you would have got through that with no problem.' Jack says, 'Me too, and I was nearly there when I saw Jim coming round the corner with an armful of watermelons!'

A tongue-tied man goes into a nut shop and the first thing he notices is that the guy behind the counter has the largest nose he's ever seen. The tongue-tied guy quickly turns his attention to the merchandise and asks, "Ess-tues me, sir?"

"Yes?" replies the clerk.

"Tould you tale me how mutsh your pisstasheos arr?"

"Pistachio's? They're six dollars a pound."

"SSit!" The tongue-tied guy goes back to browsing and then asks, "Welp, how mutsh arr your aahhmons?"

"Almonds? They're seven fifty a pound."

"SSIT! tas pensive," replies the tongue-tied man. "Welp, how bout your pikanns?"

"Pecans? They're on sale today, only four fifty a pound."

"Welp, Ssit. Just div me a pound of dose dhen."

"All right then," says the clerk as he begins bagging up a pound of pecans.

Then the tongue-tied guy says to the clerk, "Sirr, I just wanna tay tank you fo not making fun of de way I talk, cauz I tan't hep it."

The clerk replies with a smile. "Oh sir, you don't have to thank me for that. I don't make fun of anybody. I don't know if you noticed but I have a rather large nose."

The tongue-tied guy replies, "Oh, is dat your noze? I tought dat wuz your dick since your nuts are so high."

A golfer was lining up his tee shot. "What's taking so long?" demanded his partner. "My wife is watching me from the club house. This needs to be a perfect shot." "Forget it," said his partner, "you'll never hit her from here."

Walking down the high street, a woman spies a shop doorway she's never seen before. Pinned to the front is a sign: "Lady pleasing frog – inside."

Checking to make sure no one's watching, she darts in – only to find an almost bare room. "Er, can you help me?" she asks the man behind the counter. He looks up and grins widely, "Oui, mademoiselle!"

Cruising at 40,000 feet, an airplane suddenly shudders and a passenger looks out of the window. "Shit!" he screams, "one of the engines just blew up!"

Other passengers leave their seats and come running over. Suddenly the aircraft is rocked by a second blast as yet another engine explodes on the other side.

The passengers are in a panic now, and even the stewardesses can't maintain order. Just then, standing tall and smiling confidently, the pilot strides from the cockpit and assures everyone that there is nothing to worry about. His words and his demeanour make most of the passengers feel better, and they sit down as the pilot calmly walks to the door of the aircraft. There, he grabs several packages from under the seats and hands them to the flight attendants.

Each crew member attaches the package to their backs.

"Say," says an alert passenger, "aren't those parachutes?"

The pilot nods with a smile. The passenger goes on, "But I thought you said there was nothing to worry about?"

"There isn't," replies the pilot as a third engine explodes. "We're just going to get help."

God, feeling very proud of himself, tells St Peter that he's just created a 24-hour period of alternating light and darkness on earth. "That's clever, God," says St Peter, "what will you do now?"

"Oh, I think I'll call it a day," replies God.

What do you call 12 naked men sitting on each others' shoulders?

A scrotum pole

Late one night, a drunk guy is showing some friends around his brand new apartment. The last stop is the bedroom, where a big brass gong sits next to the bed.

"What on earth is that gong for?" one of the friends asks him. "It's not a gong," the drunk replies. "It's a talking clock." The guy picks up a hammer, gives the gong an ear-shattering pound, and steps back. Suddenly, someone on the other side of the wall screams, "For God's sake, you asshole... it's 3.30 in the goddamn morning!"

Deep in the forest, a tortoise was slowly padding towards a tall tree. Ever so slowly she started climbing the tree. After a few days of this, she managed to climb high enough to reach the lowest branch, but it was apparently not high enough, as she carried on upwards.

It took her a week to reach a suitable branch and then another three days to arrive at the end of the branch. Once there, she took a deep breath and hurled herself forward, instantly falling like a brick all the way down, finishing her trip with a thud in the humus.

A couple of birds had been watching the whole process for a week and the male bird turned to his mate and chirped:

"Dear, I know how much this will upset you, but we'll have to tell her she's adopted."

A little boy was lost in the supermarket. He went up to the security guard and said: "I've lost my dad."

The security guard asked him "What's he like?"

The little boy replied "Beer, kebabs and big tits."

A man is standing on his porch talking to the letterbox.

"Please let me in dear," he says, "let's at least talk about this."

"No way," says a voice from inside the house. "I've packed up my things and I'm leaving. You're an evil bastard and a sick man. My therapist says that I should leave you 'cos you're a paedophile!" The man says, "wow, that's a pretty big word for a 9-year-old!"

The priest said, "Sister, this is a silent monastery. You are welcome here as long as you like, but you may not speak until I direct you to do so."

Sister Mary Katherine lived in the monastery for 5 years before the priest said to her, "Sister Mary Katherine, you have been here for 5 years. You can speak two words."

Sister Mary Katherine said, "Hard bed."

"I'm sorry to hear that," the priest said, "We will get you a better bed."

After another 5 years, Sister Mary Katherine was called by the Priest.

"You may say another two words, Sister Mary Katherine."

"Cold food," said Sister Mary Katherine and the priest assured her that the food would be better in the future.

On her 15th anniversary at the monastery, the priest again called Sister Mary Katherine into his office.

"You may say two words today."

"I quit," said Sister Mary Katherine.

"It's probably best", said the priest, "You've done fuck-all but moan since you've been here."

A beautiful young woman is trying out skiing. By the fourth day, she feels confident enough to take the lift with her husband to the top of a gentle slope. While on the lift, stress takes its toll and the desire to visit the restroom builds up, until it becomes unbearable. Unfortunately, on top of the slope, there is nothing as far as powder rooms go, so the husband, seeing that she desperately need to go, suggests that she just uses the nearby thicket to do her business: her all-white suit would provide adequate camouflage.

The woman weighs her option and realizes that this is the only solution she has if she doesn't want to pee in her suit, so off she goes.

The woman is quite novice at skiing however and doesn't really know the position to leave her skis in and, slowly, inexorably, starts sliding down the slope. Gathering speed, she somehow manages to stay or her skis, her bottom bare and her undies wrapped around her ankles.

'And this is what happened, doctor,' a young man, laying on a hospital bed said to the surgeon. 'I was on the lift when I saw this gorgeous woman sliding backward, half naked and her pants around her ankles. I bent over to get a better view and I fell off the seat and broke my leg.'

'I see', the surgeon said. 'But tell me, how did you break your arm?'

What should you do if a Rottweiler starts shagging your leg?
    Fake an orgasm.

What do politicians do when they die?
    Lie, still!

A man walks into a bar and sits down for a beer. Now, this guy likes his beer, so when he sees a sign behind the bar that claims, 'A Lifetime's Free Beer For He Or She Who Can Pass The Test' he starts thinking this could be his lucky day.

When the owner of the bar comes in, the man says to him, "So what's this about some test, then?" and the owner says, "Well, I'll tell you this much: many have tried and many have failed my test and to this day none has passed! It consists of three parts...

"The first part is simple: just drink one whole gallon of pure jalapeño-laden tequila in one go, without shuddering or uttering a noise.

"The second part is a little more difficult: there's a vicious croc outside – pet of mine – and he's got a sore tooth. You have to wrestle him unconscious and get that tooth out using only your bare hands!

"The third part is tough too: there's a woman upstairs who hasn't had an orgasm in her seventy years on this earth, and you have to make her come!

"Complete the three and you will drink beer in this bar free to the end of your days!"

Now the man thinks that maybe it's going to be too tall an order, and he settles down for a decent evening's drinking.

After a couple of hours the beer brain takes over and he starts to think, 'You know, I reckon I could chin that "Kila, take out that 'croc and I could do that bird – hell, yes!" so he shouts for the owner to come out and watch him pass the test: "Gizza go on that tequila, why don'tcha?"

The owner puts the gallon jar of tequila on the bar and the man picks it up. He drains the whole huge bottle without saying a word and the tears stream from his eyes.

Then he walks outside and for the next twenty minutes the sound of beating, ripping and screaming come from the backyard. Then, the door is kicked open and the man is standing there with his shirt ripped to shreds, covered in mud and sweat and panting for breath.

And he says, "Now, where the hell's that woman with the bad tooth?"

Former Presidents Bill Clinton, George Bush Snr, and George Bush Jnr are travelling through Kansas.

A tornado comes along and whirls them up into the air and tosses them thousands of miles away. They all fall into a daze. When they come to and stumble out of the limousine, they realize they're in the fabled Land of Oz.

They decide to go see the famous Wizard of Oz, known for granting people their wishes.

Bush Jnr says, "I'm going to ask the Wizard for a brain."

Bush Snr responds, "I'm going to ask the Wizard for a heart."

Clinton thinks for a moment, and says "Where's Dorothy?"

Two men's shopping trolleys collide in a supermarket.

"Sorry," says the first man. "I was looking for my wife."

The second man replies, "Me, too. Let's work together. What does yours look like?"

The first man describes his wife, "She's a tall brunette with a great figure. What about yours?"

The second man thinks for a second, "She'll turn up. Let's look for yours instead."

A collection of 'Ass' emoticons:

(_!_) A regular 'nice' ass

(__!__) A large ass

(!) A tight ass

(_._) A flat ass

(_E=mc2_) A smart ass

(_$_) Money coming out of his ass

 (_^_) A bubbly ass

(_*_) A sore ass

(_!__) A lop-sided ass

{_!_} A squishy ass

(_o_) An ass that's been around

(_O_) And more...

(_x_) Kiss my ass

(_X_) Get off my ass

(_zzz_) A tired ass

(_o^o_) A wise ass

(_13_) An unlucky ass

The captain calls for the sergeant.

"I have some bad news for Private Johnston," he tells him. "His mum died last night. I'd like you to break the news to him gently, you know: he's a good guy. Tell him to come and see me."

The sergeant nods, salutes and departs for the morning roll call. "Listen up," he says in front of the men. "The company has been assigned cleaning duties in the south yard. Douglas, you are needed at the depot and Smith, at the Mess. By the way Johnston, your mother died yesterday: report to the captain." Later that day, the captain says to the sergeant: "Sarge, that was a pretty harsh way to break the news to

Johnston. Next time, be a bit more tactful when things like this happen, you know?" The sergeant nods and says that he will.

A few days later the captain receives the sad news that soldier Allen's mum died of a heart attack during the night. He sends for the sergeant and tells him to inform Allen – tactfully – of the tragedy and to send the unfortunate soldier to him. The sergeant nods, salutes, and departs.

At the roll call, when all the men are lined up, he pauses for a minute, then says:

"Right, listen up! All of you who have a mother, two steps forward! Not so fast, Allen!"

As Claude the hypnotist took to the stage, he announced, "Unlike most stage hypnotists, I intend to hypnotise each and every member of the audience."

Claude then withdrew a beautiful antique pocket watch from his coat. "I want you each to keep your eye on this antique watch. It's a very special watch. It has been in my family for six generations."

He began to swing the watch gently back and forth while quietly chanting, "Watch the watch. Watch the watch. Watch the watch. Watch the watch. Watch the watch..."

Hundreds of pairs of eyes followed the swaying watch – until, unexpectedly, it slipped from Claude's fingers and fell to the floor, breaking into a hundred pieces.

"Shit!" exclaimed the hypnotist loudly.

It took three weeks to clean the seats.

The soldiers are tired and lonely after spending weeks in enemy territory. To entertain them the Major calls for a dancer from the nearby town to entertain them. After the first dance, the soldiers go mad, clapping for five minutes.

For her second number she strips and dances in a sheer bra and G-string. This time the applause goes on for ten minutes. For her next number she dances topless, and this time the applause goes on and on. The Major has to come on stage and ask them to quieten down for the grand finale.

For her last number, she strips completely and dances naked. The Major expects the soldiers to make enough noise to bring the roof down, but ten minutes later, there is no clapping.

As the dancer comes offstage, the Major asks her, "What happened? How come there was no clapping this time?"

"How do you expect them to clap with one hand?" she says.

This is the story of a farmer's son. One morning he got up early to go and play on the farm but his mother told him he would have to do chores because now he was old enough to be helping out. The boy didn't like the thought of this much but didn't have a lot of choice. He started in the barn, where he milked the cow. When he'd finished he booted the cow up the arse. Then he went to feed the pig. When he'd finished, he booted the pig up the arse. The he went to feed the chickens. When he'd finished, he booted the chickens up the arse. Now his chores were done, he went back to the house for breakfast. His mother gave him a bowl of dry cornflakes. "What about milk and my fried breakfast?" asked the boy. "Well, you don't get any milk because you kicked the cow up the arse" said his mother. "And you don't get any bacon because you kicked the pig up the arse," she continued, "and you don't get any eggs because you kicked the chickens up the arse." At that moment, the farmer walks in as the cat walks past the door. In a bad mood, the farmer launches a kick at the cat and gets it up the arse. The boy is silent for a while, then looks at his mother and says, "Do you want to give him the bad news or shall I?"

The Game Warden, fresh out of school, spots a man walking on the bank of the lake carrying two fish in a bucket. "Can I see your fishing licence, sir," he asks. "I did not catch these fish," the fisherman says. "They are my pets. Everyday I come down to the water and whistle and these fish jump out and I take them around to see the sights only to return them at the end of the day."

"I do not believe it... You know it is illegal to fish without a licence." "If you don't believe me, then watch," the guy says as he throws the fish back into the water. "Now whistle to your fish and show me that they will come out of the water," the warden says in an ironic tone, to which the man replies: "Fish? What fish?"

A labrador, a rottweiler and a chihuahua spot a nice-looking female poodle. They rush to meet her and the poodle, aware of her charms, pouts coquettishly and tells them:

"I will go out with the one of you who can use the words 'liver' and 'cheese' in a proper sentence."

The labrador goes first, racks his brains and blurts out:

"I like liver and cheese."

"What imagination!" giggles the poodle.

The rottweiler growls and prances, then says lamely:

"I hate liver and I hate cheese."

"That's even worse than the labrador!" howls the poodle with glee.

Then the chihuahua winks at her and says: "Liver alone. Cheese mine."

A man, looking like a mechanic in stained overalls, comes into the reception of the posh local surgery, full of mothers and their children, well-to-do professional and retired people looking at him with disdain.

He approaches the receptionist and says, in a voice that is altogether too loud for this sort of place: "There's something wrong with my dick."

"We don't use this kind of language here," says the nurse reprovingly. "Please try again and be more polite this time: say you have a problem with your ear or something."

The man seems about to explode but, with visible effort, decides to just let it go. He takes a deep breath and says:

"There is a problem with my ear."

"Is there, my dear?' the receptionist says smugly. 'What kind of problem?"

The man gives her an evil grin and says: "I can't piss out of it."

Health nuts are going to feel stupid someday... lying in hospitals, dying of nothing.

A woman walks into a sex toy store and asks where the vibrators are. "Come this way," the cute woman behind the counter says, gesturing with her finger. "If I could come that way, I wouldn't need the vibrator, would I?" the woman responds.

Two blondes are waiting at the bus stop. A bus pulls up and the doors open. The first blonde steps in and asks the driver:

"Will this bus take me to New Street?"

"Sorry, it won't: you're at the wrong stop," the driver replies. The second blonde steps inside, throws her chest out, smiles devilishly and twitters:

"Will it take ME?"

After their 11th child a couple from Somerset decide that's enough. The husband goes to his doctor and tells him that he wants the snip.

"OK," says the doctor. "Go home, get a cherry bomb, light it, put it in a beer can, then hold the can up to your ear and count to 10."

The bumpkin replies, "I may not be the smartest man alive, but I don't see how putting a cherry bomb in a beer can next to my ear is going to help me."

So the man drives to London for a second opinion. The London physician is just about to explain the procedure for a vasectomy when he notices from the case file that the man is from Somerset. Instead the doc says, "Go home and get a cherry bomb, light it, place it in a beer can, hold it to your ear and count to 10."

The bumpkin figures that both doctors can't be wrong, so he goes home, lights a cherry bomb and puts it in a beer can. He holds the can up to his ear and begins the countdown.

"1, 2, 3, 4, 5...", at which point he pauses, places the beer can between his legs and resumes counting on his other hand.

Three mice were sitting at a bar talking about how tough they were. The first mouse slams a shot and says, "I play with mousetraps for fun. I'll run into one on purpose and as it's closing on me, I'll grab the bar and bench press it 20 to 30 times." The second mouse turns to him, slams a shot and says, "That's nothing. I take those poison bait tablets, cut them up and snort them, just for the fun of it." The third mouse turns to both of them, slams a shot, gets up and walks away and shouts, "I'm going home to shag the cat."

Three software engineers were in the toilet, standing at the urinals.

The first engineer finished and walked over to wash his hands. He then proceeded to dry them very carefully, using paper towel after paper towel and ensuring that his hands were completely dry. Turning to the other two engineers, he explained, "At Microsoft, we are trained to be extremely thorough." He then began to check the fit of his suit.

The second engineer finished his task at the urinal and, in his turn, proceeded to wash his hands. He used a single paper towel and made sure that he dried his hands using every available portion of it. He turned and said, "At Apple, not only are we trained to be extremely thorough, but also extremely efficient." He then started grooming his hair in the mirror.

The third engineer, rather peeved, finished and walked straight for the door, shouting over his shoulder: "At Google, we don't piss on our hands."

Bob is sitting at the coffee shop, staring morosely into his cappuccino. Tom walks in and sits down. After trying to start a conversation several times and getting only distracted grunts, he asks Bob what the problem is.

"Well," says Bob, "I think I've upset my wife after she asked me one of those questions she always asks. Now I'm in deep trouble at home."

"What kind of question was it?"

"Well, my wife asked me if I would still love her when she was old, fat and ugly."

"That's easy," said Tom. "You just say, 'Of course I will!'"

"Yeah," said Bob, "that's what I did. Except I said, 'Of course I do.'"

Young Son: "Dad, I heard that in some parts of Africa a man doesn't know his wife until he marries her. Is that true?"

Dad: "That happens in every country, son."

Did you hear about the dogs' home that got broken into?

The police still have no leads

How do you stop a snake from striking?

Pay it decent wages.

An Aussie lass visiting Britain in February stops at a red light behind a trucker. She leaps out of her car, knocks on his window and says: "Hi, my name's Cheryl and you're losing your load."

The trucker shakes his head and drives on. At the next set of traffic lights, she stops behind him, gets out and taps on his window again saying, "Hi; I dunno if you heard me. My name's Cheryl and you're losing your load."

He drives on. At the third set of lights she's still tapping on his window, saying: "Hi, mate; my name's Cheryl and you're losing your load."

Once again he shakes his head and drives on.

At the fourth set of lights, the truck driver leaps out of his cab quickly, goes over to the blonde's car, taps on her window and says, "Hi, Cheryl. My name's Dave, and I'm driving a gritter."

A young man comes into the computer store:

"I'm looking for a mystery adventure game with lots of graphics: you know – something really challenging."

"Well," replied the clerk, "have you tried Windows?"

A Welshman is shipwrecked after a big storm and ends up on a desert island with only an Alsatian and a sheep for company. There is enough food for them all and there is plentiful fresh water, too. The weather is great and they all have a pretty good time.

After a few months, the three of them get into the habit of walking up into the hills to watch the sun go down every night.

One particularly balmy night, everything is just beautiful: the sea can be heard gently lapping in the distance, the cool breeze carries the sound of the crickets chirping and everyone is happy.

The Welshman looks over at the sheep and the sheep looks back. They glance into each other's eyes and the Welshman starts to feel warm inside. The sheep continues to look at him, so he reaches out and puts his arm around the animal.

As soon as he does this, the Alsatian begins to growl, and doesn't stop until the arm is removed. The three of them continue to watch the sunset, but there is no more funny business.

After a few more weeks there is a huge storm and a beautiful woman is washed up on the beach. She is pretty ill and has to be tended night and day for weeks before she even has enough strength to talk.

After a few months of tender, loving care the woman is perfectly well again and the four of them all get along fine. The Welshman, the sheep and the Alsatian introduce the woman to their nightly ritual of watching the sun go down, and one night they are all there and it is just magical.

As before, they can hear the sea, smell the scented air and see the most beautiful sunset of their lives and as before, romance is most certainly in the air.

The Welshman is getting his warm feeling inside so he turns to the beautiful, scantily-clad maiden at his side and just nuzzles his mouth up next to her ear. She tips her head to one side to hear what he has to say, as he whispers, "You wouldn't take the dog for a walk, would you?"

One October, during a dark and stormy night, the following radio conversation took place off the eastern coast of Canada:

Americans: Please divert your course 15 degrees to the North to avoid a collision. Over.

Canadians: Recommend you divert YOUR course 15 degrees to the South to avoid a collision. Over.

Americans: This is the Captain of a US Navy ship. I say again, divert YOUR course. Over.

Canadians: No. I say again, you divert YOUR course. Over.
Americans: THIS IS THE AIRCRAFT CARRIER USS LINCOLN, THE SECOND LARGEST SHIP IN THE UNITED STATES' ATLANTIC FLEET. WE ARE ACCOMPANIED BY THREE DESTROYERS, THREE CRUISERS AND NUMEROUS SUPPORT VESSELS. I DEMAND THAT YOU CHANGE YOUR COURSE 15 DEGREES NORTH, THAT'S ONE-FIVE DEGREES NORTH, OR COUNTERMEASURES WILL BE UNDERTAKEN TO ENSURE THE SAFETY OF THIS SHIP. OVER.

Canadians: This is Rock Point Lighthouse, Newfoundland. Your call.

An elderly man lay on his deathbed. Suddenly, he smelt the aroma of his favourite cheese scones wafting up the stairs. Gathering his remaining strength, he lifted himself up from the bed. Leaning against the wall, he slowly made his way out of the bedroom and crawled downstairs, one painful step at a time.

Completely knackered, he leaned against the door gazing into the kitchen. Were it not for the agony, he would have thought he was already in heaven, as he spotted dozens of cheese scones cooling on a tray. Was this the final act of love from his wife, making sure that he left this earth a happy man? With a superhuman effort he lunged at the table, one aged and trembling hand reaching for the nearest scone. Then – "thwack!" – his hand was smacked with his wife's spatula. "Get your thieving hands off!" she shouted. "They're for the funeral!"

A little old lady walks down the street, dragging two plastic rubbish bags with her, one in each hand. There's a hole in one of the bags, and every once in a while a £20 note flies out of it on to the pavement. Noticing this, a policeman stops her.

"Ma'am, there are £20 notes falling out of that bag."

"Damn!" says the little old lady. "I'd better go back and see if I can still find some. Thanks for the warning!"

"Well, now, not so fast," says the cop. "How did you get all that money? Did you steal it?"

"Oh, no,"

says the little old lady. 'You see, my back yard backs up to the car park of the football stadium and each time there's a game, a lot of fans come and pee in the bushes, right into my flowerbeds! So I go and stand behind the bushes with a big hedge clipper, and each time someone sticks his little thingie through the bushes, I say: '£20 or off it comes!'

"Hey: not a bad idea!" laughs the cop. "By the way, what's in the other bag?"

"Well," says the little old lady, "not all of them pay."

A woman had been driving 16 hours straight when she decided she'd had enough: she was still at least six hours away from her destination, it was almost seven o'clock in the morning and she had dozed off and nearly crashing into a telegraph pole.

She decided to pull on to a side road and rest for a bit before carrying on.

She turned off the car and closed her eyes ... drifting off to sleep, precious sleep ... When an old man in a bright blue jogging suit knocked on her window, scaring her half to death.

"Sorry to wake you," he huffed, jogging in place, "but can you tell me what time it is?" The woman glanced at her watch.

"7:15," she said through the glass.

"Thank you," the jogger said, and left.

"Just my luck," the woman muttered angrily, "I'm parked on someone's jogging route."

She considered driving off and parking somewhere else, but she was too tired, so she settled back into the seat, trying to recapture the beautiful dream she was having... when another jogger knocked on her window.

"Hi, do you have the time?" he said.
The woman sighed and looked at her watch. "7:19," she said.

"Thanks," the jogger said, then trotted off. She looked down the road and saw more joggers coming her way. Irritated, she retrieved a pen from the glove box and scrawled 'I DO NOT KNOW THE TIME' on the back of a magazine. She jammed the hastily-constructed sign in the window with her shoulder and settled back to sleep.

A jogger knocked on the window just as she started dozing off. The woman pointed at the sign and shouted, "Can't you read?"

"Sure I can, ma'am. I just wanted to let you know: it's 7:27."

An atheist explorer in the deepest Amazon suddenly finds himself surrounded by a group of bloodthirsty natives. Upon surveying the situation, he says quietly to himself, "Oh, God; I'm screwed this time!"

There is a ray of light from heaven and a voice booms out, "No, you are not screwed. All you have to do is pick up that stone at your feet and bash in the head of the chief standing in front of you."

So the explorer picks up the stone and proceeds to bash the chief until he's unconscious.

As he stands above the body, breathing heavily and surrounded by hundreds of natives with looks of shock and anger on their faces, God's voice booms out again and says, "OK... now you're screwed."

A plane crashes and five men are stranded on a desert island. They are all in their early 20s and very horny.

After a month of survival John gets up and says, "I can't take it any more: I'm so horny I'm going to shag that female gorilla at the other end of the island."

He grabs himself a bag and runs off. The other four guys follow him and they quickly catch the gorilla. Each of the guys grabs a limb and John pops the bag over its head, jumps on top of the animal and starts to screw it.

The gorilla is pretty strong and doesn't put up with any nonsense, so pretty soon it gets an arm clear, and then another. It puts both of them around John's waist and holds on tight. Then it gets first one, then the other leg free as well. These become wrapped around John too. The gorilla seems to be enjoying itself and John starts to shout, "Get it off! Get it off!" One of his mates says, "You must be joking: you're on top and she's wrapped around you tightly." John says, "Not the gorilla – I mean the bag: I want to kiss her!"

Bill Clinton dies and goes to Hell. Satan, who's been waiting for him at the gate, greets him warmly.

Now it turns out that Hell is a bit full at the moment, so Bill will be replacing some lucky person, who will get to go up to 'the other place' instead.

The good news for Bill is that he gets to choose who he can replace. The Devil tells Bill to follow him as he leads him to three doorways. Satan opens the first door and Bill sees a man chained to the wall, smashing big rocks into smaller ones with a big hammer.

At the sight of this, Bill goes pale and says, "Oh, no, I couldn't handle that, no way."

The Devil opens the second door and Bill sees a man up to his neck in mud, just able to breathe and keep his head above water. At the sight of this, Bill goes even paler, and says, "Oh, no, I couldn't handle that, no way."

The Devil opens the third door and Bill sees a man tied to a pole, totally naked. Kneeling in front of him is Monica Lewinsky, giving him a blowjob.

At the sight of this, Bill gets a bit of colour back in his cheeks. "Well, I think I could handle this," he says.

"Great choice," says the Devil. "Monica – you can go now."

Two men waiting at the Pearly Gates strike up a conversation.

"How'd you die?" the first man asks the second.

"I froze to death," says the second.

"That's awful," says the first man. "How does it feel to freeze to death?"

"It's very uncomfortable at first," says the second man. "You get the shakes, and you get pains in all your fingers and toes. But eventually, it's a very calm way to go. You get numb and you kind of drift off, as if you're sleeping. How about you, how did you die?"

"I had a heart attack," says the first man. "You see, I knew my wife was cheating on me, so one day I showed up at home unexpectedly. I ran up to the bedroom, and found her alone, knitting. I ran down to the basement, but no one was hiding there, either. I ran up to the second floor, but no one was hiding there either. I ran as fast as I could to the attic, and just as I got there, I had a massive heart attack and died."

The second man shakes his head. "That's so ironic," he says.

"What do you mean?" asks the first man.

"If you'd only stopped to look in the freezer, we'd both still be alive."

Scientists have recently suggested that men should take a look at their beer consumption, considering the results of a recent analysis that revealed the presence of female hormones in beer. The theory is that drinking beer makes men turn into women. To test the finding, 100 men were fed six pints of lager each. It was then observed that 100 per cent of the men gained weight, talked excessively without making sense, became overly emotional, couldn't drive, failed to think rationally, argued over nothing and refused to apologise when wrong. No further testing is planned

Two men walking down the road see a dog licking its balls.

The first man says, "I wish I could do that."

The second man replies, "Better stroke him first – he might bite."

Officer: "Soldier, do you have change for ten dollars?"

Soldier: "Yeah, sure, buddy."

Officer: "That's no way to address an officer! Let's try it again, soldier, do you have change for ten dollars?'

Soldier: "Sir, No, SIR!"

A brain and two turds go into a pub. The barman says to the brain, "I'm not serving you; get out!" The brain asks why, and so the barman replies, "Because you're out of your head and your two mates are steaming!"

What's the difference between kinky and perverted?

Kinky is using the feather; perverted is using the chicken.

A sailor is driven off course by a storm, and smashes into a small island. The next morning, he awakes on the beach. The sand and sky are reddish. Walking around in a daze, the sailor sees red birds, red grass, red trees and red bananas. He is shocked to find that even his skin is red.

"Oh, no!" he exclaims. "I'm marooned!"

A Greek and an Italian are arguing about whose culture has contributed most to the world. The Greek guy says, "Well, we have the Parthenon."

"We have the Colosseum," the Italian counters.

"We gave birth to advanced mathematics," the Greek retorts.

"But we built the Roman Empire," the Italian challenges.

Finally the Greek says triumphantly, "We invented sex!"

"That may be true," replies the Italian, "but we introduced it to women."

A blonde is complaining to her friend about her boyfriend and men in general.

"I've had enough with men. They're cheap, they cheat on you, they don't respect you...Next time I want sex, I'll use my trusty plastic companion instead."

"Yeah, but what will you do when the batteries run out?" her friend asks.

"I'll fake an orgasm as usual."

On a train from London to Manchester, an American is berating the Englishman sitting across from him in the compartment. "You English are too stiff. You set yourself apart too much. You think your stiff upper lips make you above the rest of us. Look at me; I have Italian blood, French blood, a little Indian blood and some Swedish blood. What do you say to that?" "Very sporting of your mother," the Englishman replies.

An old woman is on a plane and is getting increasingly worried about the turbulence around her. She turns to the vicar next to her and asks: "Reverend, you are a man of God. Why can't you do something about this problem?"

"Lady," says the vicar. "I'm in sales, not management."

A redneck is walking down the road and sees his cousin coming toward him with a sack.

"What you got there?" he asks.

"Some chickens," replies his equally slack-jawed cousin.

"If I can guess how many you got, can I have one?"

"Shoot; if you guess right, I'll give you both of 'em."

"OK... five."

What do giraffes have that no other animal can possibly have? Baby giraffes!

An Essex Girl enters a sex shop and asks for a vibrator.

The man says "Choose from our range on the wall."

She says "I'll take the red one."

The man replies, "You can't, that's a fire extinguisher."

Q: Why do most women pay more attention to their appearance than improving their minds?

A: Because most men are stupid but few are blind.

A skeleton walks into a bar. The barman asks, "What can I get you?" The skeleton replies, "I'll have a pint of lager and a mop, please."

A man with a strawberry stuck up his bum goes to the doc.
The doc says: "I'll give you some cream to put on it."

A man goes into a fish and chip shop with a salmon under his arm.
He asks "Do you sell fish cakes here?"
"No," comes the reply.
"Shame, it's his birthday."

Two buddies are sitting in a singles' club and talking about another guy sitting at the other end of the bar. "I don't get it," complained the first guy. "He's not good-looking, he has no taste in clothes, drives a beat-up wreck of a car, yet he always manages to go home with the most beautiful women here!" "Yeah," replies his buddy, "He's not even very good conversationally – all he does is sit there and lick his eyebrows."

A blonde has been asked for a date and is being treated to a seafood restaurant. On her way to her table, they pass an aquarium full of live lobsters.

At the end of the meal, taking pity on the lobsters, she manages to get near the aquarium while her date is settling the bill and hides a couple of them in her bag.

"Neat," she thinks triumphantly. "I'll ask Bill to stop by the woods and I'll free the poor creatures."

A man goes to his local gym to ask about yoga classes for beginners.
The instructor asks, "How flexible are you?"
"Well," replies the man, "I can't do Wednesdays."

An Army brat was boasting about his father to a Navy brat.

"My dad's an engineer. He can do everything. Do you know the Alps?"

"Yes," said the navy brat.

"My dad built them."

Then the naval kid spoke: "Well, do you know the Dead Sea?"

"Yes."

"It's my dad who killed it!"

Why does it take 100,000,000 sperm to fertilise one egg?

Because none of them will stop and ask for directions

How do you know if there's a fighter pilot at a party?

He'll tell you.

What are woks for?

Throwing at wabbits.

One day, a man came home early from work and was greeted by his wife dressed in very sexy lingerie and high heels.

"Tie me up," she purred, "and you can do anything you want."

So he tied her up and went golfing.

A man is in a butcher's in Glasgow. The butcher is out the back, by a radiator. The man is looking at the counter and shouts, "Is that your Ayrshire bacon?"

The butcher shouts back, "No, I'm just warming my hands."

A small boy is lost, so he goes up to a policeman and says, "I can't find my dad." "What's he like?" the policeman enquires. "Beer and women," replies the boy.

A man put some tulip bulbs in his fridge to keep them fresh. A few days later his wife mistook them for onions and put them in a cheese and onion sandwich. Of course, she was horribly sick and was rushed to hospital for treatment. The man was desperate for news of his wife, so he rang the hospital.

A nurse told him she was comfortable, and was expected to be out in the spring.

A man was walking down the street in a sweat because he had an important meeting and couldn't find a parking space.

Looking up towards heaven he said, "Lord, take pity on me. If you can find me a parking space, I'll go to church every Sunday for the rest of my life and give up lager."

Miraculously, a parking space appeared.

The man looked up to heaven again and said, "Never mind; I found one."

What do you get when a grenade is thrown into a French kitchen?

Linoleum Blownapart.

A man is telling his neighbour, 'I just bought a new hearing aid. It cost me £4,000 and it's proper state-of-the-art.'

"Really?" answers the neighbour. "What kind is it?"

"Half past 12."